WOMAN INTO CITIZEN

Books by the same Author:

SYMBOLS FOR DESIGNERS

HISTORY OF CEMETERY SCULPTURE FROM ANCIENT TIMES
    TO NORMAN CONQUEST

ERIC MENDELSOHN

CIVIC DESIGN AND THE HOME

WAR MEMORIALS

THE SMALL HOUSE TODAY AND TOMORROW

EUROPEAN ARCHITECTURE IN THE TWENTIETH CENTURY

SYMBOLS, SIGNS AND THEIR MEANINGS AND USES IN DESIGN

THE NEW TOWNS—THE ANSWER TO MEGALOPOLIS
    (With Sir Frederic Osborn)

ENCYCLOPAEDIA OF URBAN PLANNING

RUSKIN'S VENICE

Woman into Citizen

by

Arnold Whittick

Introduction by
HELVI SIPILÄ

ABC-Clio
SANTA BARBARA, CALIFORNIA

ABC-Clio, Inc.
Riviera Campus 2040 Alameda Padre Serra
Box 4397, Santa Barbara, CA 93103

Library of Congress Cataloging in Publication Data
    Whittick, Arnold, 1898-
        Woman into citizen.

        Bibliography: p.
        Includes index.
        1. Women in politics—History. 2. International
    Alliance of women—History. 3. Women's rights—History
    —20th century. I. Title.
    HQ1236.W45   301.41'2   79-26516
    ISBN 0-87436-269-5

To Dame Margery Corbett Ashby in profound
admiration of her sustained and effectual activity
throughout the century for the world-wide
emancipation of women

CONTENTS

LIST OF ILLUSTRATIONS

PREFACE

The task of recording the contribution made by a vital and inflential international women's organisation to the emancipation of women throughout the world during the twentieth century is a colossal one. To do so within the compass of a single easily portable volume it is necessary to select the most significant in that contribution. What in the twilight of history is most significant is a matter of opinion, but in this work I have been guided by the advice of the prominent members of the International Alliance of Women, above all by Dame Margery Corbett Ashby, who has been a member since the Congress at Berlin in 1904, following the inauguration of the Alliance at Washington in 1902. She was president for 23 years from 1923 to 1946, and has been a very active honorary president since, having attended Congresses up to that at Delhi in 1973.

I have been a member of the Alliance for many years and attended the Congress at Königstein in 1970, taking part in debates. I have had the pleasure of knowing Dame Margery Corbett Ashby for twenty years and have enjoyed immensely her entertaining reminiscences. I have known and admired the presidents succeeding Dame Margery, having visited Hanna Ryde and Edith Anrep in Stockholm and Ester Graff in Copenhagen, while I have met many of the vice-presidents and board members. I would like particularly to acknowledge the help of Amy Bush, first vice-president (1976) who has given me the benefit of her advice and practical wisdom, of Constance Rover for appraising the work and for several valuable suggestions, of Gillian Pitt who has contributed the well informed comments of a younger generation, and of my wife who has been editor of the *International Women's News* since 1959, and is really more a participating author of this book than she is perhaps aware. Also I gratefully acknowledge the generous financial assistance for publication given by the Virginia Gildersleeve International Fund for University Women Inc. of New York.

Organisations in seventy-eight countries of the world have been affiliated to the IAW in the 75 years of its life, and in giving this account of its work on the broadest possible basis I can claim, I think, that it is the first history in English that comprehends the emancipation of women in the twentieth century as a world movement.

The varied sources of information on which I have drawn are too numerous to mention here, they are given in the notes at the ends of chapters and in the bibliography. I would, however, like to express indebtedness to the International Alliance of Women for making available to me the copies of its journal founded in 1906 and the reports of congresses since 1904. These have been valuable sources of information and are in constant demand by the growing number of students of the subject who have frequently expressed the wish for a record that this book aims to supply. I am also sensible of my debt to Adele Schreiber and Margaret Mathieson for the account of the work of the IAW that they gave in the Golden Jubilee publication of 1954 entitled *Journey towards Freedom*, where the record of much valuable work had to be summarised in a small compass.

The significant collaborating work of the IAW with the League of Nations and the United Nations and its pertinent constituent bodies deserves a fuller account than has so far been given and this is one of the aims of the present history.

It has been widely felt by many who have been engaged during the century in trying to improve the position of women in the communities of the world, and thereby increase the rights in society of all persons, men as well as women, that the momentous work of the International Alliance of Women and its great contribution to these causes calls for a fairly full record, in the interests not only of the students and researchers in social history, but of those who feel that there is still much work to be done to complete the emancipation of women.

Arnold Whittick

Crawley,
January, 1979

INTRODUCTION

Woman into Citizen is being published to mark the anniversary of seventy-five years of struggle by the International Alliance of Women for the Equal Rights and Responsibilities of Men and Women. It is also being published at a time when International Women's Year has mobilised the world to focus attention on the situation of women, in the past, in the present and in the future.

Woman into Citizen will help to achieve the goals of the United Nations Decade for Women 1976–1985, the period during which the World Plan of Action and related resolutions, emanating from the World Conference of International Women's Year are to be translated into action.

It will be a reminder of the long struggle which had to be fought before women were recognised as citizens of a country with the right to participate in the formulation of policies and the opportunity to contribute to the solution of national and international problems.

Don't let us forget that women were not granted the *right* to vote until nine years before the founding of the International Alliance and that the second country to grant this right to women did so in the year of the Alliance's first anniversary.

Although women now have political rights in all but a few countries of the world, and are, therefore, in a better position to become more active agents for change, their subordinate position in many other fields has delayed progress.

If we compare the impact of two simultaneous processes of liberation, namely the self-determination gained by a large number of developing countries through decolonisation, and the citizenship gained by women through political rights, we can observe an enormous difference in the real opportunities which they afforded. The newly independent nations were mostly able to begin restructuring their own countries according to their own political will, whereas women were seldom equipped to take advantage of their new political rights to become active participants in the political process. A great deal of inequality in the situation of men and women in the family and society still persisted, in law and in fact. Discrimination was apparent in the fields of education and training, employment and occupation and in access to economic opportunities in general. The rights of women, especially married women, were restricted in many areas of civil law, beginning from legal capacity, marriage, inheritance, income and property or guardianship, and they were thus hindered in their opportunities to make independent decisions within their own family, let alone society at large. This lack of opportunity was aggravated by the unequal division of labour in the family and lack of social services.

The history of every nation bears witness to the changes which have gradually taken place in the situation of women at the national level. We have witnessed the development of wider possibilities for education and training, better access to economic opportunities in various fields, improved maternal and child health care and other social services, changes in civil laws and gradual changes in attitudes. Much of this has been achieved with the help of continuous pressure exercised by women's organisations. The most influential groups have been those which have actively participated in politics, if they have had the political will to improve the situation of women, children and families. The dynamic participation of women in social activities even in the non-governmental field, has been enormously important as source of information and of pressure and as a mobilising force for more women to play an active role in society.

Woman into Citizen is, however, devoted especially to the role of women in voluntary organisations at the international level. What was said above about the importance of women's role in national affairs, can also be said about their role in international affairs.

The first inter-governmental efforts for the improvement of the status of women which took place during the late twenties in Latin America, were a result of pressure exercised by women's organisations in that region.

The impact of these efforts was first felt in the activities of the League of Nations and subsequently those of the United Nations.

It is thanks to these early efforts of women's organisations and groups that the principle of equal rights of men and women was embodied in the United Nations Charter among the purposes and principles of this World Organisation.

Obviously women's organisations as such did not have direct access to the formulation of this instrument. But the principle was promoted by the governments of countries with active women's groups and organisations.

When the United Nations Commission on the Status of Women was established in 1946, many non-governmental women's organisations immediately began to participate in its activities as observers. Among them was the International Alliance of Women since 1948. The members of the Commission are nominated by their governments and appointed by the United Nations Economic and Social Council and they speak on behalf of their governments, but many of them have actually come from the non-governmental organisations. This dual role of some of its members has been all to the benefit of the Commission which has thereby gained the knowledge accumulated over the years by the voluntary organisations.

The Commission on the Status of Women has in fact been one of the United Nations organs which has consistently benefited from the active participation of the non-governmental organisations in consultative status with the Economic and Social Council. The NGOs have had the right to submit written and oral statements and have thus been able to contribute a great deal to the formulation of policy decisions by the Commission. As many of them are subsequently endorsed by the Economic and Social Council and the General Assembly, the actual impact of the active women's organisations can be far-reaching indeed.

Perhaps the most exciting and recent example of this was the proclamation of 1975 as International Women's Year. The initiative came originally from a non-governmental organisation, and the members of the Commission on the Status of Women were the first ones to be convinced of its merits. When the Commission adopted a resolution to this effect, and when the General Assembly, on the recommendation of the Economic and Social Council endorsed it, the said resolution was actually to be attributed to the one non-governmental organisation.

There is no doubt that women's organisations also played a most important role in the promotion of the programme of the International Women's Year at the national and the international levels. They participated in the formulation of the World Plan of Action and related resolutions in Mexico and a large number of their members participated in the informal parallel meeting, the "Tribune".

When the General Assembly endorsed the recommendations emanating from the United Nations Conference of the International Women's Year and proclaimed a Decade for Women for their implementation, this action opened additional opportunities for the non-governmental organisations to play an active role in the promotion of the Decade in addition to the governments and their organisations.

This is tremendously important. The most crucial action has to take place at the national level. For this purpose national machineries are to be set up and they should represent various sectors of the government and the non-governmental circles. These national bureaux, commissions or committees will assist in the formulation of national short-, medium- and long-term plans and programmes with national targets and priorities. Through active participation in the work of the national machineries, women's organisations can again have a direct impact on national and international decision-making.

The national plans are expected to become an integral part of the overall national development plans. Their implementation will be reported to the United Nations to be reviewed in connection with those development plans, and further international policies will be based on them.

The non-governmental organisations are also expected to play an active role as pressure groups for the implementation of the national and international plans and progammes of the Decade for Women 1976–1985. Part of the programme for the Decade is devoted to the development of international and national standards and to the monitoring of their implementation. The technical co-operation projects, which can be financed from internal or external funds, are a vital part of the programme. A great deal of emphasis is also put on the need for continuous data collection, analysis and research. In all of these fields non-governmental organisations can again play a very helpful role. The same applies to the field of public information. They are the best promoters of women's own awareness of their rights and responsibilities.

The role of women's organisations as well as other non-governmental organisations can best be performed when they are working together. Each one has its own special goals and objectives but virtually all women's organisations have adopted the improvement of the situation of women as one of their objectives. It is the main objective of the International Alliance of Women.

International Women's Year and other recent events have, however, given full evidence of the fact that women and their organisations are no more the only promoters of the improvement of the situation of women. An enormous change in attitudes has taken place. In addition to governments and their organisations, including all the organisations in the United Nations system, a number of non-governmental organisations and institutions of all kinds have become active promoters of the Decade's programme as well as real participants in the implementation of the World Plan of Action and related resolutions.

These resolutions contain a very clear call for women to widen the scope of their activities beyond the non-governmental field, and to become active planners, decision-makers and implementors of decisions in the society at large. This is perhaps the most important provision of the World Plan of Action and the Decade's programme.

Women now have their political rights. Their contribution to the solution of national and international problems is more and more vital. Women should assume this responsibility as their priority number one. This would finally make them equal as decision-makers in national and international affairs. This could give them an opportunity not only to improve their own situation but also to share with men the responsibility for the affairs of society.

The best guarantee for the success of the Decade for Women 1976–1985 would be the maximum participation of women in the planning and decision-making bodies at the local, national and international levels in every field. The activity of non-governmental organisations could be crucial in this respect. Without carefully considered targets and strategies the inclusion of women in these bodies will not be easy. And women have to be informed and they have to be trained for this purpose.

Woman into Citizen is a report of the history of one women's organisation and its contribution to the achievement of all those rights and opportunities which many women have gained during the last past seventy-five years.

It is one of the very first publications which describes the governmental and non-governmental activities in the struggle for equal rights, responsibilitnes and opportunities of men and women at the national and international levels.

It is an invaluable review of the history of human rights and of economic and social development seen from the point of view of half of humankind. As such it will be an important tool in the promotion of the objectives of the United Nations Decade for Women 1976–1985, which are the same as those International Women's Year: equality, development and peace.

I would like to take this opportunity to congratulate the International Alliance of Women for their great contribution to the improvement of the situation of women all over the world. A great addition to them is the publication of this book.

Helvi Sipilä
Assistant Secretary-general for
Social Development and Humanitarian Affairs
United Nations

CHAPTER ONE

PROLOGUE

*The political, social and economic status of women at the
beginning of the twentieth century*

That the nineteenth century witnessed the most complete and degrading
subjection of women in the history of mankind could be plausibly argued
as there is much evidence to support the assertion. There were many
causes: the industrial revolution, the influence of the Code Napoleon, the
economic insecurity of men, and, strangely enough, the general extension of the male franchise. This increasing subjection of women accompanied the degradation of living and working conditions that came with
the industrial revolution, conditions which are vividly revealed in the report of the Royal Commission on the Distribution of the Industrial Population.[1] Catherine Bauer writing of conditions in the middle of the nineteenth century in her book *Modern Housing* says that it is "one of the great
historic ironies that the century which invented the notion of material
progress, which unfolded more scientific possibility than all the preceding
years of Western civilisation put together, was also the century which
debased human environment to about its lowest known level". It could be
added with truth that it was the century when the subjection and humility
of women reached their lowest known levels. Ethel Wood in her book
The Pilgrimage of Perseverance remarked that "the Victorian age, glorious
and prosperous, was for women the dark night of their soul".

It is difficult to discover another period when the relative position of
women was as bad as it was in the nineteenth century. During the middle
ages and up to the early seventeenth century their position in society was
in some ways similar to that of men, and in many fields they enjoyed the
same rights, so that the women's suffrage movement which began in most
countries of the western world in the nineteenth century was in some
measure a move towards the reinstatement of women to the position that
they once occupied. There was not in the middle ages the sex discrimination that arose on so many issues in the nineteenth century. During the
middle ages, women often enjoyed the same rights in property, they occupied important positions in the religious orders, in the guilds and in education. Up to the mid-fourteenth century women could occupy professional

chairs in Italian universities, which were open on an equal basis to men and women. That they generally took less advantage of their social and cultural rights than men, was because of their traditional position since the Roman civilisation of their place in the management of the home, a place however which often in the middle ages gave them an authority in social life very different from the subservient one of the Victorian age. This can be appreciated when it is remembered that in trade the workshop— the ancestor of the modern factory—was often an adjunct of the home.

The position of women in the reign of Elizabeth I appears from all the evidence to have been one of which they had fewer reasons for complaint than in subsequent centuries. Ethel Wood (op. cit.) speaks of it as a happy one for women, and remarks that the Queen herself set the standard.

From that time there was a gradual decline in the position of women in society so that in the first half of the nineteenth century they had hardly any political rights, few legal rights, and few professional, vocational, educational and cultural opportunities. There was practically no independent status for a married woman, for legally she became identified with her husband. In law, therefore, a married woman had no individual existence.

To obtain a broad, clear picture of the status of women at the beginning of this century it is necessary to consider briefly their political rights and place in electoral systems, their legal rights and the professional, vocational, educational and cultural opportunities given and denied to women during the nineteenth century.

Political rights

In 1900 in only one country of the world did women have the parliamentary vote: in the self-governing British Colony of New Zealand where women received the vote in 1893. In two American territories women had the vote earlier. Wyoming established equality of franchise for men and women in 1869, the same year as the National Women's Suffrage Association was formed in the USA. When Wyoming became a state in 1890 the enactment was confirmed. The state seal adopted in 1893 depicts a female figure of victory standing on a pedestal flanked by two men. She holds a banner inscribed with the words "Equal Rights".

A year later, in 1870, women's suffrage was adopted in the territory of Utah, which had five times as many women as Wyoming, but their vote was taken away in 1887 by an Act of Congress. It was restored when Utah became a state in 1895. In 1896 the suffrage was extended to women in Idaho which had become a state of the Union in 1890. The design of the state seal by Emma Edwards, an advocate of women's suffrage, suggests the equality of the sexes. The dexter supporter of the central shield is a female figure of justice and liberty, with scales and a liberty cap on a spear;

the sinister supporter is a miner with pick and shovel.

In 1893 the state of Colorado extended the franchise to women on equal terms with men. Thus by 1900 in four western states women had the vote. Other western states gradually followed, but the eastern states lagged behind in this progress, and were a long time following.

Three reasons for this might be suggested, one that the eastern states were more strongly influenced by the European way of life, secondly that in the tough and arduous pioneering work in the west the sterling qualities of women in contributing to that pioneering work were more readily appreciated, and thirdly the sex ratio showed a more marked minority of women than in the east. (The question is discussed in *The History of Women Suffrage* by Susan B. Anthony, Elizabeth Cady Stanton and Matilda Joslyn Gage—see bibliography.)

The first country to follow New Zealand was the Commonwealth of Australia which extended the franchise to women in 1902. The states of South Australia and Western Australia had already given the suffrage to women in 1894 and 1899. It was to take the mother country a very long time to follow these progressive examples. In Europe, apart from the Isle of Man, where the House of Keys had given women the vote in 1880, the first country to do so was Finland in 1906, then a Grand Duchy of Russia. This followed the rebellion in 1905 against Russian dictatorship, and in the reconstitution not only did universal suffrage accompany the new freedom, but 19 women deputies were elected to the Diet out of 200. Finland was the first of many countries in which the nationalist movement for liberation enthusiastically supported by women equally with men, resulted in women being given the vote. This occurred in Egypt, India, Pakistan and in the newly independent African states.

In 1901 a limited parliamentary franchise was granted to women in Norway, only a few months after its separation from Sweden, thus making it the first European sovereign state to do so. (By sovereign state is meant one that has supreme power within itself.) It was granted to all taxpaying unmarried women over 25 with a certain income at the same age as for men.[2] Finland did not become a sovereign state until its separation from Russia in 1915.

In no other country of Europe was the parliamentary suffrage extended to women until during and after the first world war. There was a limited municipal franchise for women property owners given at various times during the nineteenth century. In Sweden women paying taxes to the amount of 500 kroner (£25) received the municipal franchise in 1862, and in the United Kingdom the municipal franchise was restored to women householders in 1869, which had been taken away by the Municipal Corporation Act of 1835. Other countries followed at various times, and the dates are given in Appendix 6.

The campaign for the suffrage and equal citizenship began in organised movements from about the middle of the nineteenth century, gathering strength and reaching a crescendo in the decade before the first world war. Individual propagandists through the media of books and pamphlets were however much earlier. National histories of these movements, especially in America and England, are numerous, (see bibliography) and it will therefore be unnecessary to give more than a summarised selection of significant events.

In the extension of the franchise in England as the result of the first Reform Act of 1832, the word "male" was inserted before the word "persons". This was the first time the former word had been inserted in an act of parliament, formerly it had been assumed that the word "persons" included those of both sexes. If not the beginning of sex discrimination it was the beginning of administrative sanction of such discrimination and was the beginning of the long battle for women's franchise in Britain.

In the same year as the Reform Act the first petition for women's suffrage was presented to Parliament. It was from Mary Smith of Stanmore in Yorkshire and asked that every unmarried female with the necessary pecuniary qualifications should be entitled to vote for Members of Parliament. It was presented by "Orator" Hunt, MP, but met with no success.

Of some significance in the history of women's suffrage is the Chartist movement which began in 1838. It was an agitation for the democratic extension of the franchise with claims for equal electoral areas, universal suffrage, the abolition of property qualifications, voting by ballot, payment of members of parliament and annual elections. Universal suffrage originally meant both sexes, indeed women's suffrage was mentioned, but in the revision this was deleted and universal suffrage meant: for men only. The reason for this was that many of the Chartists thought that by claiming the extension of the suffrage for women would jeopardise the chances of men. Not, it must be noted, that they were opposed to women's suffrage, the exclusion of women was a matter of expediency. It was an attitude, not always conscious on the part of men, that was to become one of the chief opposing forces to women's franchise and had its roots in male self-interest and fear, of which many examples can be given in the professional and educational fields.

In 1851 a petition for women's suffrage from the Female Political Association of Sheffield was presented to the House of Lords by Lord Carlyle. In 1866 the most famous petition of the century for women's suffrage was presented by John Stuart Mill and Henry Fawcett, and the following year an amendment by Mill to the Government's "Representation of the People's Bill" to substitute "person" for "man" was defeated. In 1869 appeared the best reasoned advocacy of women's franchise in English: Mill's *Subjection of Women*. Although it won many converts among the more progressive intellectuals, the realisation of its advocacies was still remote. Further measures for the extension of the suffrage to women were introduced in the House of Commons in 1870, and in the years of the further Reform Acts of 1867, 1884, 1885, and 1897. In 1900 a petition for women's suffrage was presented to Parliament on behalf of 67,000 textile workers, and in 1904 a resolution for women's suffrage was carried in the House of Commons, but nothing more happened.

Thus from 1832 to 1904 women working for equal franchise, a cause which they thought just, a cause which was supported by a large body of intellectual men, was met with constant rejection. Little wonder women had a sense of frustration, and realised that stronger and sterner measures were necessary. The success of their cause was often nearly in sight, but one man more than any other obstructed progress—W. E. Gladstone. He had a successor of the same regrettable spirit in Herbert Asquith. In the words of Pethick-Lawrence, both must "bear a heavy responsibility for forcing women into revolutionary courses". But for these two men England might have been in the forefront of the democracies of the world in extending the franchise to all citizens.

What happened in Britain happened with variations in many countries of the world. As we have seen, some countries and states, New Zealand, Australia, four American states and two Scandinavian countries were in the vanguard of progress. The position of French women in society suffered from the crushing effects of the Code Napoleon which influenced French law throughout the century. In the Code the function of women was a very subordinate one, and married women, as in England, had very little individual status. Organised efforts to put matters right in the field of the parliamentary suffrage for women began during the middle of the century, but it was not until 1885 that a petition with that purpose was presented to the French Government, and not until 1901 that the first Women's Suffrage Bill was introduced into Parliament, both meeting with the same frustrating response.

Italy also suffered from the influence of the Code Napoleon but the prospects for women greatly improved after the combination of the various states into a united country in 1861. This was particularly the case in education where the tradition of equality continued, but the legal position of women was far from satisfactory. Because of the divided condition of the country before 1861 the campaign for women's suffrage began later than in England, and the first proposal made to Parliament was in 1877. Repeated efforts were also made during the eighties to obtain the municipal franchise for women but without success. By the early years of the present century there was a good deal of organised campaigning and several women's suffrage associations had been formed in the principal towns.

The story is similar in Germany, and after the founding in 1865 of the

Allgemeine Deutsche Frauenverein in Leipzig the campaign gradually gathered momentum.

Conditions in Russia were rather different, for it was hardly a democratic country in the western sense. Alice Zimmern in her excellent little book on *Women's Suffrage in Many Lands* ironically remarks that in Russia for many years woman was the equal of man for neither had any rights, and the story of women's franchise does not really begin until after the attempted revolution of 1905. Still, in some fields, in education and occasionally in the professions, opportunities were afforded to women which indicated that sometimes a more liberal spirit was at work.

A major contribution to the women's movement was made in the USA.The women's suffrage campaign began as far back as 1787 when the constitution of the United States was prepared by the representatives of the thirteen member states, but there was not a great deal of concerted positive action until half a century later. It is often claimed that when the World's Anti-Slavery Congress held in London in 1840 refused to admit the American women delegates this insult was a stir to action among American women. In the early days organisations depended on the pioneer efforts of a few women like Lucretia Mott, Elizabeth Cady Stanton and Susan B. Anthony. The founding of the National Women's Suffrage Association in 1869 was a great step forward for it was able by co-ordinated experience to give much assistance to local organisations and was a great stimulus generally.

In 1888 an International Congress of Women was held in Washington DC under the auspices of the National Suffrage Association, and a major result was the founding of the International Council of Women which had its first headquarters in Zürich. This International Council was and is a federation of National Councils or Unions of Women concerned with all social and economic questions. Its policy, as stated in Article II of its constitution, was couched in a series of negatives and it seemed little more than a general international nurse for National Councils. It was possibly consciousness of this that prompted Elizabeth Stanton, Susan B. Anthony, and a new recruit to the cause, Carrie Chapman Catt, to found an international body with the main purpose of affiliating the societies of all countries working with the object of obtaining women's suffrage. As a result of their endeavours the National American Woman Suffrage Association organised an International Woman Suffrage Conference as part of its annual convention in Washington DC in February 1902. Delegates from England, Russia, Norway, Germany, Sweden, Turkey, Australia and Chile attended. This was the gestation of the International Woman Suffrage Alliance, and an account of its birth logically commences in Chapter 2.

Legal status of women in the nineteenth century

The legal status of women in the first half of the nineteenth century was humiliatingly low and in the case of married women non-existent, certainly in England. This is testified by the circumstances of Caroline Norton's marriage, best related in her own passionate writings, and briefly narrated in Ray Strachey's *The Cause* (1934, pp. 34–40) and recounted several times since. Certain significant points might be underlined. A grand-daughter of Richard Sheridan the dramatist, she married the Hon. Richard Norton and they had three children. It proved to be an unhappy marriage and there appears to have been brutality in the husband's treatment of his wife. While Caroline was visiting her sister, her husband sent the three children with their nurse to a relative with instructions that his wife was not to have access to them. He then tried to divorce his wife, citing Lord Melbourne as co-respondent, who, by the time the case was heard, was Prime Minister. Political passions were involved in this as Norton was a Tory, his wife a Whig and friend of Melbourne. The case was so weak, there being absolutely no evidence of misconduct, that the jury dismissed the case without retiring. A significant point was that Caroline could not be legally represented because, in the eyes of the law, she had no independent existence apart from her husband.

Caroline was a writer of considerable ability, yet all her earnings were in law the property of her husband, for in those days a married woman had no property of her own. What she may have had before marriage, left or given by her father perhaps, all became the possession of her husband. Some idealists who think marriages are made in heaven might say: "Well, that is as it should be", but when it is considered how brutally and tyrannically thousands of Victorian husbands treated their wives—and the evidence is sadly voluminous—then such idealism becomes inhumanity.

Caroline set to work to alter the law so as to obtain either the custody of her children or to obtain occasional access to them. In this she was much assisted by a lawyer, Thomas Talfourd, and they together perpared a parliamentary bill. This association however prompted some scurrilous comments of a highly libellous nature from the *British and Foreign Review*. Caroline naturally wanted to sue for libel but discovered that as a married woman she had legally no separate identity and could not sue. These points demonstrate the complete and degrading legal subservience of married women in the first half of the century. The passing of the Infants Custody Bill in 1839 was the first timid step towards improvement. Subsequent measures in various fields were the Matrimonial Causes Act of 1857 (amended in 1858, 1884 and 1896) which removed some of the injustices and inequalities, but not all; the Matrimonial Causes Act of 1878 which provided for the legal separation for wives with custody of children; and the Married Women's Property Act of 1882 which placed matters of the property of husband and wife on a more equitable basis.

By 1900, however, there were still gross inequalities in the marriage partnership, in property, in remuneration for the same work, and in laws relating to nationality and domicile. Only a few improvements had been effected by that year, and the laws of England still supported the degrading subservience of women at the beginning of the present century. It would take too much space to review the legal status of women in other countries of the world. There were, of course, some differences in European countries, but the remarkable circumstance is the general similarity in the legal and moral subjection of women throughout Europe during the nineteenth century, and the gradual but slow movement towards improvement.

Professional, Vocational and Educational Opportunities

Sex discrimination in employment arose with the large scale organisation of labour consequent upon the industrial revolution, and in the professions with registration and systems of qualification. Although the nineteenth century was a great period of industrial expansion and the employment of industrial labour was always increasing, there were occasional periods of unemployment which stirred feelings of insecurity among men and prompted them to make first claims on employment in preference to women. The circumstance that women were paid at lower rates naturally encouraged some employers to engage the cheaper female labour rather than male labour, and this fermented the antagonism to women in employment.

In the early nineteenth century the opportunities for employment for women were few compared with those for men. There were some trades and industries, however, in which women were traditionally employed, such as millinery and dress-making and in the cotton and woollen mills. The constant demand for labour in the mines started the employment of women and children for auxiliary work which was often of the roughest kind in the most appalling conditions, employment which constitutes one of the blackest chapters in English economic and social history. In the report of the Commission on Mines of 1842 it was stated that "women always did the lifting or heavy part of the work, and neither they nor the children were treated like human beings", and that "females submit to work in places where no man or even lad could be got to labour in: they work in the bad roads, up to their knees in water, in a posture nearly double: they are below till the last hour of pregnancy; they have swelled haunches and ankles, and are prematurely brought to the grave. . . . The females pulled like horses through the holes in the mines with tears and in a state of exhaustion." One woman in evidence said, "I have a belt round my waist and a chain passing between my legs and go on my hands and feet". She further remarked, "I have drawn till I have had the skin off me; the belt and chain is worse when we are in the family way". Another woman said that she had a child born in the pits and that she brought it up the pit shaft in her skirt.

That is the kind of employment to which men for their profit subjected women. Fortunately as a result of these appalling revelations an act was passed (in the same year as the report of the Commission was published), prohibiting the employment of women in mines.

The conditions of employment of women in factories were also so bad that legislation was introduced in 1841 limiting the number of hours women could be employed. (But this was only in factories and did not apply to women employed in dress-making and millinery.) It was not uncommon for women to work fifteen hours a day, and on occasions, when demands of customers were exacting, to work even longer. The premises in which they worked these long hours would now be looked on with horror.

One of the social problems of the mid-nineteenth century was the provision of opportunities for women to earn their living—which many had to do or starve—and a very large number did.

The census of 1851 revealed a "surplus" of nearly a million women, and in addition the labour market indicated about $1\frac{1}{2}$ millions who had from necessity to find employment for a period before marriage and some later during widowhood. Yet the opportunities for this $2\frac{1}{2}$ millions to do so were few, and one of the reasons was that the majority of men did their utmost to restrict the vocations open to women. These difficulties occurred not only among the poorer classes and in industrial employment, but in the lower strata of the middle classes, where the search was often for some form of sedentary occupation. In the middle of the century there were a few women shop assistants, but no women clerks or secretaries. Even Queen Victoria is reported to have expressed concern about the few opportunities of employment open to women.

In the second half of the century conditions began to improve, and during the seventies women were employed as clerks and secretaries on an increasing scale. A contribution was made by the civil service. In 1855 it was placed on a more professional basis and selection was made by examination. Fifteen years later a start was made with employing women, the first department to do so being the Post Office. This, however, met with a good deal of opposition from men in the department. By 1900 the employment of women was general in offices, but always at a lower remuneration than for men doing similar work.

The history of women's endeavours to enter the professions has frequently been recalled. The prejudice against women, particularly strong in medical profession, is a little difficult to understand, but it was obviously very deeply rooted. Although the efforts of such women as Elizabeth Blackmore, Elizabeth Garrett Anderson, Sophia Jex-Blake and others have often been vividly described, and the circumstances that the very abilities of such women stirred men and particularly male students often to stronger opposition, there have not been, as far as I am aware, any thorough psychological studies of this male antagonism. That it has its roots in fear, partly of competition, partly of invasion of territory that man had thought to be exclusively his own, are obvious reasons but there are probably others. The psychology of male opposition to women's emancipation is an important subject that merits more study than has so far been given to it. Gladstone's pre-occupation with reforming prostitutes and his opposition to women's suffrage are not unrelated.

In no profession was there more of a fight than in medicine. Its history can be read in Ray Strachey's *The Cause* and in other books. In the admission of women to practise both medicine and law England was rather behind many of the principal countries of the world. Still, by 1900 equality of the sexes in the medical profession was in sight. This could not be said of the law or the church, although it was to be realised later in the former.

The inequality of the sexes and the subjugation of women is again illustrated in educational opportunities.

This subjugation was in some measure due to religious doctrine translated into superstition. For example up to the fourteenth century in Italy women enjoyed great personal liberty, and were renowned for their intelligence and influence, and in the twelfth and thirteenth centuries they entered the Universities and even had places of high honour in the Faculties. Many were famed for their achievements in learning, mathematics and philosophy. But in 1377, the Faculty of the University of Bologna decreed:

"And whereas woman is the foundation of sin, the weapon of the devil, the cause of man's banishment from Paradise, and whereas, for these reasons, all association with her is to be diligently avoided, therefore do we interdict and expressly forbid that anyone presume to introduce in the said college any women whatsoever, however honourable she be. And if anyone should perpetrate such an act, he shall be severely punished."

That decree not only closed that University, but the theory upon which it was founded: that women were responsible for the presence of sin in the world and its perpetuation closed to them all universities of Italy and Spain. More, it condemned all education for women. Under this terrible mandate, generation after generation of women, endowed with great abilities were compelled to live and die in the darkness of ignorance.[3]

This attitude to women still persisted among many men well on into the twentieth century; especially those who were the victims of superstitions emanating from some of the myths of Palestine. Woman, and the temptations she offered to man, was regarded as a major source of evil

"Women's Rights"—a meeting held
in London, May 1872. Mrs Millicent
Fawcett, founder of the Fawcett Society is seated at the extreme left of
the front row.

and must therefore be kept in subjection.

Education generally up to the middle of the nineteenth century was for
the privileged minority of the population. In England the great public
schools for boys to which the wealthy and comfortably established families
sent their sons have existed as distinctive features of English life since the
fifteenth century, yet the daughters of the same families were either educated by governesses at home or sent to a small boarding school where a
very limited range of subjects was taught. The two great universities of
Oxford and Cambridge were, of course, open only to men, and this remained the case to nearly the end of the nineteenth century.

From the eighteenth century the upper strata of the "working classes",
consisting of the more highly skilled artisans and clerks, had the opportunity of sending their children to charity schools and dame schools. In the
nineteenth century schools began to benefit from a system of state endowments, but for a long time this was mainly for boys' schools, comparatively few girls' schools benefited.

Improvements on an increasing scale began about the middle of the century and a large number of girls' schools and colleges were founded in the second half of the century. Although the disparity between the opportunities for education for boys and girls was far less in 1900 than in 1850 it was still considerable.

Several important women's colleges were founded near the middle of the century: Queen's College in 1848, Bedford College in 1849 and the North London Collegiate School in 1850. In 1869 a Women's College was started at Hitchin by that great pioneer of women's education, Emily Davies. In 1874 in accordance with the original intention it was moved to Cambridge and became Girton College. In 1871 Newnham College, Cambridge was founded. A little later, in 1879, Lady Margaret Hall and Somerville College at Oxford were opened. Other women's colleges that later became part of London University were Westfield College, Hampstead, established in 1882, and Royal Holloway College established in 1886. The establishment of the Girls' Public Day School Trust in 1872 proved to be a great fillip to the progress of secondary education for girls.

Although several women's colleges were founded and became at various times parts of universities there was a strange reluctance on the part of the old universities to admit women to their examinations and degrees. In England, London was the first, and from 1878 women could take BA, MA and BSc degrees. The younger universities were much more liberal in their attitude towards women's education than were the old die-hard universities of Oxford and Cambridge. The University of Wales founded in 1893 made no discrimination between the sexes and opened its degrees to women; and this occurred at about the same time with the four Scottish Universities of Edinburgh, Glasgow, St Andrew's and Aberdeen. This also obtained in the Royal University of Ireland, so that in 1900 all the universities of the United Kingdom with the notable exceptions of Oxford and Cambridge conferred their degrees and opened many of their courses to men and women alike. It took the older universities a long time to follow.

In America there was not naturally such a conservative traditional attitude to act as a handicap of women's education and opportunities were given to women at a much earlier date. In 1833 a co-educational school, Oberlin College in Northern Ohio, organised its degree courses for men and women alike, and in the sixties Iowa and Wisconsin Universities opened their degree courses to women. Other American universities gradually followed. Universities in Australia and New Zealand opened their courses with little sex discrimination. The University College of Otago at Dunedin in New Zealand founded in 1869 admitted women very early and produced in 1877 the first woman graduate in the Commonwealth. The University of Sydney opened its degrees to women in 1881.

Biological differences of the sexes

One of the arguments often advanced against equal citizenship and equal educational and vocational opportunities for the sexes relates to their biological differences. The physical differences produce certain differences in conditions and habits especially with offspring, but there is no conclusive evidence of any difference in mental endowments. That men have achieved more in the arts and sciences is because they have had the freedom to do so, while most women have traditionally been occupied, often very fully, with domestic tasks. The pull of the home and the care of the young is strong in women, often stronger than the development of her creative and intellectual capabilities. I can recall the case of a woman painter, one of the most distinguished of her time. She married and gave up painting to devote her energies to her home and looking after her husband and family. When she was about fifty she returned to her painting and for the last ten years of her life produced work that holds a high place in contemporary English painting. That is illustrative of many women in several walks of life, but the majority do not return to the work in which they once showed great promise, and they fulfilled themselves only in the limited sphere of the home.

I remember shortly after the second world war asking a brains trust, which was very popular in those days, whether it felt that if women played a more important part in the councils of the world that this would be an important factor in contributing to peace, as the pugnacious instinct seemed not quite so strong in women. One member of the trust, a biologist and an FRS, replied by saying that the policy decisions and the higher administrative work of the world should be done by men and in support of this quoted Darwin who had suggested that the variability in the species was greater in the male than in the female which, translated in terms of human beings, means that the extremes of creative and intellectual capacity are found more in the man than in the woman. Is there really any reliable evidence for this? We have never been in a position to decide. The truth is that communities as constituted up to 1900 have generally given opportunities only to a minority of privileged men and it has been possible to note, therefore, only the full development of the mental capacities of these privileged men. Because of the comparatively negligible opportunities given to women such development has not been possible, and civilisation has suffered.

This constitutes the fundamental reason why opportunities for citizenship, work and education should be on an equal basis for both sexes. The progress of civilisation and of democratic societies depends on the freedom of individuals to develop fully their potentialities, and they should be given the utmost assistance and opportunities to accomplish this, not only in the interests of human evolution, but in the interests of democratic states and in the fulfilment of individual talent. Only recently is this becoming possible to men and women on an equal basis in anything like a full degree. Up to the end of the nineteenth century almost, the freedom to develop individual potentialities was denied to nearly the whole of one half of humanity. In 1900 the world was in process of slowly emerging from what had been a dark age for women, but even then the suffrage was still denied to nearly all women in the world, the very few exceptions representing less than one per cent. In legal status, in employment, in the professions, some progress had been made, while fortunately in education which is often a preliminary to the others, most had been achieved. There was still a very long way to go, and the accomplishment of so much during the present century, which is nothing less than a complete revolution in the position of women throughout the world, is an achievement to which the International Alliance of Women has made one of the major contributions. Something of what it has done is told in the following pages.

REFERENCES

1   London 1940. The appalling conditions under which the mass of the industrial population lived and worked in the early and middle nineteenth century are desscribed in Part II which considers the social disadvantages of the distribution of population as it then was.
2   Roger Fulford in his book *Votes for Women* mistakenly gave the date as 1913.
3   See Carrie Chapman Catt's presidential address at the Copenhagen Congress (1906) of the International Woman's Suffrage Alliance.

CHAPTER TWO

1904—1907

The campaign for women's suffrage—Berlin and Copenhagen
Congresses

As mentioned in the first chapter the need for an international body that should stimulate and assist national women's associations to obtain the franchise for women had been strongly felt by Elizabeth Stanton, Susan B. Anthony, and Carrie Chapman Catt of the United States, and led to their organising an International Woman Suffrage Conference as part of the annual convention of the National American Woman Suffrage Association at Washington in February 1902. Delegates from ten countries attended. Susan B. Anthony presided at the conference, Miss Vida Goldstein of Australia acted as secretary, and a committee of five was formed, consisting of Mrs Fenwick Miller of England, Mrs Rachel Avery of the United States, Miss Antoine Stolle of Germany, Mrs Gudrun Drewson of Norway and the secretary. It was decided that a second meeting of the International Woman Suffrage Conference should be held in Berlin in 1904 in connection with the quinquennial meeting of the International Council of Women.

A committee of three consisting of Susan B. Anthony, Anita Augspurg and Carrie Chapman Catt prepared a declaration of principles which after discussion and amendments was adopted for presentation to the Berlin meeting.

This formed the charter of the international organisation for many years. It was as follows:

1. That men and women are born equally free and independent members of the human race; equally endowed with intelligence and ability, and equally entitled to the free exercise of their individual rights and liberty.
2. That the natural relation of the sexes is that of interdependence and cooperation, and that the repression of the rights and liberty of one sex inevitably works injury to the other, and hence to the whole race.
3. That in all lands, those laws, creeds, and customs which have tended to restrict women to a position of dependence; to discourage their education; to impede the development of their natural gifts, and to

subordinate their individuality, have been based on false theories, and have produced an artificial and unjust relation of the sexes in modern society.

4. That self-government in the home and the State is the inalienable right of every normal adult, and the refusal of this right to women has resulted in social, legal, and economic injustice to them, and has also intensified the existing economic disturbances throughout the world.

5. That governments which impose taxes and laws upon their women citizens without giving them the right of consent or dissent, which is granted to men citizens, exercise a tyranny inconsistent with just government.

6. That the ballot is the only legal and permanent means of defending the rights to the "life, liberty and the pursuit of happiness" pronounced inalienable by the American Declaration of Independence, and accepted as inalienable by all civilised nations. In any representative form of government, therefore, women should be vested with all political rights and privileges of electors.

The International Woman Suffrage Conference was held in June 1904 at the Prinz Albrecht Hotel, Berlin. It was a great success and the hall was full to overflowing. Perhaps the announcement that Susan B. Anthony, who was world famous in the woman's movement, was presiding prompted a large number of women from various countries to attend. There were delegations from seven National Women Suffrage Associations, from USA, who sponsored the conference, Great Britain, Germany, the Netherlands, Norway, Sweden and Denmark. Australia was one of the original supporting countries, but was not able to send a delegate. Representatives of associations in other countries included those from Austria, Hungary, New Zealand and Switzerland. The head of the British delegation was Millicent Garrett Fawcett (1847–1929), who had worked hard as the principal leader of the constitutional movement for women's suffrage in England for over twenty years. She was the widow of Henry Fawcett, MP who had supported John Stuart Mill in his efforts for women's suffrage in 1867 and 1869.[1]

Delegates and representatives gave accounts of the progress that had been made in their countries in securing women the vote. It was agreed that it was to the everlasting credit of the British Dominions of New Zealand and Australia that in 1904 they were the only sovereign states in the world in which women voted for national parliamentary representatives equally with men.

The major achievement of the conference was the establishment on a firm basis of the International Woman Suffrage Alliance, as it was decided

Carrie Chapman Catt, first president
of the International Woman Suffrage
Alliance, 1904–1923

to call it in the constitution. The principles formulated at the Washington
Conference in 1902 were adopted, and these were to guide the Alliance
in its work. A constitution was considered and adopted. The agreed object
was "to secure the enfranchisement of the women of all nations, and to
unite the friends of women suffrage throughout the world in organised
co-operation and fraternal helpfulness". This object was reaffirmed at
many succeeding conferences. Other matters included in the Constitution
were the qualifications for membership, meetings, officers, committee and
the usual machinery for the operation of an international association. A
particularly important item was that concerning membership in Article III.

It provided that any National Woman Suffrage Association may become an auxiliary (later called affiliate) to the IWSA and be represented by six delegates at all international meetings by payment of the specified subscription. In those countries where no National Woman Suffrage Association exists, local associations of the same kind may unite in forming a National Committee of six, which may become an auxiliary to the IWSA on the same terms as a National Association. Any person can become an Honorary Associate on payment of the necessary subscription, and have the same privileges as an auxiliary except the right to vote. And these Associates can form a National Suffrage Committee if there are no suffrage organisations in their country which can send one delegate to international meetings.

Susan B. Anthony, then 84, was elected honorary president and Mrs Carrie Chapman Catt was elected president with Dr Anita Augspurg, founder of the first German Woman Suffrage Union and Millicent Fawcett as vice-presidents.

The choice of Mrs Chapman Catt as president was a wise one. She was a very able and inspiring speaker, an indefatigable worker and willing to travel almost anywhere in the world to further the work of the Alliance.

Rachael Foster Avery became secretary and Kathe Schirmacher of Germany and Johanna Naber of the Netherlands became assistant secretaries, and Miss Rodger Cuncliffe treasurer. The constitution provided for an executive board of seven.

There was tremendous enthusiasm at this Berlin meeting. One incident indicates the infectious nature of this enthusiasm. A young woman journalist from Hungary, Roska Schwimmer, who had come to report the conference for her newspaper, who so inspired that she resolved that on her return to her country she would start a National Suffrage Society and that the Society would join the Alliance. (Roska Schwimmer afterwards became Ambassador to Switzerland during Hungary's brief revolution in 1956).

Among those who attended the conferences at Berlin was Mrs Marie Corbett, who, as a member of the National Council of Women of Great Britain, was a delegate at the meeting of the International Council of Women. Being a keen suffragist she attended the preceding meeting of the International Woman Suffrage Alliance and she took her two daughters, Margery and Cicely, with her. It was a meeting that was to decide the main course of Margery Corbett's life.

As will be seen later, her life, more than that of any other, can be identified with the work of the International Alliance of Women and with the great contribution that it has made to the emancipation of women throughout the world during seventy-five years of the twentieth century. She had the longest term as president, and in 1979 is still an active participant.

She was born in London on 19th April 1882. Her father, Charles Henry Corbett, was a very active member of the Liberal party who became Member of Parliament for East Grinstead from 1906 to 1910. Margery Corbett with her younger brother (b. 1883) and sister (b. 1885) were educated at home, a country house at Danehill in the midst of lovely woodland country in Sussex. Their three principal teachers were their father, who taught them Greek, Latin, mathematics and history; their mother who taught them music, theology and the bible; and a French governess who taught them French and history, succeeded later by a German governess when German was added to the curriculum. This provided the foundation for a good knowledge of languages which was to be of immense value to Margery Corbett in her propaganda work for women throughout the world.

Very early Margery Corbett became aware that men enjoyed an independence and freedom unknown to women, who, comparatively, were kept in subjection. Although both she and her sister were treated in the family as equals with her brother, she observed that girl friends of her own age were expected to treat their brothers as superior beings to be waited on, which was not an uncommon experience in those days. Conditions in the world outside gradually dawned on Margery as being fraught with the gravest injustice, and they represented a complete contrast to the order of things in her own home, where she and her brother had been brought up and educated on the basis of equality. Such were her father's and mother's ideas and it seemed that here was a task in life: to try to establish this basis of equality in modern society and eradicate the gross injustices which women had suffered for so long. As her horizon widened she gradually became aware that what obtained in modern England was symptomatic of what existed in varying degrees throughout modern civilisation and in most countries of the world. Margery Corbett thus became keenly interested in the women's suffrage campaign. When she was eighteen she formed with her sister and some friends a society called "The Younger Suffragists", and was appointed its secretary. They conducted the meetings on the pattern of those of their elders who had learned from experience of general elections. They greatly enjoyed their discussions conducted with youthful zest, and hopefully believed that the views of the younger generation would be of interest to men and women of the world.

In 1901 Margery's brother Adrian went to New College, Oxford, and their German governess, Lina Eckenstein, prompted their parents to send Margery to a college of a university. Margery passed the examination for Newnham College, Cambridge, and entrance was secured. The early days of both Newnham and Girton Colleges, founded in 1871 and 1874, were fraught with difficulties, for they represented pioneering efforts for women's university education. When Margery took up her quarters at the College her father was horrified that she was given only a bedsitting room, whereas

Charles and Marie Corbett. Charles Corbett was Liberal MP for East Grinstead from 1906–1910 and was a staunch supporter of the franchise for women. His wife Marie attended the launching of the International Woman Suffrage Alliance at the Berlin Congress in 1904 accompanied by her two daughters, Margery and Cecily. She is seen here in riding breeches which she designed herself and in wearing them was much ahead of her time.

her brother at New College, Oxford, had two rooms. The authorities bowed before Henry Corbett's storm of protest and gave Margery the two smallest rooms in Sidgwick Hall.

She made many friends at College. She found Mrs Sidgwick, the Principal, and Mrs Stephens, Miss Fuller and Professor Verrall inspiring teachers. Among the students she was naturally drawn to girls who had, like herself, been educated at home, and she remembers the close friendship she enjoyed with Molly Adamson (later Mrs Hamilton, who became a BBC director and Labour MP for Blackburn) and Professor Shuckburgh's daughter Dorothy, who later became Librarian at the Board of Education.

Margery Corbett left college in the spring of 1904, and the first important and significant event following this was her visit to Berlin in June with her mother and sister to attend the International Women's Conferences. They made a deep impression on her and greatly strengthened her resolve to work for women's suffrage both in Great Britain and abroad wherever and whenever the opportunities occurred.

Margery remembers being surprised during this visit to Germany at the division that existed among German women in the matter of suffrage. She had known the German women as good housewives and it appeared that there was much antagonism between the suffragists and the women who thought that their sphere was the home, especially the kitchen and children. The more conventional of the German married women were inclined to despise the suffragists, especially the unmarried ones. Perhaps the antagonism was aggravated by those suffragists who spoke of the menial duties in the home as inferior to work of a professional character. Tact is not always a quality of the enthusiast.

This antagonistic attitude of some women to universal suffrage proved an obstacle with which the suffragists had to contend. It existed among certain sections of women in all countries, and was not necessarily a matter of education because it included highly educated women as well as the industrial worker. The attitude was perhaps strongest in married women who identified themselves with, or subordinated themselves to, their husbands. Although many women were known to oppose the extension of suffrage to their own sex, it is not an attitude that could logically be adopted by those who believe in the full development of the individual involving individual responsibility.

The four years from 1906 to 1910 that Charles Corbett was a Member of Parliament were stirring times politically and Britain appeared to be much alive in such matters. I was a small boy at the time, my father was an ardent Conservative, and I can remember how often politics formed the chief topic of conversation, and how often arguments became heated. It was a time when the welfare state was being formed, and insurance, education, old age pensions and parliamentary reforms were debated, often bitterly. Debates in Parliament were vigorous and of a high level with Campbell Bannerman, Asquith, Lloyd George and Winston Churchill on the Government Benches, and Arthur Balfour, Bonar Law, Edward Carson and Austen Chamberlain for the opposition. Margery Corbett often attended the debates, peering through the grille in rapt attention for hours. She joined in the social life that was generally an accompaniment of the career of a Conservative or Liberal Member of Parliament in those days. She remembers going to many of the glittering receptions held at the large mansions of the great Liberal peers and at the Foreign Office. There were constant dances, especially in the London season, which began at the beginning of May and usually terminated at the end of July, and then society dispersed to the continent or to Scotland. Margery and her brother being good dancers enjoyed the balls, which were conducted with the prevailing etiquette. Full evening dress, with the gentlemen wearing white gloves, was essential. It was the time of programme dances when young men sought to get their programmes filled with the girls of their choice, but there were frequent and inevitable disappointments. No girl ever gave more than four dances to one man, if she wished to avoid slighting comments. Man, be it observed, was the initiator and woman generally complied with his wishes.

Copenhagen Congress

From 7th to 11th of August 1906 the third congress of the International Woman Suffrage Alliance was held at Copenhagen. Delegates from woman suffrage societies in twelve countries attended, the five in addition to the seven at Berlin being Australia, Canada, Hungary, Italy and Russia. In addition France, Finland and Iceland were represented by fraternal delegates. The principal British delegate was Millicent Fawcett, the second vice-president of the Alliance; and at this conference the Women's Social and Political Union founded by Emmeline Pankhurst and her daughter Christabel in 1903, applied for membership of the Alliance. The president, Carrie Chapman Catt, was neutral, but Millicent Fawcett opposed its admission on the grounds that she did not agree with the militant methods of the WSPU, especially as she was president of the Union of Women's Suffrage Societies that believed in, and employed, constitutional and non-violent methods. As a compromise the WSPU was admitted as a fraternal delegate. Although Millicent Fawcett did not agree with the methods of the WSPU she acknowledged that they possibly contributed to the advancement of the women's cause by bringing it to the notice of a wider public. In her speech at the conference she said that "extensions of the suffrage had been obtained not only by philosophical and scientific argument, but by revolution and by breakings of palings as well", and that "the rough methods so much commented upon by the press might very probably also prove their value".

The WSPU was represented at the Conference by Mrs Montefiors who made a speech that received much applause. She said that she represented a society of which three members were now in prison for the manner in which they had demanded the vote. She reminded her audience that years before she had helped to start the first Woman Suffrage Association in Australia and she claimed "that the woman suffrage cause in England is sure of the support of the Socialists and the Independent Labour Party".[2]

Carrie Chapman Catt, the president, in her message to the Congress at Copenhagen, gave an account of the progress of the Alliance and some indication of the advance towards woman suffrage in various countries. She referred to the high place of women in mediaeval Italy and their activities in universities, and then to the religious superstition that women were responsible for sin in the world, which closed the universities in the late fourteenth century referred to in Chapter 1.

There was discussion at the Copenhagen Congress whether the Alliance should establish a newspaper which could be used as an official organ. Most of the delegates were in favour of this and thus the discussion concentrated on the form it should take, and in what language it should be printed. A committee was appointed to consider the matter and shortly after the Congress in September 1906, the monthly journal of the Alliance, *Jus Suffragii*, was started to satisfy the need of communicating the progress made towards women's suffrage in members' countries. Printed mainly in English with parts in French, it was first published in Holland and edited by Martina Kramers, who had also become second Assistant Secretary of the Alliance. It still (1979) continues as *International Women's News* after many vicissitudes, including two world wars.

At the end of 1906, a few months after the Copenhagen Congress, Margery Corbett became secretary of the National Union of Suffrage Societies, of which Millicent Fawcett was president. She was a very active secretary and travelled throughout the country extensively from Land's End to Aberdeen and from the Rhondda Valley to the Humber, addressing meetings. She also edited the official journal of the Union. Margery Corbett was soon recognised as a naturally gifted speaker and although I heard her only in her later life, I can well understand the impression that she gave. That she could speak rapidly, lucidly and with effective sequence of points, without a note, soon won my admiration. Her natural gift of fluent public speaking was fortified by great enthusiasm and conviction, while she was much assisted by good looks, agreeable manners and good taste in dress, in which she was, however, always strictly and restrainedly in the fashion. The last three attributes are valuable and disarming in front of a hostile audience. She always remembered her father's sage advice:

"Never reform your clothes if you want to reform anything else."

There was probably some confusion among audiences on the relation of suffragists and suffragettes, and it is a confusion that has existed ever since. The comparatively mild and wholly constitutional activities of the suffragists have not received the credit that is their due partly because they were overshadowed by the more violent and dramatic activities of the suffragettes, which provided much more sensational material for the press on which it so largely lives. The distinction between the aims and activities of the suffragists and the suffragettes, and the contribution to the movement made by each, is, in spite of all the writing on the subject, still rather obscure in the public mind. The question whether to employ constitutional or militant methods to achieve the aims of a movement will constantly recur, and the precedents of history will inevitably influence future action. If the evidence indicates that one method rather than another achieved the object, that is bound to affect the political actions of enthusiasts for a cause.

The term "suffrage" originally had a religious application and meant to pray. By a logical sequence of meanings it was gradually extended to the notion of giving help and support, and from that to assent or vote in support of a cause. The term "suffragist" first appears early in the nineteenth century, meaning one who advocates extension of the suffrage. After 1884, when the suffrage had been much extended, advocacy of its further extension became associated with women's suffrage. The term suffragette" was first used when militant methods began to be employed. Women suffragists who preferred constitutional methods and disapproved of militancy were very careful to call and think of themselves as suffragists and were anxious to preserve the distinction.

In any great cause there are always bound to be differences among the various supporters and campaigners and they naturally divide into several groups and this was the case in the work for women's suffrage. What occurred in Britain is indicative of similar trends or movements in other countries, with of course considerable variations according to tradition and circumstance. In Britain work for the woman's cause was more intense than in most countries. As justification for saying this I will quote a German member of the Alliance, Regine Deutsch, who wrote briefly of its history from 1904 to 1929 (see bibliography), derived in part from the president's message to the Amsterdam Congress of 1908. Regine Deutsch said that, "the storm-centre of the warfare which waged from East to West, from Lapland to Italy, from Canada to South Africa, was England, in the throes of the revolutionary suffragette movement. From 1867 onwards, when the National Union for Women's Suffrage was founded, women had fought with increasing ardour for their cause. They petitioned the House of Commons with 52,000 signatories, including women of all

Millicent Garrett Fawcett, president of
the National Union of Women Suffrage
Societies, 1897 and vice-president of
the International Woman Suffrage
Alliance from 1904.

classes, demanding the franchise, and Bills had been discussed in Parliament, but without making any headway. At this juncture, several women decided to take drastic means to win public opinion to their cause. Thus began the Suffragette Movement, which echoed throughout the world.

These women did not ask for audiences with Ministers, but rather forced them. Delicate women did not shrink from violence; they allowed themselves to be thrown into prison, went on hunger-strike to the verge of death. They suffered for their principles as no women in any other country have done, and they evinced astounding energy, constancy, and courage."

The main difference of the two principal bodies of suffragists and suffragettes in Britain, the National Union of Suffrage Societies led by Millicent Fawcett and the Woman's Social and Political Union led by Emmeline Pankhurst, was one of method rather than of aim. They both wanted suffrage for women on equal terms with men. The suffragettes were uncompromising in this aim, and the same could be said of most of the suffragists, but unfortunately there were groups, of which that led by Lady Carlisle, President of the Women's Liberal Federation was one, who were willing to settle for something less, with various forms of compromise, and this rather weakened the singleness of purpose. The suffragists contended that the militant methods sharpened opposition to the cause of women's suffrage, but at the same time some of them, like Millicent Fawcett, acknowledged that these methods brought the issue more into the open and gave it a publicity that it would otherwise not have had. Also the suffragettes who began campaigning in 1903 remarked that the suffragists had been working for half a century and where had they got? It was obvious to them that stronger measures were necessary. History demonstrates that militant methods do get results where constitutional methods either fail or take much longer. There is much to be said for the ethical theory stoutly defended by Goethe that however good the end it does not justify unlawful or unscrupulous means. On the other hand if, in the opinion of a large section of the people, there is a wide discrepancy between the law and an ethical conception of justice, then these unlawful means can more easily be justified. The danger of such a doctrine however is that it could lead to anarchy.

Among Margery Corbett's first tasks as secretary of the National Union of Suffrage Societies was the organisation of the United Conference of Women's Societies held in February 1907, just before the beginning of the parliamentary session, for it was felt to be important not to leave Members of Parliament any excuse for refusing their support for women's suffrage especially on the grounds that women's societies were not unanimous in their demands. Twenty-seven societies were represented at this conference. The main resolution passed was that in the matter of parliamentary franchise, the law should be equal for men and women and that neither sex nor marriage should be a qualification or a disqualification, and that a bill should immediately be passed to give effect to these principles. On the day following there was a public procession of nearly four thousand women, extending for about a mile from Hyde Park to Exeter Hall.

In May 1907 there was a bye-election in the Wimbledon constituency which was traditionally a safe seat for the Conservatives. Henry Chaplin, who had been president of the Local Government Board and who was an opponent of women's suffrage, was the Conservative candidate and the Liberal Party decided not to contest the seat as it was regarded as safe for the conservatives. The Committee of the National Union of Suffrage Societies however decided to run a Women's Suffrage Candidate and Bertrand Russell accepted the invitation to stand. He called himself the Women's Suffrage, Free Trade and Liberal Candidate, but he acknowledged that he was primarily the first.

Bertrand Russell's election address of 3rd May 1907, was one of the most succinct and direct ever written. The first part concerned with women's suffrage reads:

"I come before you primarily as a supporter of the proposal to

GRANT THE SUFFRAGE TO WOMEN

on the same terms as men. I consider the exclusion of women from direct political action is unjust and inexpedient. If elected, I should urge the claims of women to enfranchisement at every opportunity."

The other three main points in the address are the "Maintenance of Free Trade", "Taxation of Land Values" and "Universal Schemes of Old Age Pensions".

These advocacies show Bertrand Russell as an advanced political thinker; that they were largely prophecies of what later occurred indicates their soundness. Considering that the North East Surrey (or Wimbledon) division was a safe Conservative seat it was no small achievement for Russell to poll about four thousand votes.

Margery Corbett, as secretary of the union that sponsored Russell's candidature, worked hard in his support. As in most bye-elections in those days there were many incidents, some of them amusing. At one meeting, when Margery was on the platform with Bertrand Russell, eggs were thrown at them and rats were let loose in the hall. Margery remarked, "poor beasts—they were more frightened than the audience".

Being secretary of the National Union of Suffrage Societies and a hard-working suffragist touring the country and addressing meetings, and also, at the same time, being a very active member of the Liberal party, was not without its difficulties. Asquith, who became Prime Minister in 1908, as a resolute opponent of woman's suffrage presented a problem to many women members of the party, who, but for the attitude of their leader, would probably have campaigned for women's suffrage. The Women's Liberal Federation which was formed in 1887 was in a difficult position in the matter. Mrs Gladstone was its first president, and according to Charles Roberts in his biography of Lady Carlisle, "it was perhaps the idea that the Federation should be to the Party very much what Mrs Gladstone was to her husband".[4] Lady Carlisle who became a member in 1890 wanted to make women's suffrage an object of the Federation but Gladstone asked her to defer the question in favour of Home Rule for Ireland, but she refused. Mrs Gladstone resigned the presidency in 1892. She was succeeded by Lady Aberdeen, who in the same year resigned to go to Canada to accompany her husband who had been appointed Governor General. She was succeeded by Lady Carlisle who immediately introduced women's suffrage as an object of the Federation. This meant a split and a section seceded and formed another society—the National Women's Liberal Association.

Lady Carlisle for many years was uncompromising in her support of women's suffrage, and the Federation would not support anti-suffrage candidates. Yet later, it appears, she began to waver, and was willing to compromise probably because of the attitude of the Liberal leader, and was willing to accept equality on the basis of property qualification as obtained in Norway, which involved exclusion of the wives of householders. This would reduce the suffrage for women to less than half the number of men voters. Lady Carlisle seemed afraid of women voters being in the majority. This modification in the demand for women's suffrage met with a good deal of opposition from many members of the Women's Liberal Federation. As apparently Lady Carlisle did not wish to antagonise the party too much, she therefore presented her demands in the modified form indicated. This seems, however, to be inconsistent with her more resolute attitude to Gladstone. Margery Corbett records that at the time Lady Carlisle was reluctant to support any policy not approved by the party. In consequence Mrs Maclaren, Mrs Corbett and her daughters and a few others broke away from the Women's Liberal Federation and formed the Liberal Women's Suffrage Group which as Margery Corbett says "was a thorn in the side of the conventional party sheep".

REFERENCES

1 Henry Fawcett (1833–1884) later became Postmaster General in Gladstone's Government from 1880 until his death. At the age of 25 he became blind as the result of an accident, and nine years later he married Millicent Garrett who became a very devoted wife.
2 The Labour Party in Britain sprang from many sources, the Fabian Society (1883), the Trade Unions, the Scottish Labour Party (1889), the left wing of the Liberal Party and others. The first distinct representation in Parliament was when Keir Hardie and John Burns were elected in 1892. The former was a believer in the equality of the sexes, and was a great supporter of the woman's cause. The Labour Party has been fairly consistent in its support of equal citizenship of the sexes.

It has gradually grown in strength during the century. After the 1906 election it had 29 Members of Parliament which increased to 40 and 42 at the two 1910 elections. After the first world war it expanded substantially and after the 1922 election it had 142 Members and took the place of the Liberal Party as the main opposition to Conservatives. Possibly the more liberal attitude of the Labour Party to equality of citizenship than that of the Liberal Party as led by Gladstone and Asquith was a contributory factor in the rise of one and the downfall of the other.

3   There is some uncertainty when the term was first used. Roger Fulford mentions that the *Daily Mail* is believed to have coined the word in 1906. (*Votes for Women*, p. 139).

4   Charles Roberts: *The Radical Countess* (Carlisle 1962), p. 116.

CHAPTER THREE

1908–1910

The campaign spreads. Amsterdam and London Congresses

The steady growth of the International Woman Suffrage Alliance and the spread of its influence was demonstrated by several more countries being represented at the fourth congress at Amsterdam in June 1908. The additional countries from which delegates of Woman Suffrage Associations came were Bulgaria, Finland, South Africa and Switzerland, while fraternal delegates came from another five countries, making 21 in all. As an indication that the Alliance was beginning to receive recognition by some Governments, delegates attended from those of Australia, Norway and the United States.

In her message to the Congress the president, Carrie Chapman Catt, paid an eloquent tribute to the campaign of the suffragists and suffragettes in England. "It must be admitted", she said, "that the English campaign stands out clearly by comparison not only as the most remarkable ever conducted for woman suffrage, but as the hardest fought campaign ever waged for any reform. There have been several organisations, and these have differed widely as to methods, yet no time has been wasted in disputes over them, and the main object has never been lost sight of for a moment. The so-called suffragettes have displayed an amazing amount of energy, of persistency and executive force. Yet the older and more conservative body of workers has been no less remarkable. Human nature is so constituted that most leaders would have 'sulked in their tents', or joined the general stone-throwing at the newcomers, whose methods were declared to be 'Setting the cause backward hundreds of years'. These English leaders did nothing of the kind; instead, with a forbearance, we may all do well to imitate, they quadrupled their own activities. Every class, including ladies of the nobility, working girls, housewives, and professional women has engaged in the campaign, and not a man, women or child in England has been permitted to plead ignorance concerning the meaning of woman suffrage. Together, suffragists and suffragettes have carried their appeal into the byways and most hidden corners of the kingdom. They have employed more original methods, enlisted a larger number of women workers, and grasped the situation in a bolder fashion than has been done elsewhere. In other countries persuasion has been the chief, if not the only, weapon relied upon; in England it has been persuasion plus political methods. 'By their fruits shall ye know them.' Already these English women have made woman suffrage a political issue. No one can understand the meaning of this achievement so well as those who have borne the brunt of hard fought suffrage battles. It has been the dream of many a suffrage campaign, but no other women have made it a realisation. When the deputation of sixty Members of Parliament paid a visit to the Prime Minister a few days ago to ask his support for woman suffrage, the zenith of the world's half-century of woman suffrage campaigning was reached."

The resolutions at the Amsterdam Congress were largely concerned with the progress towards woman suffrage in various countries. Congratulations were given to the women of Finland upon their full enfranchisement in 1906 and for the election of nineteen women to Parliament in 1907; and to the women of Norway for the complete franchise in 1907 for the majority, which was a substantial advance on the limited franchise given in 1901 with the hope that the tax paying qualification for a minority will soon be removed so that there will be complete equality with men. Finland and Norway were thus the first countries in Europe to have the parliamentary franchise for women. It was also recorded that in Germany the law which forbade women to join and to form political organisations had been repealed.

The last resolution stated in clear and precise terms that "the plain duty of women at the present hour is to secure the support and co-operation of all the forces favourable to woman suffrage, without question as to their political or religious affiliations; to avoid any entanglement with outside matters; to ask for the franchise on the same terms as it is now or may be exercised by men, leaving any required extension to be decided by men and women together when both have equal voice, vote and power".

Reports of the affiliated associations of the sixteen countries were given with two from fraternal delegates, which included a report by Margery Corbett of the activities of the National Union of Women's Suffrage Societies given briefly in the previous chapter.

Margery Corbett vividly remembers this Congress partly because she took a very active part attending in the double capacity of one of the alternates to the delegates of Great Britain and as secretary of the NUWSS. In the latter capacity she made a report to the Alliance in which she recorded some of the significant events in the history of the Women's Suffrage Movement in Great Britain since the foundation in 1867 of the Central Society for Women's Suffrage under John Stuart Mill. At this conference she made many enduring friendships. One was with the president, Carrie Chapman Catt, whose political sense, oratory and charm she much admired, and whose tremendous enthusiasm for the suffrage cause was inspiring. Another was the charming lively Dutch girl, Rosa Manus, the daughter of a wealthy tobacco merchant. Although rather plump Rosa was extremely light on her feet and joined in a display of folk dancing which the young people of Amsterdam gave at the conference. Rosa proved to be a great asset to the Alliance as she seemed to inherit her father's organising ability. She became a devoted follower of the president whom she accompanied on journeys to European countries, to the Far East, to South Africa, and to South America. She not only helped in the organisation work of the Alliance, but gave great assistance to Lord Cecil's peace campaign. Later in Germany she became a marked woman and died during the second world war in a concentration camp.

Shortly after the Amsterdam conference Margery Corbett's period as secretary of the National Union of Women's Suffrage Societies terminated. A little later she was elected to both the executive of the National Union of which she had been secretary, and of the executive of the Women's Liberal Federation. She confesses to being amusedly surprised because she had been accused of being too liberal for the National Union and too suffrage for the Federation. She was convinced that there was neither inconsistency nor conflict of loyalties on her part for she conceived herself as a better Liberal for being an ardent suffragist, and a better suffragist for being an ardent Liberal.

The London Congress 1909

The fourth Congress of the International Woman Suffrage Alliance was held in London from 26th April to 2nd May in 1909, in response to Millicent Fawcett's invitation at the Amsterdam Congress. Because of the intensified activities of the suffragists and the militant activities of the suffragettes London had become the acknowledged storm centre of the woman's movement, and it is little wonder that the London Congress attracted a very large number of delegates and sympathetic visitors from all parts of the world. Both the militants and non-militants took part. Woman suffrage societies from twenty countries were represented at this Congress by delegates of affiliated societies, the countries additional to those at Amsterdam being Austria, Belgium, Bohemia and France; and fraternal delegates added two—Servia and New Zealand—to the number of countries. Two men's societies were represented by fraternal delegates: the "Men's League for Women's Suffrage of England" and the "Dutch Men's League for Woman Suffrage".

Carrie Chapman Catt's presidential address gave a picture of the progress of the work of the Alliance and of the woman's movement throughout the world in the preceding years. She was able to record that in most of the eighteen affiliated nations continued vigorous efforts and encouraging advances were being made towards woman suffrage, but she also had to admit setbacks, particularly in two countries, Russia and Finland, mingled however with hope of renewed efforts for woman's cause in these countries.

In Russia the setback was due not so much to any new resistance to the campaign for woman suffrage, but to a resurgence of state oppression. She said that, "When our Russian sisters entered our Alliance three years ago" (Union of Defenders of Women's Rights, St Petersburg, became affiliated at Copenhagen Congress 1906) "there was a temporary lull in the oppressions of the Russian Government, and movements of philanthropy, education and reform, long overdue, sprung up all over the Empire like mushrooms in a night, and the hearts of the people were filled with the hope that freedom had come at last. But the respite was brief, and directly, the old exodus to Siberia began once more; the scaffolds were again brought into requisition and hangings for minor crimes, and for no crimes, took place continually. The man, or the woman, who had spoken too loudly for that liberty, which one day the world will recognise as the inherent right of every human being, was mysteriously silenced. The police now have orders that they may open all letters going into Russia or coming out of it; the despatches are censored so that we do not know the truth; meetings in general are forbidden. The government gives out the report that peace now reigns, and the people are content. Yet, in the last three years there have been something like 3,500 sentences to death, and the majority have been condemned for offences which in other lands would be punished as misdemeanours and some, for acts which no other land would recognise as a violation of public order. Yet, even in this land, our women are working, and there are signs of progress. During this last year the women of Russia for the first time in their history called and held a great Congress. It is true the government, in the midst of its absorbing duties of regulating the households of the land, and the thoughts and opinions of the people, found time to censor the programme so thoroughly that every topic the women wished most to discuss was cut out. It is true, that they forbade the Congress to invite any foreigner to attend the meeting— if there is anything of bitterness in what I am saying, it is due to the fact that I could not go to that Congress—and further, it stipulated that if any foreigner should come without invitation, she should not be permitted to express even a little greeting to the Congress. Yet, for one whole week hundreds of women sat together in convention, and the press of St Petersburg, as well as that of the provinces, was filled with the news of that wonderful phenomenon, a woman's congress. The people were amazed at the ability, the brilliance and the intelligence manifested by the women. Just at its close, at the very last moment of the last day, a woman arose and introduced a resolution on behalf of that thing, which I suppose, is the most sensitive question in Russia, the condemnation of capital punishment. At once the great audience sprang to its feet, and with wild waving of hats and handkerchiefs, clapping of hands and shouting of voices, the resolution was unanimously adopted before it was put, and the act so amazed and startled the police who had been put in charge of the meeting, that it was all over before they knew what had happened. As soon as scattered wits could be collected the police pronounced the meeting dissolved, but the quick-witted chairman responded, 'Ah, it is unnecessary, the meeting has already been dissolved!' And so it lived out its appointed time and came to an end without the record of having been dissolved by the police.

"When these women, with their hearts and brains aflame with the spirit helpfulness and hope which they had received in St Petersburg, went home to their own provinces and asked permission to give a report of the Congress about which the press had been talking so much, the Governors in most of the provinces forbade them to do it. Every page of history teaches the lesson that whenever free thought and free speech are suppressed the fact has never failed to breed rebellion, and yet, the tyrants of the world, even those of the twentieth century, walk open-eyed along that same path to their own inevitable downfall. We give our sympathy and extend our fraternal greeting to our Russian sisters; and beg them to remember that progress never forgets a race nor a people. It is unthinkable that these conditions in Russia shall much longer withstand the onward swelling tide of human rights; and so we bid you, men and women of Russia, be of good cheer, for the day of your deliverance is surely near at hand."

These words proved to be prophetic, and they indicate some of the conditions that led to the revolution within the following decade.

The setback in Finland was due rather to the spread of Russian tyranny to that country.

Mrs Catt referred again to the work of suffragists and suffragettes in England, and implied that there were other centres where storms were gathering. In England, "There has been no lull in the storm, but there have been whirlwinds and cyclones of endeavour in many other parts of the world, and within the past six weeks a thousand women have marched to the parliament of Canada carrying a big petition; two thousand have gone to the legislature of Massachusetts; a thousand to the legislature of New York; as many more to the legislature of Illinois. In South Africa there is a great campaign, and all the way around the world there is now such vigour of endeavour that I think we can only say the storm is spreading."

Later in her address she spoke of the widespread opposition of trade unions to the employment of women in many trades and said that, "Trade

unions in a number of countries make serious and most harmful discriminations against women", which was an early indication that in addition to
securing woman suffrage there were still many battles to be fought before
anything like sex equality could be achieved.

There were twenty-one resolutions at this Congress most of which were
expressions of satisfaction at the progress made by the Alliance since its
inception, and congratulations to nine affiliated countries on the advances
made in various ways towards the goal of woman suffrage. There was certainly cause for satisfaction that the number of national societies that were
members had risen from eight in 1904 to twenty-one in 1909. Among
the resolutions was a welcome to "the formation in various countries of
men's leagues for woman suffrage, actuated by a genuine love of justice
and a purely unselfish purpose, thus for the first time bringing the force
of direct political power into the service of our movement". The final
resolution at the Amsterdam Congress concerned with concentration on
the main task of securing the franchise for women was re-affirmed. The
name and object of the Alliance remained the same but Article III concerned with membership was considerably amended.

An important addition introduced at this Congress was a bye-law which
stated that the "Alliance by mutual consent of its auxiliaries, stands
pledged to observe absolute neutrality on all questions that are strictly
national; to respect the independence of each affiliated association, and to
leave it entirely free to act on all matters within its own country".

The committee entrusted with the revision of the constitution was not
satisfied with its work, and requested the privilege of reporting further
changes in wording to the Stockholm Congress 1911. These changes were
however very minor. The constitution was still further amended in a few
details at the Budapest Congress in 1913 and an outline of the main
changes then adopted is given in the next chapter.

A motto for the Alliance was proposed and adopted: "In essentials
unity; in non-essentials liberty; in all things charity", and it was agreed to
have the motto in Latin for international purposes, instead of as Dr Anna
Shaw proposed to have it in one of the official languages (French or English). Dr Shaw was right—a living language would have been better.

Several men attended the London Congress and took part in discussions.
The two men's societies, already mentioned, each sent two fraternal dele-
gates; Mr Willy Pogary, was one of the delegates for Hungary, Mr Thomas
Haslam, was a fraternal delegate for the Irish Women's Suffrage and Local
Work Association—and Mr Charles Shaw for the English Adult Suffrage
Society. At one of the sessions Mr Herbert Jacobs, chairman of the Men's
League for Women's Suffrage announced, in the course of an address, plans
for an international league and club in London for woman suffrage,
an announcement which, as can be imagined, was greeted with much

applause.

The most spectacular event of the Congress was the procession of women engaged in various trades and professions, which took place on the evening of the third day, 29th April. It was arranged by the London Society for Women's Suffrage. The women carried emblems of their trades and marched from Eaton Square to the Albert Hall. The official report comments: "It was a wonderful inspiration to the brave bands of pioneers from other lands to see the long procession march with fluttering flags and swinging lanterns along the darkening streets, greeted now with sympathy, now with jeers. As the procession entered the Albert Hall, and trade after trade, profession after profession, filed past the platform on which were seated women of all nations, the enthusiasm reached its height. It would be impossible to give a list of the groups, but especially notable were the chain makers from Cradley Heath, who toiled for about 4s per week of sixty hours. The common remark that the movement is an amusement for rich women was once for all disproved as the factory workers and cotton operatives, in their distinctive dresses, swung into the vast arena. The group of doctors in their gorgeous robes was loudly cheered, as were the nurses and midwives who followed, while teachers of all branches of the profession closed the long line." Margery Corbett found herself near the head of the procession and when it was about to start a woman ran forward and filled her arms with arum lilies, and so decorated she marched to the Albert Hall. She remarked that as the procession moved through part of clubland some of the men who filled the windows jeered, until a contingent of army nurses in scarlet capes came by and then the men stood and saluted.

Among the speakers at this Albert Hall meeting at which Millicent Fawcett presided, were Mrs Chapman Catt, the president, Ramsay MacDonald, Mrs Philip Snowden, Miss Frances Sterling, and Dr Anna Shaw. The last mentioned, who was a minister of religion of Moyland, Pennsylvania, and who was a very active member of the Alliance, preached a sermon to men only on the previous Sunday afternoon at the Men's Meeting, Whitfields, Tottenham Court Road. It was a crowded meeting—probably some went out of curiosity. Another event of particular interest was the reception on Saturday evening at St James' Hall by the Men's League for Women's Suffrage.

Both the suffragists and the suffragettes, the constitutionalists and the militants, joined together in this conference, for their aims were precisely the same, if their methods were different. On one evening the Social and Political Union organised a meeting at the Albert Hall at which they explained militant methods. Even if most of the members of the International Woman Suffrage Alliance disapproved of unconstitutional methods they yet admired the courage and tenacity of the militants.

CHAPTER FOUR

1911–1914

*Stockholm Congress. Women in Asia. Budapest Congress.
Crescendo*

At the sixth Congress of the Alliance at Stockholm in June 1911, the number of countries represented by delegates of associations affiliated to the Alliance rose to twenty-four, the two new affiliates being from Bohemia and Servia. A considerable number of fraternal delegates attended. As each country could be represented by twelve delegates and twelve alternates, and several had that number (USA) or very nearly so, there was, with the fraternal delegates, a gathering of over 300. One unusual and very welcome event at the Congress was the presence of ten men delegates representing men's associations working for woman suffrage from France, Germany, Great Britain, Hungary, The Netherlands, Sweden and the United States.

Among the twelve British delegates was Chrystal Macmillan who went as proxy for Millicent Fawcett, the first vice-president of the Alliance, Mrs Philip Snowden and Mrs Corbett Ashby (for Margery Corbett married Arthur Brian Ashby, a solicitor, six months before the Congress in December 1910). In her presidential address Carrie Chapman Catt gave a report of the progress of woman suffrage in several countries. She began rather amusingly by referring to the debate upon the Woman Suffrage Bill in the Swedish Parliament that had taken place a few weeks previously in which a university professor said, "in a tone of eloquent finality: 'The woman suffrage movement has reached and passed its climax; the suffrage wave is now rapidly receding.' To those who heard the tone of voice and saw the manner with which he spoke, there was no room for doubt that he believed what he said. With patronising air, more droll than he could know, the gentleman added: 'We have permitted this movement to come thus far, but we shall allow it to go no further.' Thus another fly resting upon the proverbial wheel of progress has commanded it to turn no more. This man engages our attention because he is a representative of a type to be found in all our lands: wise men on the wrong side of a great question—modern Joshuas who command the sun to stand still and believe that it will obey."

Mrs Catt recalled that at the time of the first Congress at Washington in 1902 there were five countries with nationally organised movements for woman suffrage: in chronological order: The United States, Great Britain, Australia, Norway and The Netherlands, which comprised the world's organised movement. Now, in 1911 there are twenty-four auxiliary national associations and they could adopt the proud boast like that of the British Empire and say that now the sun never sets upon woman suffrage activities.

Selma Lagerlöf the famous Swedish writer, spoke at the Congress. Two years earlier she had received the Nobel prize for literature and was to become, in 1914, the first woman member of the Swedish Academy. Mrs Catt commented that Selma Lagerlöf may vote for a municipal or county councillor, but with all her genius she is not permitted to vote for a Member of Parliament.

The theme of Selma Lagerlöf's speech was home and the state. She spoke of the home as woman's contribution to civilisation, her small masterpiece from which she had not excluded men, and which stood as the safeguard of security and happiness, the shelter of compassion and love. The man-made state, on the other hand, with its crime and misery and menace of war had been made without woman's co-operation. Until man and woman join hands to build it together it would not succeed. Of some relevance to its theme was that during this visit to Sweden Margery Corbett Ashby had observed that many Swedish women were already accomplished and experienced in performing the triple duties required by home, profession and public work, and many had succeeded admirably in combining the three and living in consequence, rich and full lives. It is not so difficult to find this in many countries in 1979, but it was not common in 1911. Lt-Col Mansfeldt of The Netherlands was able to announce at this Congress the formation of an International Men's League for Women's Suffrage, with himself as secretary and Mr E. F. W. Kehrer as treasurer.

At one of the sessions the question of the relation of woman suffrage to party politics was discussed. It is a theme that has recurred often since. Margaret Hodge of Australia emphasised the advantage of a non-party attitude both before the suffrage is gained and afterwards. By taking this line all parties consider women, and it leaves women free to vote on principles rather than for party reasons. One result of this non-party attitude, she said, has been an improvement in the type of candidate, because it is recognised that women will not vote for a candidate of unsuitable character for party reasons. This advice of Margaret Hodge should be for everybody, men as well as women. It would discourage membership of a party and is closer to true democracy. Mrs Philip Snowden explained the difference of policy of the different suffrage societies in Great Britain. She explained that the WSPU (the suffragettes) worked against the candidate nominated by the government in power, but the policy of the Auxiliary to the Alliance the NUWSS (the suffragists and constitutionalists) was to support the candidate, whatever may be his party, who promises to further the cause of woman suffrage in Parliament. She said that a weakness in the campaign was that women in the political parties will not put woman suffrage before party questions. In the interest of both the woman's cause and democracy any propaganda for women should be independent of party politics. In a despotic state where there is practically only one party, which is identified with the state government, then allegiance to any political party hardly arises; but such a government is hardly consistent with the principles of democracy that the Alliance supports.

Accompanied by Dr Aletta Jacobs, president of the National Suffrage Association of The Netherlands, Mrs Chapman Catt devoted the time between Congresses to travelling in Asia to discover, as far as possible, the place of women in the progressive activities of that vast continent. This marked a great extension of the activities of the Alliance. Hitherto these had been concentrated mainly on the western world, on the countries of North America and Europe, but in this tour there was an attempt to comprehend the women of the orient.

Mrs Catt gave some of the impressions of the life of women in Asiatic countries and of the prospects of improved status in her presidential address at the Budapest Congress. "The tangible results of our trip", she said, "are that we are connected with correspondents representing the most advanced development of the woman's movement in Egypt, Palestine, India, Burmah, China, Japan, Sumatra, Java, and the Philippine and Hawaiian Islands, and also in Turkey and Persia, which we did not visit. As to the effect upon the movement in the countries visited, we shall claim little more than that we have blazed a trail which we may point out to other women willing to carry the inspiration and sympathy of our movement to the women of Asia. They, knowing the way, will be able to accomplish much more than did we. It is our earnest hope that the other women, comprehending the unity of the women's cause, will be led to carry our greetings to the women of Asia, who just now need the encouragement which Western women, emancipated from the most severe mandates of tradition, can give in practical advice to these women, who for many years must continue to struggle under conditions which obtained in our Western world some generations ago."

The impressions Mrs Catt gave of the life of women in Oriental countries and of their reactions to the life to which they were condemned did not accord with the generally accepted notions usually spread by men. "The women of the Orient", she said, "have never been the satisfied, contented sex the world has believed them. Authors, European and Oriental, have declared that the women of this or that Eastern nation were the happiest in the world. Men said so, and we believed them. It was never true. Behind the purdah in India, in the harems of Mohammedanism, behind veils and

Rosa Manus who from the early years of the IWSA to the second world war was one of the most untiring workers for the emancipation of women. She organised the Paris Congress in 1926 and was a vice-president of IAW from 1935 to her death in 1945 (see pages 150–151). A brilliant linguist she became Carrie Chapman Catt's constant companion in her world tours.

barred doors and closed sedan chairs, there has been rebellion in the hearts of women all down the centuries. There, compelled to inactivity, they have been waiting, waiting for a liberator. Like captive birds many have beaten their wings in despair against the unyielding walls of their cage; but now and then a bar gave way, a woman escaped, and whenever she did she made her protest."

Many of her other impressions are worth recalling which bear out some of the traditional erroneous notions propagated by men, who she said, "may honestly believe that women should be cloistered and veiled, silent, and subject; but when a national interest arises which needs aid, all through the ages, such men, black, brown, white, or yellow, have forgotten their reasons, and become not only willing but anxious that women should come out of the cloister, take off their veils, break their silence, and cease their servility. At such times they encourage women to plunge their nimble fingers into the nation's fire and to bring out the roasting chestnuts of the nation's liberty. These men then take the chestnuts, and send the women back to the cloisters and veils, the silence and servility. Just now Asiatic men, not a whit more selfish than Western men have been and will be, are beginning to desire a taste of those chestnuts, and all the surveillance is weakening in consequence. Women are organising, speaking, working. It is our business to encourage these women to demand their share of the chestnuts when they have been won. . . ."

Mrs Catt spoke of the influence of religion in the life of Oriental peoples which is far stronger than in the West, and this has contributed to the subjection of women, due partly to a traditional misunderstanding of religious doctrines, in which she included Christianity. "As leaders of Christianity a generation ago, under 'the higher criticism' movement, publicly repudiated the misinterpretation of the Christian Scripture concerning women, which had been accepted for centuries, and sought a loop-hole through which they might pass from under the blighting edicts of St Paul; and as the most enlightened Jewish Rabbis are now pointing to the fact that the Oriental status of women in the Jewish Scripture has no place in these modern times; so Brahminism, Buddhism, Confucianism, and Taoism, the great religions of Asia, are alike repudiating the seclusion and oppression of Eastern women as no part of their dogma. All declare that the Mohammedans alone are responsible for it. Under the banner of the Crescent, war was waged everywhere, they say, until no woman's life or virtue was secure, and they were driven to seek safety behind the walls of their homes. What had been a necessity in time became established custom, and no one asked its origin. With all these religions disclaiming responsibility for the subjected position of women, and all bestirring themselves to right past wrongs, it is left for the Mohammedans to defend themselves against the charge which all the others lay at their door. . . . A princess of Turkey has made a careful study of the Koran, and is an acknowledged scholar in Arabic. She has declared that she finds nothing which demands a secluded life for women."

Mrs Catt spoke of the influence of theosophy on modern Hinduism, and of that of the Bahais on Mohammedanism and gave her impressions of the woman's movement in China. She gave first a picture of the traditional life of millions of Chinese women. "For centuries", she said, "Chinese women have been sold at an early age into wifehood, or concubinage, to husbands they had never seen. Many such women rode in the red sedan-chair of the marriage procession to the door of the husband's house, and never again passed over the threshold until carried to their graves. Utterly illiterate, and trained to belief in the most absurd superstitions; accustomed to hear the most scathing ridicule of their sex as the opinion of the wisest philosophers and religious leaders of their land, their environment reduced them to the most abject dependence. With feet bound so that they could neither walk nor exercise, natural growth and health were impaired, and the dangers of maternity greatly increased. Among the poor, little girls were commonly sold into slavery, where they served master or mistress until the marriageable age, when they were sold again into wife-hood or prostitution, with a comfortable profit to the first owner. The murder of female infants was common, and the sad lot of the Chinese women seemed the most soul-deadening and pitiful in the world.

"Yet, for reasons difficult to understand, they bear the reputation of always having been the most spirited women in Asia. A curious custom existed there, and whenever a woman reached the point when she could endure her life no longer, public opinion permitted her to seek a quiet spot and to pour out her wrath to her heart's content. As there are not many quiet spots in China, the roof of her own home or the banks of a river were favourite resorts. We saw a few of these exhibitions of women pro-testing against the inevitable. At first we thought them insane, not un-derstanding what they said. We recognised a mighty flow of language, eloquent and indignant tones, and afterwards learned that they were merely 'freeing their minds'. There were always many men who paused to listen, and we never saw one laugh at the women. I am inclined to think that this opportunity to let off restrained and accumulated rebellion has had a tendency to preserve the spirit of the women; and that the eloquent condemnation of every hampering custom of their lives, which these in-dividual women had been pronouncing for centuries, has had a wholesome educational influence upon the men."

She then went on to give her impressions of women's gradual emergence from this traditional bondage and their movements towards obtaining the suffrage and improving their status in the numerous and varied Chinese communities. She spoke of their valuable services in the revolution of

1911–12 which won for them the recognition by many influential men of their abilities. The emancipation of women in China really started from this revolution which changed the government from a monarchy to a republic. Mrs Catt remarked that The Manchus had granted legislative assemblies to each province, and that when the revolution ended "elections for new members of these assemblies were ordered, and during the transition each province was permitted to conduct these elections according to its own rules. The revolutionists of the great Province of Kwantung decided to reserve ten seats in their assembly for women, and to permit women to elect them. Universal suffrage was temporarily established, men voting for the men members, and women for the women members. Few, if any, men or women outside the revolutionary society voted. The ten women were elected. One, a young Christian, resigned. It was our understanding that the others were Confucianists. They were women of mature years and educated. Some were teachers, and several were the wives of prominent merchants of Canton. We had the privilege of seeing these women sitting in the assembly, and of talking, by means of interpreters, with several of them. We found them dignified, self-respecting, intelligent women, with an abiding faith in the new China and the coming emancipation of Chinese women."

She mentioned, however, that no other province seems to have given women a vote in these elections, but the theoretical belief in woman suffrage was held, with however, the declaration that women were not yet ready. But she was able to express "every confidence in the permanence and the ultimate success of the woman's movement in China". It was through such efforts as those of Mrs Catt and Dr Jacobs that the activities of Chinese women were beginning to register internationally, and it is symptomatic of this that the National Chinese Woman Suffrage Association became an affiliate of the Alliance at its Budapest Congress.

Earlier in her address at this Congress in 1913 the president said that at that time apart from the Spanish American Republics there were only a very few countries in the world without organised suffrage movements, only three in Europe: Greece, Spain and Luxemburg, and only four in the rest of the world: Liberia, Turkey, Persia and Japan.

The new affiliates at the Budapest Congress, in addition to China, were Galicia, Portugal, Roumania and Servia, although of these only Galicia and Roumania sent delegates to the Congress at which twenty-four countries were represented, and a total of nearly 400 attended. Among the twelve delegates from Great Britain were Kathleen Courtney, Chrystal Macmillan, Maud Royden and Mrs H. M. Swanwick. This was the only Congress not attended by Margery Corbett Ashby, but her mother, Marie Corbett, attended as a Fraternal Delegate for the Forward Suffrage Union, and her sister, Mrs Corbett Fisher, as an alternate.

Again Mrs H. M. Swanwick gave the report of progress in Great Britain and she began by saying that "many and great have been the disappointments and delays which British suffragists have had to endure, but never before this year has a Government covered itself with disgrace by breaking, without shame or apology, the most sacred promises that were ever made to voteless women; promises made as long ago as 1908, and repeated and enlarged upon by liberal speakers during the whole of the intervening five years".[1]

At previous Congresses the resolutions were all concerned with the progress in various countries towards woman suffrage, and with congratulations for the advances made, and of the policy of the Alliance in this field. At the Budapest Congress white slave traffic was discussed and a resolution agreed. The first vice-president, Millicent Fawcett, introducing the discussion, said that till the last few decades no efforts had been made to deal with the hideous evil of the compulsory subjection of women for the pecuniary benefit of men. The first efforts synchronised with the women's movement. Mrs Catt proposed that the Alliance requests (1) that governments here represented (Australia, Norway, California, Oregon and Washington) should institute an international inquiry into the extent and causes of commercialised vice; and (2) that women's suffrage organisations in each country should ask their governments to institute national inquiries on the same lines, and that women be included in the work. She supported this with numerous powerful arguments, and poured scorn on the too easily propagated idea that such vice was a necessity and necessary for the health of men. Degrading commercial enterprises can always create arguments for their contemptible activities. All those who took part in the discussion agreed with Dr Alexander Gieswien, MP, of Hungary that something must be done to awaken people from the apathetic attitude towards this great social evil. The resolution was carried unanimously.

At this Congress the constitution was further revised. The name and object of the Alliance remained the same, but there were several new provisions for membership, one being to meet the conditions existing in Oriental countries, "where no woman suffrage organisation exists, because the status of women renders woman suffrage agitation impracticable". In such cases a committee of not less than ten persons formed to forward the woman's movement, may become auxiliary to the Alliance.

Martina Kramers of the Netherlands announced at the Congress that owing to ill health she would have to relinquish the editorship of *Jus Suffragii*. The Congress requested the new board to choose her successor. Mary Sheepshanks was appointed temporary editor and the country of publication was transferred from the Netherlands to Great Britain, at the Headquarters office, Adam Street, Adelphi, London.

By 1914 at the outbreak of war the Alliance had completed the first ten years of its activities since it was formerly constituted at Berlin in 1904, after its inception at Washington in 1902. At Berlin eight countries co-operated, and by 1914 this had grown to twenty-four from all parts of the world with the exception of Latin America. In the period the campaign for woman suffrage had greatly widened and intensified and few countries were without a national woman-suffrage society of some kind, while some had several such organisations. Yet the actual achievement was disappointing, because during the period only in two countries—Finland and Norway—did women receive the parliamentary franchise, making a total, with New Zealand and Australia, of four throughout the world. Yet it was felt that in 1914 the women of several countries were nearing success, and in some it merely needed a change of government, because the generality of people were beginning to accept it as an inevitable change and step in progress. That the war accelerated these changes as in many other things the countries of the world were soon to realise.

In Great Britain which was the storm centre of the world in the campaign for woman suffrage, especially during the later part of the period, the vacillations of Asquith did not promise an early realisation of the hopes for women's suffrage and during the first half of 1914 prospects were no brighter than they were at the time of the great International Conference of 1909. Still, the suffragists continued to work hard for their cause, while the suffragettes were becoming more violent and uncompromising.

The activities of both suffragists and suffragettes reached a crescendo in this period, partly because of the frustrations caused by the indecisions and procrastinations of the Government and Parliament during these years. It is the primary background against which must be seen all those who worked so hard for woman's suffrage at this time. Margery Corbett Ashby's very active participation may be taken as an example of the untiring efforts of the suffragists (as opposed to the suffragettes who have had much more publicity). She had all the fire and enthusiasm of youth, but was old enough to have benefited from experience. Her activities were both national and international. The former had become a world focus and an inspiration in the international field.

In this national effort Margery was principally active as a member of the executive of the National Union of Women's Suffrage Societies, the most powerful of the constitutional agitators. It was a remarkably well organised association which at this time went from strength to strength. Propagandist meetings that it arranged all over the country amounted to over fifty a night, and over 400 self-supporting societies formed the Union. It thoroughly merited in those years the tribute paid to it by Ray Strachey in *The Cause* (p. 324), still the best history of the women's movement in Great Britain up to 1930.

The account of this pre-first world war period of the Alliance should not be concluded without some reference to the women who made its success possible in these early years. The major work was done by the president, vice-presidents, and secretaries of the Alliance, and by the presidents and secretaries of National Woman Suffrage Societies. The Alliance, as previously mentioned, was very fortunate in having Carrie Chapman Catt as president, who seemed to spend all her time since the Alliance began in the campaign for woman suffrage throughout the world, visiting very many countries to awaken women to a fuller and more responsible life, and presiding at every Congress. She was ably assisted by Millicent Fawcett who was vice-president throughout this decade, and who was the leader of the suffragists in Great Britain. Dr Anita Augsberg was also a vice-president at the time of the Berlin and Copenhagen Congresses. At London, Stockholm and Budapest, Annie Furuhjelm of Finland was another vice-president, and at the last Congress at Budapest Anna Lindemann of Germany and Marquerite de Witt Schlumberger of France also became vice-presidents. The first secretary of the Alliance was Rachael Foster Avery of the United States who remained so for the first three Congresses. She was succeeded by Martina Kramers, who had previously been an assistant secretary and was the founder and first editor of the monthly journal of the Alliance, *Jus Suffragii*. All these women helped to construct the solid foundations on which the Alliance worked. That it greatly expanded its influence and activities and helped to achieve many of the aims of the women's movement during the century are due to no small measure to the thoroughness of this early work.

REFERENCE

1   Mrs Swanwick's account of the discussions in the British Parliament on Women's franchise is given in the Report of the Seventh Congress of the International Woman Suffrage Alliance at Budapest, June 1913

CHAPTER FIVE

1914–1918

Women's Organisations and the First World War

Just before the outbreak of war on 31st July 1914 the International Woman Suffrage Alliance delivered a manifesto to the Foreign Office and foreign embassies in London which was signed by Millicent Fawcett, first vice-president, and Chrystal Macmillan, recording secretary, on behalf of 26 countries and 12 million women calling upon governments "to avert the threatened unparalleled disaster" pointing out that "the fate of Europe depends on decisions which women have no power to shape", although they realise their "responsibilities as the mothers of the race". The manifesto pointed out that "in none of the countries immediately concerned in the threatened outbreak have women any direct power to control the political destinies of their countries". The text of the manifesto is given in Appendix 2. The attitude of the National Union of Women's Suffrage Societies was similarly to deplore the war. An eloquent article expressing the attitude of the National Union by Mrs Swanwick, its secretary, appeared in *Jus Suffragii* for 1st September 1914, an extract from which is also given in Appendix 2.

Since war could not be averted it was considered the duty of the NUWSS to help the country to the greatest possible extent, and it "offered its services (and with 602 societies and branches all over the country, it will be seen that those services are worth having) for the relief of suffering caused by the war". Already a month after the outbreak of hostilities a very large number of women members of these societies were working on local relief committees. Because of its efficient and democratic organisation the NUWSS and its member Societies were able to give a great deal of valuable help, in all kinds of ways, the offices, organisers, secretaries and staff together with its weekly paper the *Common Cause* were all kept going, because in this way it was felt that the organisation could best serve its country. The Women's Social and Political Union led by Emmeline Pankhurst and her daughter Christabel on the other hand closed its offices and ceased publication of its journal *The Suffragette*. The Pankhurst's statement on behalf of the WSPU approved of Great Britain's intervention in the war (its official attitude is given in Appendix 2).

The International Woman Suffrage Alliance resolved to continue its activities as far as the difficulties of a European war would permit. One means of doing this was through its monthy journal *Jus Suffragii*. Difficulties of distributing the journal in Europe inevitably occurred, but a great deal of assistance was given by Swiss members and those of the Scandinavian countries. An emergency committee of the Alliance composed of Millicent Fawcett, Carrie Chapman Catt and Chrystal Macmillan met monthly in London, and the Alliance constituted itself as an International Women's Relief Association, whose help was accepted by the American Embassy in London. It was able to do much valuable work in the early part of the war in helping refugees from Belgium and in the repatriation of large numbers of women and young children.

Both the suffragists represented by the NUWSS and the suffragettes represented by the WSPU thought of the war as an opportunity to show what women could do. The contribution they made to the war effort has been told many times[1] and many think that their magnificent work during the early years of the war was the main reason for the success of the cause of women's suffrage in 1918. It is enough here to record that women embarked on many activities several of which were absolutely strange to them. They took over men's work in a large number of occupations thus releasing men for the forces. In some cases women had to be trained for the work and there were sometimes difficulties of adjustment, but once these were overcome women showed that they could mostly do the work as well as men, in some cases not quite so well perhaps, in other cases better. There was some resistance in industry, agriculture and offices to women taking over men's jobs, especially by the trade unions. When it was found that women could do the jobs just as well as men, there was a natural fear that men might find it difficult to get back their jobs. Government assurances of reinstatement necessarily had to be given. Employers were generally much impressed with the way women acquitted themselves, it came as a surprise to many, and it converted many of the cause of women's suffrage. Ray Strachey records that a shipbuilder was heard to say publicly that he would be prepared to build the largest ironclads by women's labour alone (*The Cause*, p. 344).

At the time of the outbreak of war Margery Corbett Ashby and her husband were staying at her parents' home at Danehill as members of a gay party during that lovely weekend of August Bank Holiday. I remember the beautiful weather that the country was enjoying, as very many people inevitably did, when the alarming news came. Margery's father had been deeply disturbed by the events of the previous fortnight as he had premonitions perhaps of Germany's intentions, but he did not share these forebodings with the gay party in his house. In those days it was not uncommon to think of war as out of date and as remote as the dinosaur; it might survive as tribal conflicts or as part of colonial adventures, but surely not between civilised nations. Thus the news that Servia, Austria-Hungary, Germany, Russia and France were all in a few days at war, that Germany had invaded Belgium, the country that Britain was pledged to defend, came with the more startling suddenness. Life for most people in Europe changed overnight.

At the outbreak of war Brian Ashby immediately joined his regiment, while Margery stayed with her parents for a time, and then returned to her home at Richmond where their son was born on 1st November. Later she joined with other women doing war work first working in a hospital and then on the land at Woodgate Farm.

In 1917 discussion of women's suffrage again arose but this time without the violence of the suffragette activities. It was occasioned by the need to revise the electoral register as the annual revision had been suspended in 1914, while the movements of population resulting from the war necessitated an entirely new register which should be related in some measure to war service. The National Union of Women's Suffrage Societies revived its insistence on the inclusion of women's suffrage in any new franchise bill. A consultative committee of surviving suffrage societies was formed to ensure united action, and the affiliated societies of the NUWSS sent deputations to Members of Parliament, while Millicent Fawcett and others at headquarters interviewed Cabinet Ministers. One thing they made plain: if the new legislation that was envisaged was merely a provision for re-registration then the NUWSS could hardly advance the claim for women's suffrage in the midst of war as it would be introducing a new issue, but if the new legislation was intended to change the basis of the franchise then they were justified in advancing the claim as vigorously as possible, and the war work done by women, so widely appreciated by liberal minded men, was cited. It was obviously the intention to change the basis of the franchise on the lines of the 1913 bill so that the parliamentary vote would be based on citizenship and residence and no longer on property. In the autumn of 1916 an all-party conference was appointed presided over by the Speaker to make recommendations for a bill. It reported early in 1917. Many reforms were proposed which included suffrage for women over thirty or thirty-five. Although the proposal was a tremendous step forward there was opposition to this age limit especially as large numbers of women on war work were under thirty. After the matter was thoroughly discussed by women's organisations throughout the country the NUWSS told the Government that women's organisations welcomed and would support the bill if the age limit were thirty and not thirty-five. The second reading of the bill in the House of Commons was carried by 320 to 40, and at the Committee stage the women's suffrage clause was passed by 385 to 55. The passage in the House of Lords was not quite so triumphant but was carried by 134 to 71 with 13 abstentions. Thus victory was won at last with the Representation of the People Act, 6th February 1918.

In her book *Rapiers and Battleaxes*, Josephine Kamm asks to which of the two women, Emmeline Pankhurst, whose name is a household word, or Millicent Fawcett, whom few remember, do British women owe the vote? "Or do they, as many people maintain, simply owe it to the War?" It is a difficult question to answer but probably all three factors contributed, and it would be true to say that the thousands of workers for the cause contributed to this result. But if one had to select an indivdual who perhaps contributed as much or more than any other and who should be selected as the symbol of this achievement I would select Millicent Fawcett. Previously when I was impressed with the ability, resolution and fighting spirit of Emmeline Pankhurst, when I realised that she was the stuff of which the early Christian martyrs were made, I felt that women's suffrage in Britain was due more to her efforts than to any other single factor. But now with more knowledge and viewing the matter more dispassionately in the light of all the evidence it seems to me that the long, persistent efforts and the leadership of Millicent Fawcett was unsurpassed among individual contributions. The great organisation of the NUWSS, of which she was the leader, was kept in being during the war, and when the question of women's franchise again arose in 1916 this organisation was ready to remind the Government of the claims of women and to press for the inclusion of women's suffrage in the Representation of the People Act. Yet Emmeline Pankhurst has become the historic symbol of this achievement. A monument to her was erected in the precincts of the Houses of Parliament, and she appeared on the postage stamp at the fiftieth anniversary. As the events recede more into historic twilight I think the silhouette of Millicent Fawcett will become stronger.

After the war ended on 11th November 1918 there was just time for a general election before Christmas, and to enable women to stand for Parliament a bill was rushed through for this purpose. It was the intention of the Government to maintain the coalition for the work of reconstruction and therefore it sought the votes of the electorate with candidates pledged to support the coalition as it was felt that it was not the time to return to party politics.. This appeared to accord with the mood of the country, and therefore the prospects for the Independent Liberal Party and the Labour Party were not bright.

Margery Corbett Ashby received a telegram asking her to stand as a Liberal candidate for the Ladywood Division of Birmingham against Neville Chamberlain. She thought it an impossible request. As there was a committee meeting of the NUWSS on the day she received it she took it with

Margery Corbett Ashby was a Liberal
Candidate in the Ladywood Division,
Birmingham, at the General Election
in 1918. She is seen here answering
a question regarding soldiers' pensions. The Conservative Candidate was
Neville Chamberlain, later Prime Minister.

her and waved it at the meeting as a joke. She was rather taken aback at
the unanimous opinion of the committee that she should accept. On re-
flection she felt that however hopeless the result it was important to get
public opinion to accept women candidates. She therefore wired acceptance, and went to Birmingham to meet the Liberal Association. The prime
mover was Mr Hobman, the editor of the *Birmingham Gazette*, and Margery was adopted unanimously as the Liberal candidate. Being a Liberal
candidate under Asquith's leadership she did not, of course, receive the
Lloyd George Coupon.

The odds against her were overwhelming. In addition to not being a
coalition candidate she was fighting the election against a member of the
Chamberlain family in a Chamberlain stronghold. It is true that Neville

Chamberlain's appointment as Director of National Service in 1916, from which he resigned in the following year, owing partly to adverse criticism, had not been very successful, but that was a small factor in relation to the others mentioned. Seen in relation to the pre-war campaign for women's suffrage it may appear a little surprising that Margery accepted this candidature not only because of the small prospect of success, but because the leader of the discredited section of the liberal party, Asquith, had done more than any other man to oppose woman suffrage and he had done so in an iniquitous manner. That women over thirty now had the vote was not due to him but in spite of him.

Having helped her father on the several occasions when he was candidate at East Grinstead the technique of electioneering was familiar to Margery. In her election address she gave prominence to supporting the idea of a League of Nations, and she said that "Just as our common sense makes us agree to live together under a common rule of law and order within the nation, so I believe their common sense will teach the nations to live together in future". Among other matters to which she gave prominence was, progress with the social services, that had begun with the Liberal administration, and, in spite of the opinions of her leader, equal citizenship between men and women. She made a special point of equal pay for work of equal value with a sound minimum for all. Among the messages of support that she received was one from her uncle, Sir Julian Corbett the eminent naval historian. He said "When two hundred years ago Abbe de St Pierre after the War of the Spanish Succession produced the first complete scheme for a League of Nations, he showed it to Cardinal Fleury, the Minister of France, at the Peace Conference. The Cardinal was sympathetic but shook his head. 'Sir', said he, 'you have forgotten the preliminary conditions. You must begin by sending a troop of missionaries to turn the hearts of kings and princes.' It is no longer the hearts of kings and princes we have to turn, but the hearts of peoples, and it is to the women we look for the missionaries." In contrast to this, Margery became aware as the campaign developed of the poisonous doctrine of "squeeze the Germans and hang the Kaiser" that gradually gained impetus and moderate opinion found little support.

Many women would not vote out of loyalty to their husbands in the Forces overseas whom they thought could not vote. They did not appear to be aware that arrangements were made for their husbands to vote by post. (I was in the army in France at the time and although under 21 I had the privilege of the soldiers' vote.)

In the climate of opinion at the election and the circumstance that Margery Corbett Ashby was a Liberal Party candidate under the discredited Asquith leadership it was a little surprising that she polled as many as 1,552 votes. Of the seventeen women candidates at the election only one was successful, Countess Markievicz, who was elected as a Sinn Feiner for South Dublin, but like the other Sinn Feiners she did not take her seat. Otherwise the woman who did best was Christabel Pankhurst who was Coalition candidate for Smethwick. All the other women candidates with the exception of Mrs Lucas were either Liberal, Labour or Independent. Local committees supporting the Coalition being mostly Conservative or Unionist were reluctant to adopt women candidates. 484 Coalition candidates were elected, 57 Labour and only 26 Liberals under Asquith's leadership. This result indicates the difficult fight that Liberal women candidates had at this election.

REFERENCE

1 See principally *The Cause* by Ray Strachey (1928), *Rapiers and Battleaxes* by Josephine Kamm (1966) and *Women on the Warpath* by David Mitchell (1966).

CHAPTER SIX

1919—1922

The Peace Conference, women police, election campaigns and Congress at Geneva

Initially no representation of women and women's interests appears to have been contemplated at the Peace Conference in Paris, the plenary sessions of which began on 18th January 1919. Thus the Central Committee of the *Union Française pour le Suffrage des Femmes* decided to invite to a conference in Paris delegates of the Allied countries affiliated to the International Woman Suffrage Alliance with the purpose of obtaining consideration of the position of women in the world and of representation of women at the Peace Conference. Three delegates and three alternates were invited from each country, the three delegates from Britain being Millicent Fawcett, Mrs Oliver Strachey and Rosamund Smith. The conference was held at the Lyceum Club in Paris from 10th to 16th February. President Wilson received delegates on the evening of the first day. Millicent Fawcett was the spokesman and explained the reasons which determined the Conference of IWSA to ask for his support. President Wilson fully approved of the representation of women's interests at the Peace Conference and proposed the appointment of a Special Commission of Plenipotentiaries to inquire into and report upon those questions of interest to women which are of international importance. It should be specially advised by a commission of women to be appointed by the Inter-Allied Suffrage Conference. Clemenceau on hearing of the proposals from a delegation of the women's conference thought it would be better that women should enter directly into the Commissions of the Peace Conference and he said to the delegation, "Address a demand for this personally to me, and I promise that I will present it to the Congress".

The Supreme War Council of the Allies[1] decided in favour of the course proposed by President Wilson and on 11th March Mme Siegfried, the president of the National Council of French Women, was informed "that women's organisations could be heard by commissions occupying themselves especially with questions touching on women's interests". Millicent Fawcett could not attend the Peace Conference for this purpose, and she asked Margery Corbett Ashby to deputise for her, as the representative of the National Union of Suffrage Societies. Margery agreed but had some misgivings about being given so important a task, but her fluent French and German gave her some confidence. The first commission to receive a delegation 18th March was that on international labour legislation presided over by Samuel Gompers, the American labour leader. The women's delegation asked that all posts in or in connection with the International Labour Organisation should be equally open to women as to men, and that Germany should be invited to join. Suzanne Grinberg, who was secretary of the Inter-Allied Suffrage Conference, put these points to Samuel Gompers. When Mme de Witt Schlumberger, one of the French delegates, who wore several medals for war service, pleaded that Germany should be invited to attend the first meeting of the International Labour Organisation, Gompers said: "You, a Frenchwoman, ask this?" She replied firmly, "Disease and labour problems know no frontiers." The request was finally agreed to, but too late for the German delegates to attend the first meeting.

Among the points in the resolutions submitted by the delegation to this committee on international labour legislation were a maximum of 44 hours per six days week; a minimum wage in accordance with the cost of living, and equal pay for equal work for men and women, and prohibition of child labour below the age of 15. Margery Corbett Ashby put an additional resolution on the protection of maternity, especially rest at confinement with payment of wages.

The delegation to the Commission of the League of Nations was received three weeks later on 10th April. This commission was presided over by President Wilson who received the delegation from the Inter-Allied Suffrage Conference and the International Council of Women led by Lady Aberdeen, who made a short speech followed by Margery Corbett Ashby and other delegates, asking that the resolutions be given full and sympathetic consideration. These resolutions covered the moral, political and educational aspects of women's life. Those on the moral status of women sought:

1. "To suppress the sale of women and children."
2. "To respect and apply the principle of woman's liberty to dispose of herself in marriage."
3. "To suppress the traffic in women, girls, and children of both sexes, and its corollary, the licensed house of ill fame."

Conditions that made such petitions necessary were widespread in many countries at the time of the Peace Conference. That it was the concern of a Peace Conference was emphasised by Suzanne Grinberg who said that such a conference must recognise not only the rights of nations, but also of individual citizens.

The political resolutions were:

1. "That the principle of woman suffrage should be proclaimed by the Peace Conference and the League of Nations so that it may be applied all over the world as soon as the degree of civilisation and democratic development of each nation shall permit."
2. "That in all plebiscites to decide the nationality of a state women as well as men should be called upon to pronounce on the fate of their country."

In presenting these two petitions it was pointed out that "no-one can esteem himself authorised to speak in the name of the people so long as women are excluded from the political life of countries", and that it is "unjust that they can take no part in decisions determining a future of which they, without a share in the responsibility, must bear the consequences". It was also stated that "the status of women has ever been recognised as the criterion of freedom in states" to which could have been added Shelley's question "Can man be free if woman is a slave?"

On the subject of education it was recommended:

1. "That an international commission or a permanent international bureau of education should be provided for and included in the Peace Treaty."
2. "That women whose role is every day more active in the educational sphere should be called to sit on this commission or bureau on the same terms as men."

While thanking the Commission for granting the request of the delegation for women to take their place with men in the League of Nations, Margery Corbett Ashby asked the members of the commission when returning to their countries to "insist that your Government nominates women as members of the council, of the commissions, and of the bureau, as this right has been granted them. See, too, that women are chosen from among those whose names are recommended by women's societies in a democratic and representative way; for it may happen that a woman nominated by a government may represent more the opinion of the government than that of the women of a country." It is gratifying that in the Charter of the League of Nations the representations made by these delegations of women were apparently heeded. Article 7 (3) of the Covenant states that "all positions under or in connection with the League, including the secretariat, shall be open equally to men and women"; while Article 23 (a) is concerned "with fair and humane conditions of labour for men, women and children" and 23 (c) with "the supervision over the execution of agreements with regard to the traffic in women and children".

Women Police

In this spring of 1919 Margery Corbett Ashby visited Cologne to see Frau Lindemann, a board member of the International Woman Suffrage Alliance, so as to revive contact with the woman's movement in Germany. While there she became aware of the shocking conditions in Cologne occupied by British troops, and was very much concerned at Frau Lindemann's account of these conditions. The British troops were mostly the young conscripts, for the older men who had fought through the war had been brought home. Because of the acute inflation from which Germany was suffering these young soldiers were finding girls and champagne dirt cheap, for girls came in from the hungry countryside. One consequence was that venereal disease was rising sharply, and stringent army medical examinations were proving useless.

When Margery Corbett Ashby returned to England she interviewed a high official at the War Office. After giving an account of conditions in Cologne she said that if the War Office did nothing she would rouse all the women's organisations and the churches, and she asked the War Office to send someone out to investigate. The official replied: "Will you go?" Margery hesitated. She would have liked an experienced social worker to be sent, but she had a premonition that if she refused no-one would be sent, so she agreed to go provided that Commandant Allen, founder of the Woman Police, also went. This was agreed and they flew to Cologne. The Army Chiefs there were a little taken aback as they apparently rather expected militant extremists. Good relations were soon established.

Margery asked for an interview with the Mayor of Cologne, and was taken to the City Hall by a very smart aide-de-camp. Before entering the Mayor's room Margery turned to the aide-de-camp and thanked him and went in alone. He was rather astonished at what seemed a dismissal, but Margery knew that she would get nothing from the Mayor with an army officer present—a useful psychological appraisal of a delicate situation.

Margery found the Mayor much harassed and disturbed by the worsening relations between the city and the occupation troops and grateful for any help in securing better understanding. Both Margery and Commandant Allen worked hard to achieve this. Interviews were held with social organisations, they visited prostitutes in prison and they patrolled the streets at night. Both the Chaplain and army chiefs were worried at the staggering figures of venereal disease. An army doctor, however, told Margery that this was a medical problem and she replied "when the army and civic authorities have failed in their duties".

On returning to England they made four proposals to the War Office·

1. Women police should be sent out.
2. Propaganda, and adequate facilities should be provided for banking soldiers' savings.
3. Chaplains should give lectures to the troops.
4. Steps should be taken to meet girls arriving in Cologne unaccompanied and to send them home.

These measures were accepted and a number of women police were sent out under Miss Harburn. The army laid down that women police should deal only with the German girls, but not with the soldiers, who would resent them. The experienced women police disregarded this instruction completely and successfully, and it was observed by Miss Harburn that the soldiers and women police were soon on the best of terms. The Chaplain gave a series of addresses to the soldiers and savings arrangements were made. Relations between the city and the troops gradually improved, and VD figures dropped.

The success of the measures in Cologne resulted in a request from the German Government that British women police should train some of the German women social workers. This was done, but the German women police were not integrated into the ordinary police force as in Britain, they did not wear uniform, they had no power of arrest and were used in preventative social work among women and girls. They were, however, so successful within those limitations that some years later at the Berlin Congress (1929) the appointment of women police in all countries was strongly urged.

Geneva Congress 1920

The first post-war Congress was to have been held in Madrid in May 1920, but owing to a misunderstanding[2] it was held instead at Geneva in June 1920. Delegates from 31 countries attended including many from governments.

The Alliance was at the outset able to place on record its "gratification that since it last met in 1913 women in twenty-one countries of the world have been enfranchised making a total of twenty-five; that women sit on many legislative bodies of the world; and that the Council, Assembly, Commissions and Secretariat of the League of Nations are open equally to women as to men". Representatives of these twenty-one countries proudly told the stories of their enfranchisement.

Up to the Geneva Congress the Alliance was guided in its activities by its object adopted at the second Congress at Berlin in 1904 and by its charter drafted at Washington in 1902 and adopted at the first Congress in 1904 (See Chapter 2). At the Geneva Congress agreement was reached on a restatement of the object: "To secure the enfranchisement of the women of all nations by the promotion of woman suffrage, and such other reforms as are necessary to establish a real equality of liberties, status and opportunities between men and women." The original object adopted in 1904 was concentrated on acquiring woman suffrage, this revised object really included sex equality in practically all fields of political, social and economic life. Also a new charter of woman's rights was agreed at this Congress as follows:

Political Rights
1. That the suffrage be granted to women, and their equal status with men upon legislative and administrative bodies, both national and international, be recognised.

Personal Rights
2. That women, equally with men, should have the protection of the law against slavery such as still exists in some parts of Eastern Europe, Asia and Africa.
3. That a married woman should have the same right to retain or change her nationality as a man.

Domestic Rights
4. That on marriage a woman should have full personal and civil rights, including the right to the use and disposal of her own earnings and property, and that she should not be under the tutelage of her husband.
5. That the married mother should have the same rights over her children as the father.
6. That the children of widows, if left without provision, should have the right to maintenance by the State, such maintenance to be paid to the mother as guardian.
7. That research for the father of a child born out of wedlock should be authorised; that such a child should have the same right to maintenance and education from the father during the period of dependency as a legitimate child, and that an unmarried mother, during the period when she is incapacitated, should also have the right of being maintained by the father of her child.

Educational and Economic Rights
8. That all opportunities of education, general, professional, and technical, should be open to both sexes.
9. That women should have the same opportunity as men for training and for entering industries, professions, civil service, and all administrative and judicial functions.

10. That women should receive the same pay as men for the same work.
11. That the right to work of both married and unmarried women be recognised; that no special regulations for women's work, different from regulations for men, should be imposed contrary to the wishes of the women themselves; that laws relative to women as mothers should be so framed as not to handicap them in their economic position, and that all future labour regulations should tend towards equality of men and women.

Moral Rights
12. That a higher moral standard, equal for men and women, should be recognised; that the traffic in women should be suppressed; the regulation of vice and all laws and practices differentiating against women, or any class of women, in this matter be abolished.

Among the Congress resolutions was support for the League of Nations (4). It was recommended that a conference of women should be summoned annually by the League of Nations for the purpose of considering questions relating to the welfare and status of women. This work was considered so important that a special secretary was appointed in connection with it and because of Margery Corbett Ashby's experience of the League she was appointed to this position.

Other resolutions were concerned with (5) Prostitution and Venereal Disease, (6) the Economic Crisis, (7 & 8) the Deportation of Women and Children, and matters concerned with the operation of the Alliance. The items of the first mentioned are worth recalling. The Congress affirmed its belief that:

1. (a) A high moral standard equal for men and women should be recognised.
   (b) That laws which strike at women without touching men are in-ineffective and unjust.
   (c) That the regulation of prostitution in any form should be abolished.
   (d) That education in sexual matters should be extended.
   (e) That numerous centres for the free treatment of venereal disease should be established.

2. Since the regulation of prostitution is an important contributing cause of the continuance of this traffic in women, this Congress declares for its abolition, both nationally and internationally. It therefore urges the League of Nations to adopt the following policy:

   (a) To recommend to its constituent States the abolition of the State regulation of prostitution.

(b) To grant mandates for the administration of undeveloped countries, subject to the condition that within the mandatory territory there shall be no regulation, segregation, or official toleration
of prostitution.

Margery Corbett Ashby had the arduous task of recording secretary to
the Congress, which was to have been performed by Chrystal Macmillan,
the second vice-president, who had an eye infection and who asked Margery to do this. So from an unimportant junior delegate, that she expected
to be, Margery took a very hardworking major part in the Congress, especially as, in addition to recording, she acted as interpreter for Carrie Chapman
Catt, the president, who did not know French or German. Taking minutes
and translating speeches into two languages was heavy work, but very
inspiring.

The Congress had its difficulties, chief among them was the co-operation of representatives of hitherto enemy countries. The Belgian delegation
refused to work with the German and did not attend, and the French
would do so only on condition that the German delegation apologised
for war atrocities. Marie Stritt, a German Government delegate, said
she could not make such an apology. A peace meeting was arranged
by a Swiss delegate, Emile Gourd, at which Frau Adele Schreiber-Krieger,
a recently elected German Member of Parliament, appealed to the French
delegates. In neither country, she said, had women political influence in
declaring or conducting the war, but they and their children had suffered.
She believed that everywhere women had the deepest fellow-feeling for
their sisters in other countries and the co-operation of all women was
needed for the maintenance of peace. This declaration was accepted by the
French and friendly relations were established.

Among other British women at the Geneva Congress was Lady Astor,
the first woman Member of Parliament[3] who went as a Government delegate, Maud Royden and Miss Picton Turberville. On the Sunday of the
conference Maud Royden conducted the service in the Cathedral of St
Peter, preaching from the pulpit of Calvin, the first woman to do so. In
the afternoon Miss Picton Turberville preached at the Anglican Church.
Both sermons made a deep impression on the delegates at the Congress
and Margery recalls the thrill of listening to the two preachers in these
surroundings. A letter of appreciation from "L" in *Jus Suffragii* (July 1920)
emphasises the essential rightness of women to preach the gospel. Those
who have been fortunate enough to have heard Maud Royden preach will
not quickly forget the experience. She was always simple, direct and sane
without the unrealistic extravagances that mar so many sermons. With the
earnestness of her utterance in her clear soft voice her face acquired a
saintly beauty. Margery became very friendly with Maud Royden at this

Maud Royden standing at the door of
St Peter's Cathedral, Geneva, where
she preached to the IWSA Congress on
6th June 1920.

conference, a friendship that was to ripen when together they went to
India some years later to the All India Women's Congress in Karachi. An-
other valued friendship that started at Geneva was with Mlle Emilie
Gourd, the president of the Swiss Verband fur Frauenstimmrecht, and
Margery recalls the many visits she paid to Emilie's delightful house at
Pregny and to her flat in Geneva. Emilie Gourd belonged to a strict Cal-
vinist family, and to Margery Corbett Ashby she presented an interesting
combination of puritan ways with the most progressive views.

Two things stood out strongly in Margery's mind at the Geneva Congress: one was the large number of countries which had given votes to women in recognition of war service, while in many countries women were also Members of Parliament, showing that the tide had turned; and secondly this was the first meeting of French and German women since the war, working together in friendly collaboration.

The new board elected at this Congress consisted of Carrie Chapman Catt, the president; Marguerite de Witt Schlumberger (France), Chrystal Macmillan (Great Britain), Anna Wicksell (Sweden) and Anna Lindemann (Germany) vice-presidents, Margery Corbett Ashby (Great Britain) recording secretary, Katherine Dexter McCormick (USA) treasurer, Margherita Ancona (Italy), Eleanor Rathbone (Great Britain), Antonia Girardet-Vielle (Switzerland) and Adele Schreiber-Krieger (Germany). Among the candidates who later withdrew were Kathleen Courtney and Maud Royden.

The first meeting of the newly elected board was held from 25th November to 5th December in the same year (1920) at the Savoy Hotel in London. Among the events in connection with this board meeting was a celebration on 29th November at the Central Hall, Westminster of the American women's suffrage victory that had occurred three months earlier. Millicent Fawcett presided and the principal speaker was Carrie Chapman Catt who said that the winning of New York State to the suffrage cause was the final factor in American women's success, and she remarked that "the women's movement in Great Britain and America had travelled along on strangely parallel lines, one country shooting forward at intervals, and then the other". Among the other speakers were Marguerite de Witt Schlumberger of France, and Adele Schreiber-Krieger, MP in the German Reichstag. Lady Astor, MP, proposed a resolution "that this meeting demands that the women of the United Kingdom should be granted the vote on the same terms as men, and calls on the Government to introduce a measure to this effect in the next session". Alfred Noyes, the well known poet, supported this resolution in an effective speech.

Lady Astor gave a dinner to the board on the following day at her beautiful house (later the Arts Council) in St James's Square. For this board meeting Margery Corbett Ashby industriously continued as recording secretary. One of its immediate actions was to telegraph the Assembly of the League of Nations, then in session in Geneva, asking that a woman should be appointed to the Permanent Mandates Commission consisting of nine members. The position was made clear in an article by Margery Corbett Ashby in *Jus Suffragii* for March 1921, which is given in Appendix 3.

At the next board meeting in Geneva from 9th to 11th July 1921 it was reported that from the names of suitable women submitted for the Mandates Commission the Council of the League had nominated Anna Wicksell, of Sweden, and that all the members of the Mandates Commission had received the Geneva Congress resolutions on prostitution and venereal disease, and on regulation in the mandatory areas.

REFERENCES

1   The Supreme War Council which first met in Paris in January 1919 consisted of ten, two representatives from the United States, France, United Kingdom, Italy, and Japan. Later this was superseded by the Council of Four consisting of Clemenceau (France), Lloyd George (United Kingdom), Wilson (USA) and Orlando (Italy).

2   The misunderstanding which transferred the venue of the Congress from Madrid to Geneva arose from the IWSA being represented as working against the Catholic Church. How this misconception gained credence in ecclesiastical circles in Spain is a mystery. It was pointed out in the journal of the IWSA (March 1920) that there were many Catholics in the affiliated societies of the IWSA and that the Catholic Woman Suffrage Society in England was one of its warm supporters. An acknowledgement of the groundlessness of the allegations was asked for by the IWSA but was not as far as I am aware, received.

3   Countess Markievicz who was the first woman Parliamentary candidate to be elected did not take her seat and thus strictly did not become a Member of Parliament.

CHAPTER SEVEN

1923–1925

The Rome Congress 1923. Participation of Mussolini

In the summer of 1922 the Coalition Government under Lloyd George showed signs of breaking up owing to the revolt of the Conservative Party, with the result that a general election took place in November with a full return to party politics. Preparations had been made by the various parties for this election, and Margery Corbett Ashby was nominated as Independent Liberal candidate for the Richmond Division, a Tory stronghold. She accepted not because she thought that there was the slightest chance of being elected, but because she wanted to help to familiarise the woman parliamentary candidate in the public mind. It was unfortunate for the chances of the Liberals at this election that the party was so divided, between what were called the National Liberals under Lloyd George and the Independent Liberals under Asquith, whereas the Conservative and Labour parties had a far greater degree of unity.

This general election was a severe disappointment to women for although there were about 25 candidates the number elected was still only two: Lady Astor and Mrs Wintringham, who had been previously successful at by-elections.

GB

Rome Congress 1923

It had been decided that the next Congress of the IWSA should be held in Rome in the spring of 1923, and in preparation for this conference Margery paid a visit to Rome early in October where she met Carrie Chapman Catt. On her return she attended a board meeting in London in preparation for the Congress. She said at this meeting that after her visit to Rome she felt that a congress there might be a real turning point in the movement for Italian women's enfranchisement. She pointed out that there was a great lack of rank-and-file support in the women's movement in Italy, and she thought that nothing less than this great World Congress would bring in this support. Among the difficulties of the movement in Italy were the violent political differences and the strong religious cleavage which made it difficult for women of different faiths to work together. As it turned out the Congress received considerable sympathy and support from the new Italian Government under Mussolini.

The number of countries with societies affiliated to the Alliance had risen from 28 at the Geneva Congress in 1920 to 38 at the Rome Congress. With fraternal and government delegates the number of countries represented was 43 (See Appendix 4).

There was considerable dramatic interest in holding the Congress in Rome in May 1923 (12th–19th). Six months earlier, on 30th October, the attention of the world was focused on Mussolini's famous march on Rome and the formation of the Fascist Government. And a little before the Congress the 2,000th anniversary of the foundation of the Roman Empire (taken from the beginning of the dictatorship of Julius Caesar whom Mussolini idolised) had been celebrated. Margery and her colleagues were spectators of some of these Fascist celebrations—among them the great procession of young Fascists headed by Mussolini.

Mussolini had consented to be patron of the Congress which he opened, attended by his bodyguard, on 12th May. After referring to its principal object in his speech of welcome, Mussolini stated "that the Italian public spirit and the tendency of our policy offer no preconceived opposition to the enfranchisement of women", and that he felt authorised to declare that the Fascista Government, if nothing unforseen happens, will undertake to grant to several categories of women the right to vote, starting from the administrative vote". He believed "that by granting women the right to vote, first in municipal and next in political elections, no disastrous effects will ensue, as is predicted by some pessimists, but very probably it will have beneficial consequences, because woman will bring to the exercise of this new right her fundamental qualities of foresight, balance and wisdom". He said later in his speech "That everything which attempts to raise the moral position of women will have the cordial support of the Fascista Government."

Perhaps the most important event of this Congress was the resolution of Carrie Chapman Catt not to stand again as candidate for the presidency and the election of a successor in whom all the affiliated countries of the world could have confidence. Carrie was one of the founders of the Alliance, she worked for the idea of its formation at Washington in 1902, and was elected its first president at Berlin in 1904. Since then she had been an untiring missionary throughout the world in the cause of woman suffrage, in the Far East, in Europe, in South America. She was a great inspiration to the many member societies of the Alliance, and had made many persuasive representations to numerous governments. In the course of her long speech at the beginning of the Rome Congress, to which Mussolini listened attentively, she said that Italy, the proud equal of the great nations of the world, was now in the minority in the matter of woman suffrage and that the Congress dared "to hope that it will be your Government, most honoured, most excellent Signor Mussolini, that will lead this land of ancient renown, into the modern majority".

It was difficult for many at the Congress to think of the Alliance without the leadership of Carrie Chapman Catt, and Margery Corbett Ashby recalls that her resignation cast a deep shadow over the proceedings. Although she was still only 64 she had not enjoyed good health in recent years and with her strenuous life for the cause and her many travels it was not surprising that she felt a little tired and felt also that the reins should be passed to a younger woman. There was also the factor that she wished to devote her energies to the work of peace and disarmament, by taking an active part in the American conferences on the "Cause and Cure of War". The choice of her successor was not easy. The first vice-president was Mme Marguerite de Witt Schlumberger of France, but she was 72 and obviously too old and the second vice-president Chrystal Macmillan of Great Britain was in her late sixties. Of the other vice-presidents both Anna Lindemann of Germany and Anna Wicksell of Sweden were both as old as Carrie Chapman Catt, while in the case of the former there was some reluctance to elect a German woman as president while the latter was fully occupied as a member of the Mandate Commission of the League of Nations. The choice of the majority fell on the hard-working recording secretary, Margery Corbett Ashby who appeared to have all the qualities necessary for world president; she was comparatively young, 41, a little younger than Mrs Carrie Chapman Catt when she became president, yet old enough to have had considerable experience, for she had been with the Alliance since the beginning in 1904; she was a brilliant speaker, was fluent in three languages, English, French and German, with a working knowledge of Italian and, perhaps most important of all, she was diplomatic and got on well with people. With all these qualities it is not surprising that hers was the first name that occurred to the majority when the nominations were considered. She was nominated by France, and supported by Great Britain, Italy and other countries. When urged to accept Margery had doubts. She was married to a young barrister and had no financial resources for travel, so she telegraphed the position to her father and received the laconic reply "take it". Others had been nominated but these withdrew. It would not be correct to say that the vote for Margery was unanimous, as there was one vote cast against her by Chrystal Macmillan, who explained to Margery afterwards that she did this because she did not consider that Margery was a good enough feminist.

In the early years of the Alliance the suffrage for women throughout the world was seen as the first major step in the equality of the sexes, but when in 1920 that had been secured in many countries in the world there was still much work to be done to secure equality in education, in the law, in professions and trade. Thus when Carrie Chapman Catt asked at the Geneva Congress whether the emancipation of women was complete and whether there was other work to be done, there was a unanimous reply at the Congress that the work was not yet complete, for apart from obtaining woman suffrage in countries where it had not yet been obtained, it was necessary to promote other reforms to secure real equality of liberties, status and opportunities between men and women.

Thus as women were enfranchised in more and more countries the scope of the Alliance broadened to comprehend more fields of social and political interest. This is reflected in the increased number of resolutions on diverse subjects adopted at the Rome Congress. Subjects not strictly on the question of equality of the sexes, yet matters of much importance in the future general welfare of peoples and the survival of civilisation, such as means to preserve peace, were deemed to be within the province of Alliance activities.

To cope with the extended activities of the Alliance and to make resolutions on an increasing number of subjects based on research and knowledge, committees or commissions began to be appointed on special subjects, with terms of reference implied by their titles. The first four of this kind were set up by the Board of the Alliance between the Geneva and Rome Congresses as follows:

Equal Pay and Right to Work—Chairman: Ray Strachey, later Dr Ancona.
Equal Moral Standard—Chairman: Marguerite de Witt Schlumberger.
Nationality of Married Women—Chairman: Chrystal Macmillan.
Status of Wives and Mothers—Eleanor Rathbone.

The first three resolutions at the Rome Congress were concerned with furthering woman suffrage, international relations and the League of Nations. It was stated in the last mentioned that the League of Nations will have no real value if it does not include all the nations, and the Congress urged that it "should secure in the shortest possible time the adhesion of all those countries of the world that are not yet members". It underlined a principal weakness of the League: that some of the most powerful nations never became members.

The fourth resolution was concerned mainly with women's rights to work and equal pay for equal work, which was included in the new charter of the Alliance adopted in 1920 at Geneva. All avenues, it was contended, should be open to women and they should receive equal pay with men for the same work. In this resolution the right to work included married women. This in 1923 represented very advanced thinking, very different from traditional notions in the matter. The fourth paragraph of the

Margery Corbett Ashby, president of
the International Alliance of Women,
1923–1946.

resolution containing this provision is:

"That the right to work of all women be recognised, and no obstacle
placed in the way of married women who desire to work; that no special
regulations for women's work, different from regulations for men, should
be imposed contrary to the wishes of the women concerned; that laws
relative to women as mothers should be so framed as not to handicap them
in their economic position, and that all future labour regulations should
tend towards equality for men and women."

The fifth resolution concerned with moral questions was mainly a reiteration of the resolution on prostitution and venereal disease at the Geneva Congress, which was quoted in the last chapter. The sixth resolution on the nationality of married women was new. Its main requirement was "that a married woman should be given the same right as a man to retain or to change her nationality", that because of the different laws of different countries it is essential to deal with the question internationally, and the Congress therefore requested its auxiliaries to approach their governments to call a conference of governments throughout the world to adopt a convention embodying the principle stated. The Alliance drew up a model convention at this Congress (See Report of Ninth Congress of IWSA, pp. 79–81).

The seventh resolution was concerned with the economic status of wives, mothers and children (including illegitimate) and declared that such improvements in the laws of countries should be made to secure to the married woman a real economic security and independence. The resolution also stated that allowances for children should be paid to the mother; and that husband and wife should each have complete control of their earnings except in the care of the home and children where there should be equitable division of income. Other matters covered in this resolution were rights of widows and fatherless children and of unmarried mothers and illegitimate children.

Other resolutions that were new were concerned with slavery (8), child marriage (9) and dangerous drugs (10). The first recommended to the League of Nations that a commission of investigation should be formed to enquire into the forms of slavery and quasi-slavery including the selling of women and girls for any purpose including marriage. Child marriage was considered by the Congress to be one of the great obstacles to the physical and intellectual development of women where it exists and that the League of Nations should be asked to consider the matter of the age of consent which, in the opinion of the Congress, should be 16 preferably 18. On the matter of dangerous drugs the Congress pointed out that "the present excessive world wide use of narcotics constitutes a grave danger to the human race" and recommended to its auxiliaries to urge their national governments to limit the use of such drugs to medical and scientific purposes, and to support the League of Nations by means of international co-operation to exterminate illicit traffic in dangerous drugs. That was in 1923; in 1979 such action is still very necessary.

Five international committees were appointed at the Rome Congress, four were a continuation of those existing, but with slightly different titles, and a new committee on illegitimate children with Adele Schreiber-Krieger as chairman. Chrystal Macmillan and Eleanor Rathbone continued as chairman of their two committees, Fru Julie Arenholt became chairman of the Equal Pay Committee and Dr Paulina Luisi of the Equal Morals Committee.

At the conclusion of the Congress members marched in procession through Rome to present a petition on women's suffrage to Mussolini. They had been warned that there might be trouble, but this warning was brushed aside by Carrie Chapman Catt who was an old campaigner. She and Margery Corbett Ashby marched at the head of the procession with the latter's young son, Michael, who was then 9, between them. The Italian tricolour banner and the gold and white banner of the Alliance were carried in front, and the procession won much cheering from onlookers. Arrived at their destination the two leaders were received by Mussolini who was sitting at his desk at the far end of a huge room in what Margery described as his favourite Napoleonic posture with lowering face over folded arms. But Carrie Chapman Catt, used to meeting heads of governments, was not intimidated, and the resolution concerning woman's suffrage was presented to Mussolini. Margery remembers that Mussolini spoke good English and he promised that Italian women should have the municipal vote. A bill was quickly introduced to implement this, but it was not until 1945 after Mussolini's death and after the second world war that Italian women obtained the parliamentary vote. A witty Italian remarked to Margery after the Rome Congress: "Why do you bother to ask for equality for men and women in Italy, we already have it, neither has any rights."

The task of being president of a very active world organisation appeared a little forbidding at first to Margery Corbett Ashby but she was encouraged by the good will and help of the newly elected board. She greatly valued the asistance of Kathleen Bompas who agreed to stay on as secretary and this was the beginning of 23 years of close friendship between them. Margery records that she owed much to Kathleen Bompas's enthusiasm for the cause, her shrewd good sense and delightful sense of humour.

The election of Margery Corbett Ashby as president of the Alliance gave much satisfaction to prominent women and women's organisations in Great Britain. The Women's National Liberal Federation passed a resolution, moved by Lady Bonham Carter and seconded by Lady Simon congratulating Margery and expressing satisfaction that an English Liberal should have been chosen to occupy this high position.

In the autumn of 1923 Margery was again an Independent Liberal candidate at the general election, this time in the Richmond constituency and although unsuccessful she secured over 8,000 votes, an improvement on her previous performance. Also in the autumn election of 1924 she was a Parliamentary candidate, this time for the Watford Division. At this election the Conservatives swept all before them, securing 414 seats, and the two Liberal parties combined obtained only 39 seats, a drop from 151 in

Rome Congress of the IWSA 1923.
Opening session in the presence of
Mussolini. On the right of the speaker
is Carrie Chapman Catt.

1923, one of the greatest blows the Liberal party has received. It has never
recovered. If Margery had been a member either of the Conservative or
Labour Parties she would probably have been a Member of Parliament, but
it is doubtful whether her work could have been as valuable for women in
the twentieth century throughout the world as it was by means of the
high position she occupied. Still, history is not written with "ifs".

The first board meeting of the Alliance after the Rome Congress was
held in Paris in March 1924 in the apartment of Marguerite de Witt Schlumberger, a vice-president of the Alliance and president of the *Union Française
pour le Suffrage des Femmes* since 1912. The board discussed many important matters, among them the question of equal pay of men and women
for the same work and positions. This was introduced by Fru Arenholt,
chairman of the Equal Pay Committee, but owing to the different conditions in different countries and the widespread divergence of views it was
decided that Fru Arenholt should prepare a detailed report embracing all
aspects of the matter for a later meeting.

Not long after this board meeting the Alliance suffered a serious loss by the death of Marguerite de Witt Schlumberger in the following September. In a tribute to Marguerite published in the *International Women's News*, Carrie Chapman Catt spoke of the brilliant battle she had waged in France for women's suffrage. Her loss was all the greater because France was not very progressive in its attitude to women's suffrage; it was a little inhibited in the matter by veneration for the Code Napoleon, and energetic, influential and able women workers like Marguerite de Witt Schlumberger could ill be spared.

Visit of the president to the USA

After becoming president of the Alliance Margery Corbett Ashby realised that she should take an early opportunity of visiting the USA, the cradle of the Alliance, where Carrie Chapman Catt had gathered round her able political campaigners, and from which work and money had been forthcoming. She felt that it was imperative she should get to know personally the prominent American women workers for the suffrage. She was greatly assisted in this resolve by receiving invitations to attend the annual convention of the American Association of University Women on 9th April 1925 at Indianapolis, and the annual meeting of the League of Women Voters. There was also the task of representing the Alliance at the Quinquennial Congress of the International Council of Women in Washington. She sailed on 17th March and remembers receiving a delightful welcome on landing in New York by Dean Virginia Gildersleeve, the president of the University Women's Association. She made a tour of many universities. On one occasion she spoke at a foreign policy luncheon where the revision of history textbooks was discussed, and she became aware of "those tiresome people who prefer national glorification to accuracy". She gave lectures at Philadelphia, Pittsburg, Columbus, and vividly remembers the University of St Louis, on a spendid hill crowning with learning the incredible wealth below. Here she had her first experience of speaking in a college chapel, later addressing an argumentative yet very friendly audience at the College Club. The small daughter of her hostess was at this meeting, whose dialect Margery Corbett Ashby found difficult to understand, and at the end of Margery's address the small daughter said, "What queer talk comes out of Mrs Ashby's mouth".

From St Louis Margery returned to the Convention of University Women at Indianapolis and listened to the discussions of educational problems, from the standard of university learning to the education of the mother and the pre-school child. She felt the contrast between USA and Britain in this respect (this was 1925). The USA was then determined to give a university education to as many as possible of her sons and daughters,

Rome Congress 1923. The beginning of the procession through Rome of delegates to the Congress to present a petition for woman suffrage to Mussolini. Leading the procession are Carrie Chapman Catt and Margery Corbett Ashby.

whereas Britain had been content to give it to those whom it had hoped would afterwards lead the nation. Margery thought that the two nations could learn from each other: the USA, she reflected, lack the leaders and statesmen and Britain the high level of general education among the mass of citizens.

She then went to Chicago, and south again to the Colleges of Hood at Frederick and Goucher at Baltimore where she had interesting conversations with the students on their system of self-government. Discipline was in the hands of the girls themselves, and the faculty acted in disciplinary matters on their advice. It seemed to work well but threw great executive responsibility on the leaders, who had double work if they were keen students.

Later Margery attended the League of Women Voters Convention at Richmond among the beautiful and low-voiced people of the South, as she described them. They discussed numerous problems of citizenship, particularly how to induce men and women to vote for the percentage had been diminishing for years.

At the conference of the International Council of Women in Washington, where she represented the Alliance together with Mrs Chapman Catt and Dr Aletta Jacobs of Holland, a large number of resolutions were passed concerned with the involvement of women in the work of the League of Nations, with peace and disarmament, with equal moral standards, and traffic in women, education, the welfare of children, equal pay for equal work and several other matters some of which demonstrated alas the slow emergence of women from subjection.

Before returning home Margery talked with Alf Smith, the popular Governor of New York State, who had appointed women to many important posts. Visits to Boston and Cambridge, the places nearest in spirit perhaps to England, concluded her tour, and she returned after two months tired and exhilarated.

CHAPTER EIGHT

1926–1928

Paris Congress and Peace Study Conference

Forty-two countries were represented at the tenth Congress of the International Woman Suffrage Alliance held at the Sorbonne in Paris in the early summer of 1926. Of these, thirty-seven by delegates of national auxiliaries, five by fraternal delegates, while five auxiliaries were unable to send delegates. Associations from seven more countries became members of the Alliance at this Congress: Bermuda, Cuba, Luxembourg, Peru, Porto Rico, Turkey and the Kingdom of Serbs, Croats and Slovenes. It opened on Sunday evening, 30th May, with greetings from the French Government and the Municipality of Paris, followed by Margery Corbett Ashby's opening speech as president, and with speeches by women from various parts of the world, Asia, Africa and the two Americas, concluding with one from Lady Aberdeen, the president of the International Council of Women.

Margery Corbett Ashby's first Congress speech as president was notable, She said many things that needed to be said, and said them well, and it demonstrated very clearly why she was chosen president at Rome three years earlier. As much that she said is just as applicable in the seventies as in the twenties it is worth quoting extracts from her speech. She re-stated the objects of the Alliance and reminded her audience that, "the woman's movement exists in every country where civilisation is based on justice, peace, and liberty. Its goals are Equality, International Understanding and Peace.

"We work", she said, "to sweep away those ancient superstitions, customs and laws which hamper women's free development. This is an hourly task for all of us, so stubbornly are these superstitions rooted in daily life. Until they are gone, we do not know to what heights women may not rise.

"We work for women's education, free and equal, varied and profound, not only for the education of school and university, but for equal opportunity in technical and professional training, in travelling scholarships, and in professional posts. Without favour, but without handicap, we ask for equal access to all professions and to all branches of industry with equal pay for equal work. It is here perhaps that women are meeting most hostility today. The economic situation in all countries has been gravely affected by the war and much of the burden of unemployment falls upon the women as workers or as wives, for the theory that men can protect women is, alas, cruelly inadequate today.

"Besides let us frankly face the fact that many women who believe in social, moral and political equality do not yet see the need for industrial equality. Yet as an alliance and as individuals we must hold our faith whole and complete. For only when real equality is attained can we discover what are the true differences of function and capacity. Differences outside the obvious one of motherhood appear more and more to be differences between individuals rather than true sex distinctions.

"The demand for equal responsibilities must not wait for the granting of equal political rights or for equal education. Our civilisation is so complex that women are needed in every branch of social work for which they show admirable capacity. No woman is so busy in her home or her profession that she cannot by a better adjustment of her time spare some energy to work for her neighbours, her town, and her country. . . .

"The woman's movement seeks to deepen woman's sense of responsibility and to widen her sphere of activity from the home to the city, from the city to the nation. We do not rest there. The League of Nations permits us to complete the circle and the work beyond our own frontiers for the peace and welfare of the whole world."

Later in her speech she emphasised that it was not enough for women to secure the suffrage on terms equal with men, but that they must continue efforts to obtain equality in all spheres of economic and social life, and to eliminate all discrimination against women.

"It is hard enough," she said, "to win the vote; it is far harder to achieve a real equality of liberties, status and responsibilities. It requires good organisation and great vigilance to watch all new parliamentary legislation and remove from it discriminations against women, to educate public opinion towards the need for reform in such matters as the marriage laws, health administration, the treatment of child offenders, opportunities for training equal for boys and girls.

"As soon as women are voters the political party machines can be trusted to undertake their political education with zeal as remarkable as it is tardy. But women's organisation must show the woman voter how she in turn can educate her party in all those social reforms which add to the health and happiness of the race."

This emphasis on the broader field of women's endeavours led her earlier to suggest that because enfranchisement had been secured for women in so many countries that the name of the Alliance was antiquated and hampering in twenty-five countries, and that a title that will show the purpose of the Alliance to the free woman voter should be adopted. The title was, therefore, discussed at the Congress and was changed to The International Alliance of Women for Suffrage and Equal Citizenship, thus indicating its wider, more comprehensive aims.[1]

The position at this date, 1926, of women's suffrage throughout the world was that Australia, Austria, Burma, Czechoslovakia, Denmark, Finland, Germany, Iceland, Ireland, Luxembourg, Netherlands, New Zealand, Norway, Poland, Sweden, USSR and USA had given the parliamentary franchise to women on equal terms to men. In a few countries—Belgium, Canada, Hungary, United Kingdom and India—women had a limited franchise compared with men, while in the rest of the world, including such important countries as France, Italy, China and Japan, women had not received the parliamentary franchise. Still, it was felt at the Paris Congress that this was a matter of time, it was attended by a certain inevitability, which could not be said about all the many fields of citizenship.

Among the public meetings that were held in connection with the Congress was one on the evening of 3rd June, which was addressed by several prominent men from many countries giving their support to the women's cause and testifying to the value of women in parliament and to their more active participation in public affairs. Among the distinguished speakers was Edouard Benes who was at that time Foreign Minister of Czechoslovakia, and Pethick Lawrence. Incidentally Marie Curie attended the Paris Congress. She brought her first radium with her. Miss Tovey records that all the lights were put out and the whole assembly saw the radium glowing.

As in all large international organisations covering many subjects related to a central purpose, much of the work is done by the committees or commissions. These had met in Paris during the preliminary days of the Congress and they were responsible for the more important resolutions (2 to 8) which were subsequently adopted as follows:

1. Woman Suffrage.
2. Peace and the League of Nations.
3. Like Conditions of Work for Men and Women.
4. Equal Moral Standard and against the Traffic in Women.
5. The Unmarried Mother and her Child.
6. The Nationality of Married Women.
7. Family Endowment or Allowances.
8. Women Police.
9. Women in Diplomacy.
10. Civil Rights of Married Women.
11. Women in Prison Administration.
12. Cooperation of National Auxiliaries.

In the resolution regarding women's suffrage protest was made against the inequality of the franchise in Belgium, Canada, United Kingdom and Hungary, and it called upon the governments of these countries to remove this injustice by the immediate granting of the vote to women at the same age and on the same terms as men. Two years later, on 2nd July 1928, this was achieved in the United Kingdom, with the passing of the Representation of the People (Equal Franchise) Act. There was very little opposition.

Like conditions of work for men and women

The resolution concerned with like conditions of work for men and women amplified the resolution at the Rome Congress and took the form of a declaration of principles. Most of these principles are now (1979) widely accepted although they are by no means all fully applied. The belief was expressed "that all avenues of work should be open to women, and that the sole consideration in regard to work should be the physical and intellectual suitability of the workers".

Although the resolution on "Equal Moral Standard and Against the Traffic in Women" repeated many of the contentions of resolutions on this subject at the Congresses at Geneva and Rome, there were a few new points. One (5) was that in all questions of public morals the functions of the police and the functions of the health authorities shall be absolutely separate; that (8) "the age of consent shall be eighteen years" and that (10) biological instruction and the principle of the moral and social responsibility of every individual of either sex should be available in all systems of public instruction in every country.

The unmarried mother and her child was a new subject for a resolution which showed that a good deal of thought had been given to the matter. Some of the principal points were that "all welfare measures must tend to keep mother and child together at least during the entire physiological period of motherhood"; that "All state welfare must aim at the re-establishment of the economic independence of the mother, to try to make her self-supporting, and enable her to contribute towards the maintenance of the child. In consequence the fact of her motherhood should not deprive her of her work or employment"; every man should be made to "share the moral and economic responsibility for his illegitimate child"; and "every unmarried mother should have the right to claim the protection of the state, even before the birth of her child".

In the resolution concerned with "The Nationality of Married Women" satisfaction was recorded with the recent progress towards the legal acceptance of a woman being given the same right as a man to retain or to change her nationality. It recorded with special satisfaction that these rights with minor variations were given to married women in Russia (1918), United States (1922), Belgium (1922), Roumania, Sweden and Norway (1924) and Austria 1925), while there were encouraging signs that this would occur in France, Britain and Finland. The resolution also included a declaration on the Nationality Report of a League of Nations Committee of Experts in which the subject was discussed in many of its aspects.

The New Commission on Family Endowment was under the chairmanship of Eleanor Rathbone, and in the resolution the principle of family allowances, which had already been accepted in many European countries and in Australia, was welcomed, although there was no insistence on the precise forms that they should take. Whichever system was adopted it was stated that certain principles should be common to them all, one of which was "that the allowance is not part of the remuneration of the wage-earner, but a recognition of the value of the child to the community" and "the allowance should be paid to the mother".

The Congress was followed by a board meeting at Geneva in the September of that year, the purpose of which was partly to implement decisions taken at the Paris Congress. The resolution adopted at Paris that a permanent peace committee should be formed was implemented at the board's Geneva meeting, by establishing the "Committee for Peace and the League of Nations" with Ruth Morgan, from New York, as chairman. Another new committee was for women police with Anna Lindemann as chairman following a resolution at Paris which was designed to continue and further the recommendations discussed in Chapter 6. In connection with the peace committee an office of the Alliance was opened at Geneva for close contact with the activities of the League of Nations, the location of which was criticised as being too far away, resulting in a change in the summer of 1927 to an office only three minutes' walk from the *Salle de la Reformation*, (where meetings of the Assembly were held). This was done at the instigation of Emilie Gourd who lived at Geneva and who had maintained valuable links with the work of the League since she became a member of the board in 1923. At the board meeting in Prague in May–June 1927, a proposal of the Committee for Peace and the League of Nations to hold a study conference at Amsterdam in the autumn, on aspects of the maintenance of peace, was supported by the board with several useful recommendations.

Peace Study Conference

The study conference duly took place at Amsterdam in November 1927, attended by many members of the board and over ninety representatives of the auxiliaries of Australia, Czechoslovakia, Egypt, France, Germany, Great Britain, Holland, Hungary, Ireland, Roumania, South Africa, Spain,

Sweden, Switzerland and the United States, while most of the important women's international organisations appointed fraternal delegates. The approach to the subject was based on two main themes: (1) Economic causes; and (2) Political causes of unrest. The addresses, discussions and resolutions were grouped under these main headings.

According to Ruth Morgan, the chairman of the Peace Committee, who presided at the first session of the conference and who wrote a short report for *International Woman Suffrage News*, the delegates to the conference "were quite certain that prosperity and peace were dependent upon free trade", and she commented that this was "a strange doctrine to prosperous, protected America—but the knowledge they brought to this decision was keen and hard to dispute as far as Europe was concerned". It was questionable whether the suggested limitation to Europe was valid, because America, as subsequent events demonstrated was very much involved in the economic conditions of Europe. Carrie Chapman Catt, who took part in one of the discussions at which Margery Corbett Ashby presided, reminded the conference that there were many other continents in the world besides Europe, and it behoved those who wanted peace to look to South America and Asia before they made world plans. As subsequent events were to show one of the causes of the second world war was the economic depression of the early thirties, which was aggravated by unsatisfactory economic relations between Europe and America The determination of the conference "to know more profoundly about disarmament, security, and above all, arbitration; impressed experts who had come to explain matters".

Senor de Madariaga told the conference that Grotius, the sixteenth century Dutch lawyer, believed in two authorities only, the Bible and the Salamanca doctors, one of whom, Victorio, said "that if a citizen of any country were asked by the majority to take part in an unpopular war, such a citizen was at liberty to refuse to co-operate, and that if one individual citizen found in his heart and conscience a conviction that a war waged by his country was wrong it was his duty to refuse to fight in that war". This is a long way from the more recent nationalism typified by the saying: "My country, right or wrong."

Not all members of the Alliance were agreed about these excursions into propaganda for peace. For example, Nina Boyle, who was an energetic champion of women's interests and who had presented an International Charter of Women's Rights and Liberties to the Inter-Allied Conference in Paris in 1919 which was enthusiastically adopted, wrote an indignant letter to the *IWS News* under the title "What is the Alliance?" (January 1928), in which she saw with dismay "that our Alliance has finally struck its flag to the two most dangerous rivals and foes of feminism—peace and the social reformers" and she spoke of "the improper use of the bureau and its organisation for purposes of a peace conference, which has nothing to do with our declared principles". She spoke further of the "crudities about peace at any price". Later in her long letter she asks, "Are we feminists, or are we pacifists?" Nina Boyle obviously saw in these efforts for peace a diversion of the main activities of the Alliance and she said so in no uncompromising terms.

Margery Corbett Ashby replied to Nina Boyle in the next issue of *IWS News* and she took the opportunity of answering the question that headed Nina Boyle's letter. "The Alliance", she wrote, "is a body of women who are united for the object of securing full equality with men in every conceivable respect and over every field of interest and work; and further to direct the energies of the new woman citizen in public life." And then she made the telling point in reply to Nina Boyle that, the greatest freedom won by women is surely precisely this equal right with men to effective interest in the whole of life", and she reminded Nina Boyle of the declaration at the Paris Congress that work for peace should be undertaken, and that the special committee appointed for the work received a special donation given by a keen pacifist, which could not be diverted to any other purpose.

Nina Boyle replied in a further letter (April 1928) in which she uncompromisingly stuck to her guns. She thought, "that the women's movement has been betrayed, and that those of us who have honourably refrained from bringing our imperialism into the movement, are deeply wronged by those who will not refrain from dragging in their pacifism. And," she added, "I do not wish to belong to a pacifist organisation." With regard to Margery Corbett Ashby's point about funds being allotted for the work of a peace committee of the Alliance, she replied, "that moneys should not be accepted for objects other than the pursuit of our campaign". This was a valid point, to which the president replied, however, that money for a peace conference could not be accepted until after the national societies had signified their approval of such work.

Carrie Chapman Catt joined the controversy with a leader in the following issue, (June 1928) in which she pointed out that the Alliance consisted "of women fully enfranchised responsible citizens, whose methods can no longer be those of petition and protest but of political action; and of those women who stand where all stood fifteen years ago". In brief the Alliance consisted of the franchised and unenfranchised women and at that date they could roughly be divided almost equally into those two divisions. The enfranchised women, although helping internationally the women of countries that had not yet the vote, had yet, at the same time, progressively to go forward and in the words of Carrie Chapman Catt if they merely "expend their time on the old programme, they are condemned . . . for having failed in the administration of political duties for which a little time ago they had campaigned", and she contended therefore that the Alliance, "must take action concerning the great problems of the world, since the enfranchised women are equally responsible now with men in their respective countries for all questions".

Nina Boyle was not alone in her antagonism to this peace propaganda of the Alliance, for a long letter of support came from Helen A. Archdale, who replied, not very convincingly, to both presidents and indulged in some exaggerations. She attempted definitions and distinctions of humanism and feminism—(working for peace comes under the former) and expressed regret that, the IWSA has deserted feminism for humanism, knowing that each such extravert to humanism is rejecting feminism". Edith How Martyn had also expressed some sympathy and understanding with Nina Boyle's point of view, although holding that the Alliance was right in the course it had adopted. She was, however, critical of the Amsterdam Conference. There was she said, "a lack of genuine discussion" and "time was wasted in listening to speeches which might have been printed and circulated. There was too much timidity, the mention of population sent a shiver through the audience though the number and distribution of the world's population is an important factor in world peace", but she added, "that it was well worth while, and the results are beneficial both to feminism and world peace."

Margery Corbett Ashby expressed regret that Nina Boyle should leave the Alliance on this issue, "instead of working through it by getting her own national societies: the National Union of Societies for Equal Citizenship, the Women's Freedom League and St Joan's Social and Political Alliance to unite in bringing forward a practical resolution for Berlin in 1929" (see later).

It must be admitted that the president's attitude was rational and conciliatory, and very much in the interests of the Alliance. If one strongly disagrees with a policy of an association of which one is a member the alternatives are, if one is not to remain merely a passive member, to resign or try to influence the association in some measure to one's point of view. Nina Boyle chose the former, Margery Corbett Ashby advocated the latter. There can surely be little doubt which is the democratic course to pursue.

Nina Boyle's attitude was, of course, that the main purpose of the Alliance was to concentrate on securing equality of women with men in citizenship and all fields of social and economic life, and not be diverted to causes, however laudable, common to both men and women like peace, who should therefore have an equal say in the policies related to such major interests. In Nina Boyle's opinion, however, and others who thought with her, it was beyond the immediate object of the Alliance. Carrie Chapman Catt's point that women should take part in the political duties for which they had campaigned to do is valid, but it contained as far as the

Alliance was concerned a risk of a diffusion of activities at the expense of the main work of the Alliance. This alternative of exclusive concentration on the main objects of the Alliance, of equality of citizenship and in all fields of ecenomic, social and cultural life of men and women throughout the world on the one hand, and of participation in all the matters that concern a citizen, was to confront the Alliance very often in the course of its activities, and it is not easy to determine the best course. Nina Boyle and her supporters would obviously advocate the former, while Margery Corbett Ashby and Carrie Chapman Catt and their supporters, who were the large majority, would support the latter. There is this important aspect of the matter in their favour; by engaging in activities beyond the immediate objects of the Alliance women can demonstrate their abilities, as they certainly did in the peace study conference, and in this by showing their capabilities demonstrate to men their right to full citizenship. Still, too great diffusion of activities could, with limited resources, have the undesirable effect of restricting the work on the main task of sex equality.

REFERENCE

1 The changed name formed part of the revised constitution and appears for the first time in the report of the Tenth Congress 1926. A curious circumstance is that *International Woman Suffrage Alliance News* continued to be used as the title of the journal until the early thirties. It was then changed to *The International Women's News* with the sub-title of "The Monthly Organ of The International Woman Suffrage Alliance" and this continued up to the second world war in the summer of 1939. As the result of an agreement reached at the meeting of the International Committee at Geneva in October 1945 a further change was made at the Interlaken Congress in 1946 to "International Alliance of Women – Equal Rights – Equal Responsibilities", a title which has remained (1976).

CHAPTER NINE

1929

The Jubilee Congress, Berlin

In April 1928 at the beautifully situated Sussex home of Mrs Marie Corbett, the president's mother, a board meeting was held to discuss mainly the arrangement for the next Congress in 1929, which would be the jubilee year of the Alliance. It was logically decided to hold this in Berlin which was the scene of the first Congress in 1904.

Shortly after this board meeting Margery Corbett Ashby and Mme Malaterre-Sellier, a vice-president of the Alliance, visited Greece, Bulgaria and Yugoslavia. These periodic visits by the president and other members of the board to the members of affiliates and leaders of women's movements in various countries of the world, were valuable in providing continual mutual stimulus, and the international leaders were able to learn at first hand the special difficulties for women in each country. For example it was observed by Margery Corbett Ashby that in a country like Yugoslavia that political differences are greatly complicated by provincial differences of tradition, custom and religion. The international body to which these conditions and difficulties are reported can sometimes offer suggestions and solutions of problems beyond the scope and experience of national bodies, especially of small and politically inexperienced countries.

In November 1928 a board meeting was held in Berlin mainly in preparation for the Congress in the following June. Immediately following this a further meeting of the peace committee was held in Dresden, and the president and members of the board who attended moved hurriedly from Berlin to Dresden. The president recorded that they "completed the last item on a full board agenda and packed hurriedly for the evening train to Dresden where our energetic leaders Frau Krantz and Frau Ulich Beil held a committee meeting with us until midnight" and she added, "Delegates take notice and don't imagine that a Congress prepared with such energy will be a rest cure or a sight-seeing expedition. Take your rest cure before you start".

The Berlin Jubilee Congress that took place from 17th to 24th June 1929 was one of the most successful ever held by the Alliance. This was in part due to its being held in the Germany of the very democratic Weimer Republic. It was also the first time a Congress had been held in a country where women enjoyed the franchise on equal terms with men, and where there were a fair number of women members of the Federal Parliament as many as 35 having seats in the Reichstag. Also it was the first large international conference to be held in Berlin since the war, and this would account in some measure for the enthusiasm for it gave the German people the feeling that they were being brought back to international discussions.

The Congress was held in the large Staatliche Gestsale. A speech of welcome was given by Carl Severing the Reichminster for Home Affairs. There were 336 delegates of affiliates from 42 countries, and a considerable number of alternates, fraternal delegates, observers and invited representatives of various women's organisations throughout the world, while the public attended in large numbers at the public meetings. Although the Staaliche Gestsale held 4,000 people many could not gain admission to the opening meeting, while at the peace meeting on 21st June, at which Ruth Morgan presided, in addition to the 4,000 people hundreds more listened in adjacent halls to broadcasts of the proceedings.

In her presidential address Margery Corbett Ashby dealt partly with the theme that civilisation to be fully mature must provide opportunities for all, women as well as men, to develop their full potentialities, but women especially had been prevented in the recent past from doing this. "Women can only give of their best", she said, "when they are spiritually and economically free"; and later: "The problems of life are infinitely complicated by our conquest of space and time. We must have every ounce of ability developed in each man and woman if countries are to survive. We dare no longer waste capacity and leadership by depriving any man or woman of the self-reliance and self-discipline bred by freedom and responsibility."

At this Congress eighteen resolutions were adopted beginning with a re-statement of policy. As this re-statement contains five paragraphs really summarising the main points of five of the principal subsequent resolutions it can usefully be given in full:

"1. *Woman Suffrage.*

The Congress instructs the board of the Alliance to inform all unenfranchised self-governing States of the fact that women are now enfranchised on equal terms with men in 25 nations with unquestioned advantage to the men, the women and the nations concerned, and to urge the enfranchisement of women in these states in order that 'government by the people' may everywhere include all the people.

Berlin Congress 1929. A parade of
young women members of IAW affili-
ates·holding the flags of their countries.

"2. *Peace and the League of Nations.*

The Congress declares that it is the duty of the women of all nations
to work for friendly international relations, to demand the substitution
of judicial methods for those of force, and to promote the conception of
human solidarity as superior to racial or national solidarity; that the
entrance of women into political life is necessary to promote the cause
of peace; that this peace should be based on a League of Nations, which,
leaving each nation its autonomy and its liberty of action, establishes a
lasting harmony between peoples.

"3. *Economic Rights.*

The Congress, realising that economic necessities and the desire and
right of women to work and to secure for themselves the means of life,
has made them important and irreplacable factors in production, demands:
That all avenues of work should be open to women and that education for
professions and trades should be available for women on the same terms

as for men; that all professions and posts in the public service should be open to men and women, with equal opportunities for advancement; that women should receive the same pay as men for the same work; that the right to work of all women be recognised and no obstacles placed in the way of married women who desire to work.

"4. *Moral Rights.*
(*a*) The Congress declares:
That the same high moral standard, based on respect for human personality and inspired by responsibility towards the race, should be recognised both for men and women, and that the laws and their administration should be based on this principle:
The Congress therefore demands that traffic in women should be suppressed and that regulation of prostitution and all measure of exception taken against women in general, or against any group of women, should be abolished.
(*b*) In view of the declaration of principles voted by the Congress and considering that traffic in women and procuration in general are the consequence of a double moral standard between the sexes, the Congress appeals to women throughout the world to base all their work on these principles.

"5. *Legal Rights*
The Congress demands that the married woman should have the same right to retain or change her nationality as a man has; that on marriage a woman should have full personal and civil rights, including the right to the use and disposal of her property; that she should not be under the tutelage of her husband and.should have the same rights over her children as the father."

The fifth is, of course, the subject of very full resolutions on the nationality of married women given at the Rome and Paris Congresses.
In the tenth resolution on equal status for women under the law, the second clause was concerned with giving to the mother equal rights with regard to children, and in the case of divorce or separation the interest of the child should determine the guardianship.
The fifteenth resolution stated that the age of marriage in all countries should be not less than 18 for boys and 16 for girls, and that affiliated Societies urge this point of view upon their respective countries, and that the mandates committee of the League of Nations should give due consideration to this recommendation in the case of mandated countries.
At this Congress some direction was given to the board on the constitution of the international committees that do so much of the fundamental work of the Alliance between Congresses, and who prepare the principal

resolutions. The board was empowered to set up international committees, but the necessity of limiting the field of work to subjects directly related to the objects of the Alliance was emphasised. The Congress thought that the chairman of each committee should have expert knowledge of the committee's subject; that one national representative of each affiliated country, should be chosen to serve on the committee for her expert knowledge of the subject, who is at the same time in agreement with the policy of the Alliance; and that where a subject is so technical that it forms the basis of professional women's organisations, a member of such organisation should be invited to serve on the committee as an additional expert. It will be seen, therefore, that with affiliates from forty countries, each supplying an expert on the subject of a committee, a very wide collection of information was possible providing many diverse aspects of a question. Several committees were able to produce large and comprehensive reports on their subjects, although their organisation was often a little difficult.

In this Jubilee year of the IAW what turned out to be a very successful enterprise for women in Great Britain—the Townswomen's Guilds were founded. (See Note 2 at end of Chapter 18).

CHAPTER TEN

1930–1935

Women's efforts for peace and disarmament

Probably the main activities of women's political, social and economic organisations throughout the world in the early thirties were directed to the maintenance of peace and to disarmament. These organisations, both national and international, combined, on a scale never previously known, to influence governments and peoples towards policies of disarmament.

Conditions in the early thirties prompted such endeavours. There was a vague and growing apprehensiveness of another world war, which the international efforts towards peace and disarmament had done little to assuage, and it is not surprising that so many women and women's organisations felt that their essential aim at that time should be to dedicate all their endeavours to maintain peace by every possible means. It was not an easy aim, because the dissatisfactions of many countries with the peace treaties following the first world war, the failure to conform to agreements between nations, and the world economic depression causing widespread unemployment, hardship and discontent, were hardly conditions conducive to success. The difficult conditions hardened the efforts

In spite of several international pacts for peace,[1] there was no general confidence that enough had been done to avert war. It was widely agreed that the first practical essential was to secure international agreement on disarmament. Although this was advocated by almost every country, each country naturally considered that this must be conditioned by its own security. Here was a difficulty for opinions differ on the necessary security for each country. Yet every nation felt that a real effort must be made and thus a world disarmament conference was arranged by the League of Nations in 1931 to commence in February 1932. This prompted great activity among women's organisations to prepare a peace and disarmament campaign in preparation for this conference.

In Chapter 8 mention was made of the study conference on the maintenance of peace at Amsterdam in November 1927, organised by the Committee for Peace, of the International Woman Suffrage Alliance, and the League of Nations which studied the economic and political causes of unrest. It will be remembered that this caused a little dissension in the ranks of the Alliance, on the grounds that the Alliance should not be diverted from its main purpose of securing equality of the sexes by engaging in peace propaganda. This provoked the response both of the president, Margery Corbett Ashby, and Carrie Chapman Catt, that it was an additional purpose of the Alliance to engage, and to encourage women to engage, as effectively as possible, in all the activities of life and particularly in the great problems of the time of paramount interest to mankind. That peace and disarmament were among the chief concerns of mankind in the early thirties, was sufficient justification for all women's organisations to participate as fully as possible in the furtherance of such activities. By standing aside and doing nothing the Alliance would have merited the severest criticism.

In view of the impending disarmament conference the peace committee of the IWSA organised a further conference in May 1931, this time at Belgrade not very far from the scene of the incidents that allegedly led to the first world war. The conference was organised on a world-wide scale and delegates from a large number of countries addressed meetings and took part in the discussions, including those from USA, France, Italy, Germany, and representatives of other international women's organisations.[2] Several men were present including Commander Adams who represented the League of Nations, and Admiral Drury Lowe from Great Britain. Ruth Morgan, (USA) chairman of the peace committee presided, and Margery Corbett Ashby, President, took an active part. Following the speeches of welcome by Mlle Stebi, president of Zenski Pokret (the Yugoslav alliance for women's rights) and Dr Stojadinovic, Deputy Mayor of Belgrade. Ruth Morgan made the opening speech, in which she defined the aims of the conference as disarmament, economic conditions, and co-operation among the women of the world. She reminded the conference that governments had taken solemn pledges in the Treaty of Versailles, the Covenant of the League of Nations, and the Briand-Kellogg Pact.

Commander Adams on behalf of the Secretariat of the League of Nations gave an outline of the work of the commission, appointed by the League in 1925, to make a preparatory study with a view to a conference for the reduction and limitation of armaments, a commission which included representatives of non-member states, USA and USSR. The commission had several meetings. A notable decision at the fifth session was that the Soviet plan for complete and universal disarmament was rejected. At the sixth session the German delegate dissociated himself from the work. These two items were not a good augury for future work. The aim of the commission was to produce a draft convention as a framework for the disarmament conference.

Some telling points were made at the Belgrade Conference by two delegates from Great Britain, Mrs Innes and Admiral Lowe. The former said eloquently, "We must not forget that by delaying disarmament we are fostering, in the nations forcibly disarmed by the treaties at the end of the War, a sense of injustice, in the removal of which our national honour is involved. The plans for reduction of armaments envisaged in the Covenant of the League of Nations were to be subject to revision at least every ten years. Eleven years have passed and the plans are just made in outline. How that outline is to be filled in will be settled at the disarmament conference which is to meet in February 1932. The disarmament conference offers an opportunity such as has never before been open to the human race in all its troubled history. We of this generation have an opportunity to make a decisive step forward in the abolition of the age-long curse of war. Will that opportunity be taken?"

Admiral Lowe who had spent 35 years in the Royal Navy had left in 1921 and devoted the ten years to work for peace and to prevent another war. He referred to the futility, waste and devastation of war and said that the purpose of the disarmament conference should be, "to secure a general reduction in armaments by all the armed nations and not an increase in the armaments of the nations disarmed by the Treaty of Versailles. The promise made then to Germany that the reduction in armaments would be general must be kept."

Admiral Lowe also referred to the resolution to be proposed at the forthcoming Congress at Budapest of the International Federation of League of Nations Societies: "That it is indispensable for the League of Nations officially to recognise the principle of equality in regard to disarmament as between the defeated and the victorious powers, and that the disarmament conference in 1932 should begin to make this equality a reality."

The Belgrade Conference passed three resolutions: on disarmament, on international economic co-operation and on participation of women at the forthcoming disarmament conference. In the first resolution it was stated that, "The Treaty of Versailles disarmed some nations as the first stage of universal disarmament. The Covenant of the League of Nations solemnly promised disarmament and the Briand-Kellogg Treaty denounced war. The failure to realise a large reduction in armaments would be a violation of treaties and might lead to new catastrophies. If, on the other hand, the Governments, represented at the conference of 1932, secure a genuine beginning in armament reduction the guarantees of peace will be greatly strengthened. And the governments will do so if the peoples, of which women form a large part, oblige them to do so."

The second resolution stated that, "the economic world-crisis demonstrates the failure of the old methods of commercial and financial rivalry, supports with all its force the efforts made by the League of Nations to secure a system of international co-operation. It demands that the decisions of the economic conferences shall be put into practice, and especially asks its affiliated societies in Europe to intensify their efforts to this end, since it is certain that a Europe economically unorganised is a menace to world peace."

The third resolution declared, "that women should form part of the official delegations to the disarmament conference in February 1932, and calls upon women in all countries to urge upon Governments the necessity for this participation".

Shortly after this Belgrade Conference eleven (later increased to fifteen) women's international organisations united to form a disarmament committee with headquarters at Geneva. Mary Dingman was the president and Rosa Manus, the secretary. At its first meeting the committee passed a resolution giving its wholehearted support for the disarmament conference and to help in organising the vast and growing public opinion in its favour and to stimulate awareness of the world-wide cry for disarmament and security. The committee arranged for a council of the ablest women from all countries to sit through all the meetings of the disarmament conference, and organised a world wide petition. It worked in a spirit of optimism and hoped for a measure of participation by women especially as the Assembly of the League of Nations had asked the Council "to examine the possibility of increasing the collaboration of women with the work of the League".

The Disarmament Conference began on 2nd February 1932, and most countries of the world were represented, but the main discussions were between the principal powers, USSR, USA, United Kingdom, France, Germany and Italy. The British delegates were Ramsay MacDonald, the Prime Minister, Sir John Simon, the Foreign Secretary, J. H. Thomas, Dominions Secretary, Lord Hailsham, Secretary for War, Lord Londonderry, Secretary for Air and Sir Bolton Eyres-Monsell, First Lord of the Admiralty, with Margery Corbett Ashby as substitute delegate. The choice of the last mentioned was partly in response to the representations of women's organisations and partly the attitude of the League of Nations to encourage the participation of women. Margery Corbett Ashby received congratulations from many women's organisations and prominent persons on her appointment. Other women delegates at the Disarmament Conference were Dr Emma Woolley for USA, Winnifred Kydd for Canada, Dr Paulina Luisi for Uruguay and Mme Szelaqowska for Poland.

On 6th February, four days after the commencement of the conference, the international committee of the world women's organisations presented the petitions, with over eight million signatures, to the conference. It is worth quoting Adele Schreiber's vivid report of this event given in *The International Women's News* for March 1932.

"On the morning of February 6th women from all parts of the world met at the Palais Eynard and from there marched off to the Batiment Electoral, where the plenary sessions of the conference take place. In front were the five acting officers of the international committee, Mary Dingman, Mrs Dreyfus-Barney, Kathleen Courtney, Rosa Manus and Mme Guthrie-d'Arcis, followed by the 15 representatives of the organisations represented in the international committee, all wearing white ribbons across their shoulders which showed in golden letters the names of the organisations, and all wearing a white armlet with the golden word "Pax". Then came the long procession of the representatives of 56 countries, 4 for each being allowed, so that more than 200 women with their white and golden ribbons marched up to the conference. The president of the international committee, Mary Dingman, of the World's Young Women's Christian Association, went up to the speakers' chair and delivered a profound, deeply felt address, a warm appeal to the delegates of all nations to realise their duty and their responsibilities. After this impressive speech, Kathleen Courtney and Rosa Manus read the names of the countries represented and the number of signatures they brought. Woman after woman marched up depositing before the platform her package of petitions. They piled up higher and higher, making a thrilling sight and, as Dingman had pointed out in her speech, this was not mere paper, but "behind each of these names stands a living personality, a human being, oppressed by a great fear, the fear of the destruction of our civilisation, but also moved by a great will for peace, that cannot be ignored and must not be denied.

"We women had opened the procession, but afterwards came the representatives of other world-wide organisations, craving for peace: Mr Mueller spoke for the churches, for those who in all creeds want to abolish war, understanding that it is opposed to the gospel. The 45 millions of women embodied in the organisations which Dingman represented were re-enforced by another 25 millions of Catholic women, for whose will to peace Mme Van Steenberghe-Engeringh was the speaker. A young Frenchman and a young American, delegates of the international students' organisations, moved all hearts by expressing their abhorrence of war, the horror they had of being compelled to kill their brethren, to kill women and children, to extinguish civilisation. Lord Cecil was spokesman of the International Federation of League of Nations Societies.

"The Belgian Minister Vandervelde spoke for the millions of workmen organised in all countries in the Second International for the toilers and the millions of unemployed, and declared: 'We have not come here to beg and to beseech. We have come to formulate claims. The people are sick of waiting, they demand not words, but acts'. The last speaker, the Frenchman, Jouhaux, represented the international trade unions, one of the great forces which can oppose war.

Mrs Bessie Rischbeith, OBE, one time
president of the League of Women
Voters of Western Australia and a
staunch supporter of the International
Alliance of Women serving on the
board during the thirties and later
becoming an honorary vice-president.

"None in the hall failed to be deeply impressed with the whole ceremony."

After the demonstration of these widespread endeavours and hopes,
the almost complete failure of the Disarmament Conference can only be
regarded as one of the saddest events in modern history, for the failure was
a prelude to large scale rearmament and the second world war. Why did

it fail and who was mainly responsible? It is difficult to resist the conclusion that the uncompromising attitude of some of the delegates, particularly those of the United Kingdom and France, was one cause of failure, while far too much attention throughout the conference was paid to
the military experts. If Nazi Germany was the powerful aggressor resulting
in the second world war, it can also be said that the uncompromising attitude of the United Kingdom and France at the Disarmament Conference
contributed, together with the economic depression, to making Nazi Germany possible.

Much time was wasted at the conference in determining what were
aggressive weapons and what defensive, and in the discussions on what
armaments should be reduced or prohibited, the disputants showing a
tendency to call those arms in which they were strong and wanted to keep
defensive, and those in which others were strong aggressive. The USSR
and the USA made the most sweeping proposals for disarmament, the
former suggesting the complete disarmament by all countries and the latter
a general reduction by a third. Italy was only prepared to disarm provided
its neighbour, France, disarmed equally. The United Kingdom, claimed
that it had to a large extent already disarmed and was unwilling to accept
further reduction. Germany's was the crucial attitude. Germany, its delegates contended, was already disarmed, and they proposed a general disarmament to its level. They asked that the Great Powers should, with
Germany, accept the limitation implied in the Versailles Treaty, and the
Covenant of the League. If other countries claimed the right to possess
armaments on the grounds of security, Germany also claimed such rights.
The proposals were all based on the principle of equality.

As expressing what many German women felt about the prospects of
the Disarmament Conference and the factors that should guide it, the
memorandum sent to the International Woman Suffrage Alliance by its
German auxiliary is typical. In this memorandum[3] it is stated that, "The
universal and voluntary disarmament of the nations which took part in
the world war, was to be the coping stone of the building, of which the
foundation had been laid by the disarmament of Germany under the Versailles Treaty". Reference was made to Point 4 of Wilson's 14 points,
which reads, "Adequate guarantees given and taken that national armaments will be reduced to the lowest point consistent with domestic safety".
The German women's memorandum gave "domestic" safety as "internal
security" and states that in article 8 of the League Covenant, "internal"
is changed to "national", which gave room for many interpretations and
of much political manœuvring. It is an example of vague wording which
was one of the unsatisfactory aspects of the League Covenant. The memorandum demanded "Equality of methods of disarmament and of rights to
armaments necessary for security for all members of the League of

Nations".

The refusal of the right of the German Government to equality, so that if other nations did not intend to disarm to Germany's level, then she claimed the right to rearm to their level, resulted in its withdrawal from the Disarmament Conference, early in 1932. This created a crisis for without German participation the conference was doomed to failure. The deadlock was overcome by the United Kingdom, United States, France and Italy conceding equality in principle, although its application could not be made at once, but in stages. These concessions brought Germany back to the conference at the end of the year, but it was felt by many observers that this was too late. It was between Germany leaving the conference and its return that the Nazi party made headway at the elections, from 107 seats in 1930 to 230 seats in July 1932, and became the strongest party. Shortly after Germany's return to the conference in December 1932, the von Schleicher government was replaced by the Nazi government in February 1933. In October of that year Germany finally left the conference because of proposed delay in the implementation.

Mrs Corbett Ashby resigned from the Disarmament Conference in March 1935, at the time of an adjournment. She was doubtful of its resuming after the adjournment, and if it did it would be for very little purpose. That and the White Paper on Rearmament[4] were the main reasons for her resignation. She was bitterly disappointed in the failure of the conference. The reasons for this failure she stated in no uncertain terms in her letter of resignation to the Prime Minister.[5]

On her resignation she received many letters of sympathy from persons actively concerned for the preservation of peace. Lord Robert Cecil expressed admiration for her patience, and said, "You were thoroughly justified in which you did—in holding on until you felt that the last fragment of a chance of doing anything effective had disappeared". In his letter, Professor Gilbert Murray said, "You could not really approve HMG's general policy, while on the other hand you were the one member of the Delegation in whom believers in a League policy had real confidence". He said further that, "Things look very grave and I feel the trouble lies deeper than in the badness or weakness of any particular government. In the whole matter of disarmament it seems to me that the fighting services dominate policy in practically every country".

One conclusion could reasonably be formed as a guiding thought for any further peace or disarmament conference: it is that military representatives should attend such conferences only in an advisory capacity, they should be treated as technicians, and in no sense as policy makers.

Although they represented a national government it is questionable whether the British Government delegation was the best available, and whether it gave the time necessary and worked as thoroughly as it might have done. Ramsay MacDonald, the leader, did not attend at the opening of the conference, and he attended very little throughout. Margery Corbett Ashby records the lack of general harmony and efficient communication, not only between delegates of different countries, but within each delegation. She records one incident as an example. One afternoon Ramsay MacDonald drove round the lake with the head of the United States delegation, who told him of a proposal that his Government was making and which he would repeat formally. Ramsay MacDonald returned to London that evening without communicating the US proposals to Sir John Simon, and the other members of the delegation. When later the proposal was made formally, the British delegation having no prior notice, Sir John Simon in indignation tore up the paper on which it was communicated and there were angry words between the UK and US delegations; Margery thought they would come to blows.

This chapter on the Disarmament Conference may appear a little aside of the main theme, but it is included because it is an example of women's participation in international affairs of prime importance in the early thirties. That the participation had little real effect compared with militiary interests was no fault of the women. Some might reflect sadly that if their influence had been much stronger there might have been no second world war, but one does not write history with ifs.

REFERENCES

1   Among the most important of these were the Locarno Pact 1925 and the Briand-Kellogg Pact 1928.
2   Among them the International Council of Women, the Women's International League for Peace and Freedom, the International Federation of University Women, the International Co-operative Women's Guild, and the Ligue Iberique des Femmes Hispano-Americaines.
3   See the International Women's News, November 1931.
4   The White Paper relating to Defence was issued on 11th March 1935 (Cmd. 4827) and presented to Parliament by the Prime Minister, Ramsay MacDonald. In this White Paper it is stated that "the course of events has rendered unavoidable an increase in the total Defence Estimates". Reference was made to the initiative taken in many matters by the British Government. It was pointed out however, that the Disarmament Conference had virtually come to a standstill and that further negotiations would be hampered by Germany not only re-arming openly on a large scale, despite the provisions of the Treaty of Versailles, but had given notice of withdrawal from the League of Nations and the Disarmament Conference, and a similar notice had been given by Japan. "All the larger Powers, except the United Kingdom were adding to their armed forces."

Later it is stated that "HM Government have noted and welcomed the declarations of the leaders of Germany that they desire peace. They cannot, however,
fail to recognise that not only the forces but the spirit in which the population,
and especially the youth of the country, are being organised lend colour to, and
substantiate, the general feeling of insecurity which has already been incontest-
ably generated. Nor is the increase of armaments confined to Germany. All over the
world, in Russia, in Japan, in the United States of America and elsewhere armaments are being added to."

5   Letter of resignation from the Disarmament Conference from Margery Corbett
Ashby to Ramsay MacDonald, Prime Minister.

Dear Prime Minister,
   The publication of the White Paper has convinced me that I can no longer allow
myself to be associated with the policy of HM Government at the Disarmament
Conference.
   Your invitation to me to serve was utterly unexpected and I was wholeheartedly
grateful to you for the opportunity to work loyally for general limitation and reduction of armaments which I then believed to be HM Government's policy.
Though the French had given notice of a concrete proposal, the honour of opening the Conference was by common consent left to the United Kingdom as a recognition of our unique responsibility and leadership. Our opening speech contained
no indication of considered and constructive policy and was received with amazed
disappointment.
   In the next few months we opposed in turn the proposals of France, Italy, the
United States and of the eight European Powers led by Spain and contributed
nothing more than formulae which amplified verbally the premature description
displayed in immense letters over its building "Conference for the limitation and
reduction of armaments".
   In spite of repeated warnings of the inevitable consequences of delay no formula
for equality for Germany was put forward by us until Germany had left the
Conference. It was in March 1933 thirteen months after the opening of the Conference that you yourself described the first constructive proposals of HM Government "as a plan of work". Briand and Brunning had disappeared and the whole
political situation of Europe and the Pacific had changed for the worse. In spite
of this delay, your lead then given, the energetic action of the smaller countries,
and the immense awakening of public opinion everywhere still drove the Conference forward.
   At this supremely critical juncture with the Conference at the height of its
activity, and when the various commissions had produced valuable constructive
results and much agreement, your invitation to the Powers to hold the economic
Conference in London in August 1933 dispersed its members never to reassemble.
From that moment as was inevitable the Conference ceased to have any effective
existence.
   For nearly three years I did my utmost to urge HM Government to support any
practical scheme for mutual security and defence, since almost every European
country considered mutual protection the indispensable basis for any reduction

in armaments. We consistently opposed every suggestion put forward by the political commission.

We now launch such a scheme independently of the Conference when Germany has rearmed and use our self imposed obligations under it as the reason, not for general reduction, but for national increase. If Germany joins us will she equally need to increase her armaments to protect if need be Austria against Italy and Poland against Russia?

In face of such a policy, if I left the delegation, I should feel less useless to the cause of Peace.

Lastly at a time when Anglo-American co-operation is essential to world peace, we, alone with Italy, nullify their proposal for an Arms Traffic Convention by refusing to accept "inspection on the spot", to which France too attaches immense importance.

Yours sincerely,
Margery Corbett Ashby.

CHAPTER ELEVEN

1932–1935

*Economic depression. The survival of the International Alliance
of Women. The Istanbul Congress*

In the period between the wars, 1919–1939, the western world (Europe and America) experienced a series of economic booms and depressions, the latter of which had a disruptive effect on the social life of most countries, producing large scale unemployment with its miseries, and the curtailment of numerous valuable social and cultural activities, while such conditions are a major cause of strife. First there was a boom immediately after the first world war from 1919 to 1920; this was followed by a slump from 1921 to 1923, then there was a period of steady economic progress and reconstruction from 1923 to 1929, reaching boom conditions in some countries especially in the USA in 1929. This was followed by the very severe depression of 1930 to 1935, which contributed to sowing the seeds of another world war.

Most countries were severely hit by the depression with the notable exception of USSR. Industrial production and international trade declined sharply, most markedly in the central European countries and USA. Taking an index figure of 100 for industrial production in 1928, in 1932 it had declined to 61 in Germany, 54 in Poland, 59 in Czechoslovakia, 66 in Austria and 58 in USA. All this meant serious unemployment which was worst in Germany and USA, and nearly as bad in Great Britain. In Germany it rose from a little over a million in 1928 to 6 millions in 1933, and in Great Britain from about $1\frac{1}{4}$ millions in 1928 to nearly 3 millions in 1933. Other countries were similarly affected with the notable exception mentioned. For Europe as a whole unemployment rose from approximately 3,400,000 in 1928 to 13,600,000 in 1933, and in addition many of those who were fortunate to remain in employment had to accept reductions in salaries and wages. It is obvious that such conditions deprived social, cultural and ameliorating activities of many usual sources of finance, and made their continuance extremely hazardous.

However, after the very successful Congress of the International Alliance of Women in Berlin in 1929, economic reconstruction seemed to hold hopes of progress and there was promise of prosperity. The Alliance thus began preparations for its twelfth Congress in April 1932. Athens was to be the venue. In the Alliance journal for August 1931, under the title "Call to the Twelfth Congress", it optimistically invited "its affiliated societies in 44 countries, those applying for affiliation, all women's organisations, whether national or international, which are in sympathy with its object, and all men and women who support its programme.

"After 28 years of work, after victories for suffrage (municipal or parliamentary) in many countries, after the magnificent Congress held in Berlin in 1929 to celebrate the 25th anniversary of its foundation, the Alliance is to hold its twelfth Congress in a country where women have as yet but a limited political freedom, though that country—Greece—may be claimed as the cradle of democracy. No place could be better chosen as a meeting-ground for the women of East and West; thither all may bring their contribution to world civilisation and renew the bonds of a union destined to surmount every obstacle which still opposes the equality of the sexes."

But alas, shortly afterwards the board of the Alliance at its meeting in Geneva, in September 1931, was forced by the adverse economic conditions to cancel the arrangements for the Athens Congress. It was felt that the difficulty of raising an adequate fund for expenses might seriously affect its success while it might be difficult for many of the auxiliaries to send proper delegations. It had been necessary to obtain the consent of affiliated societies to postpone the Congress beyond the three year period laid down in the Alliance constitution. Such was the effect of the depression that it was also impossible to fix a date for a postponed Congress. There was, of course, much disappointment, but there was the consolation that it would enable "all those societies working in support of the Disarmament Conference to give all their energy to that important work".

Meanwhile at the Alliance board meeting in July 1932, in London, financial difficulties were discussed. Support for the three year periods had been obtained to some extent at the preceding Congress, but the absence of a Congress in 1932 aggravated the financial difficulties, while the Leslie Commission which had previously given generous support to the Alliance had been wound up. Yet, it was the unanimous feeling that the work of the Alliance must continue; but it could only be done on a greatly reduced budget, and the board was faced with the necessity of cutting expenditure to a minimum. One of the main items of cost was the excellent journal of the Alliance, and even after many economies, income from its sale and advertisements was not sufficient to meet outgoings. The only alternatives, therefore, were to reduce its size drastically or cease publication. The latter was too painful to contemplate if the Alliance was to survive, because the journal was one of the principal links of the numerous affiliated societies throughout the world with headquarters, and with each other, and without this valuable means of communication the Alliance would be threatened with extinction. It was therefore decided to continue publication with a reduced size, which meant as seen in the issue for October 1932, a reduction from 16 pages to 8. It was regrettable because the value of its international service would be much reduced. For twenty-six years *Jus Suffragii* had been one of the best women's international journals, giving a great amount of information of the activities of women in the cause of equality of citizenship throughout the world. Yet when the board decided to continue with a reduced size rather than cease publication much more than the journal survived.

Another important decision at this momentous London board meeting of July 1932, which the president, Margery Corbett Ashby, left her work with the Disarmament Conference to attend, was to hold a special meeting of the presidents of affiliated societies at Marseilles in the spring of 1933. The main purpose of such a meeting was for a discussion of the financial and other problems which confronted the Alliance during the period of world-wide economic depression and to determine the most urgent work for the Alliance, the methods to be employed to carry it out, and the means for the purpose.

The conference took place from 18th to 23rd March 1933. In addition to meetings of the board and the presidents of affiliated societies, there were three well attended public meetings on women's suffrage, traffic in women, and peace and disarmament.

To determine the essential work of the Alliance and the means for carrying it out, delegates from 24 countries attended. After considerable discussion the conference formulated items in a general resolution that indicated the paths that the Alliance should follow in the immediate future. It was also possible to record in this general resolution that the auxiliaries were prepared to back the Alliance with generous financial assistance. The first clause of the resolution was a reaffirmation of the policy and work of the Alliance since the Geneva Congress in 1920, and included, in addition to universal woman suffrage, equal moral standards, equal economic rights, equal civil rights of men and women, and the maintenance of peace as the necessary basis for effective work.

Nothing was resolved that had not previously been agreed at an Alliance Congress. It was however confirmation and support for the continuation of the work and was, therefore, heartening. The result enabled the board to make preparations for the twelfth Congress. At its meeting in Brussels in November of the same year (1933) it was decided that a Congress should be in the spring of 1935 at the very latest, and that it should be held in the Near East as providing a meeting place between East and West. This decision was followed by an invitation from the Turkish Society affiliated to the Alliance, the Türk Kadin Birligi, to hold the Congress at Istanbul at Easter (18th–25th April) 1935.

Before this Congress the president, Margery Corbett Ashby, attended the All-India Women's Conference at Karachi in December 1934, accompanied by Dr Maud Royden. As a prelude to the conference a manifesto was issued addressed to all the candidates in the elections for the legislatures, which stated that the conference requests "the removal of all such customs and legal, educational and social disabilities that deny to women or to any particular class or community equal opportunities and facilities for free and unfettered service and moral, material and physical advancement".

Subjects discussed at the conference were child marriage, traffic in women and children, and the need for free compulsory primary education. It was proposed that legislation should be introduced and fully implemented (apparently a necessary requirement) prohibiting child marriage. Margery Corbett Ashby was told during her visit that one mother in four dies in childbirth, and that it is child murder not child marriage.

On the return journey home in January 1935 Margery visited Palestine, Syria, the Lebanon, Egypt and Istanbul where she spent ten days, partly in preparation for the Congress in April. She talked with Dr Anna Brachyahoo, vice-president of the Palestine Jewish Women's Equal Rights Association, and later with Mrs Mogannam, secretary of the Arab Women's Union, and discussed with her the possible affiliation of the Union to the Alliance. Unfortunately, it seemed impossible for Arab and Jewish women to work together and to subordinate their political differences to the common cause of their improved status in their respective communities.

Margery Corbett Ashby spent the ten days in Istanbul with Rosa Manus, then the second vice-president of the Alliance. They were greatly impressed with the Yildiz Kosk, a pavilion in the grounds of the former Sultan Abdul Hamid's palace, which was provided for the Congress by the Turkish Government. Margery was lyrical in its praise. "We were lost in surprise and admiration", she said, "not only at its beauty but at its perfect adaptation to Congress needs. Neither Rome, Paris nor Berlin can boast of a similar congress hall, committee rooms, restaurant, post-office and even baths"; and Latife Bekir, the president of the Turkish affiliate who was acting as host, had previously remarked that, "it is difficult to imagine a more romantic setting".

During this visit of preparation Turkish women had still not been given the parliamentary vote, although it appears to have been promised several times. In 1930 a measure was introduced to be submitted by the government to the Grand National Assembly to establish direct universal suffrage. It was stated in Jus Suffragii in January 1931 that municipal suffrage was given to women in Turkey and there was a promise of the parliamentary vote in 1931. Three years passed, however, without anything being done, but in December 1934 the National Assembly amended articles X and XI of the Turkish Constitution so that men and women will have equal franchise for the Assembly (Parliament) at the age of 22, and equal eligibility at the age of 30. Still, one could not be absolutely sure that this was not another promise with an uncertain date of implementation, and the circumstance still obtained in early 1935 that Turkish women had not the vote. During her visit to Istanbul Margery Corbett Ashby remarked to the Mayor of the city that it was a pity "that women will come from all over the world to modern Turkey, and find Turkish women still without the vote". Her remark was conveyed to the President, Kemal Ataturk, and before the Congress opened, women had the parliamentary vote on the same terms as men, and there were seventeen women members of parliament.

Congress at Istanbul 1935

Affiliated societies from thirty-one countries were represented at the Istanbul Conference by delegates and fraternal delegates. Two important countries were unfortunately not represented, Germany and Italy, and the affiliated societies of both could no longer operate for political reasons. If the adjectives of Nazi and Fascist are added the reason is apparent. Dr Ada Sacchi, the president of the Italian Society, had been retired by the government and was therefore unable to go to Istanbul.

The Congress was welcomed by the Governor of Istanbul and the President, Kemal Ataturk, sent a message in which he said that, "the exercise of civil and political rights by women was a necessity for the happiness and prestige of mankind". Messages were also received from Eleanor Roosevelt, wife of the President of the United States, and from Carrie Chapman Catt who, because of illness, was unable to attend. In the course of her message the latter recalled the origin of the Alliance, how it began in Washington in 1902 and was confirmed in Berlin in 1904. Then "the future looked dark and unpromising, and many suffragists believed the new organisation to be a foolish step. The belief was common in most countries that women would never vote. At that date they voted only in New Zealand, a state in Australia, and one state in the United States. Now, thirty-one years later the women of half the world have the vote.

"When we met in Washington, in 1902, Turkey was represented by Dean Fensham of the Istanbul Girls College. Then Turkish women lived behind closed doors and no one knew to what they aspired. Now they vote and sit in the parliament. This, I regard as the most remarkable change in a century. I congratulate the Turkish women upon their newly won freedom and express my sincere gratitude to Kemal Ataturk, the brave ruler who has brought about their liberation."

At the outset of her presidential address, Margery Corbett Ashby, in-

dicated a double task that confronted women of the world, (1) freedom
for women; and (2) peace for mankind. She mentioned that women will
bring to problems of citizenship and nation-building their special contribution and special experience. In amplification of this she said:

"Men say there have been no great women sculptors or painters, archi-
tects or musicians. May not the answer be that women's creative force is
expressed, not through marble and stone, colour and harmony, but through
social adjustment and experiment? Certainly in those countries where
women vote, there has been better housing, better nursing, better education, better social insurances, a greater urge towards peace. a deeper sense
of social responsibility. But to achieve these great objects woman must be
developed to her fullest capacity. She must decide for herself where her
highest duty lies, what education and preparation she needs for her development and work. Since boys and girls inherit equally from their parents, a
woman may have her father's characteristics, a man his mother's; only by
freedom and responsibility can each individual achieve his or her full
growth. This does not imply anarchic selfishness nor deny the doctrine
that the family is the unit of the state. But it does imply that the family
depends on two equal partners, that it is more important that it should
be a spiritual unity than an economic one. We therefore stand for the full
and free development of women, against all hampering customs old or
new, equal and free, though not necessarily identical education, equal
status under the law, equal economic and professional freedom. Our newly
extended powers we shall dedicate to the welfare of the family and the
peace of the world."

It might be said in parenthesis that the contention of many men about
the inferiority of women in· the arts and sciences, implied in the first part
of this quotation, would less easily be held in the seventies than in the
thirties, because it is dawning on mankind that there is no achievement
in the arts and sciences that is beyond the capability of women, equally
with men. The difference in the past has been the greater opportunities
in these fields enjoyed by men, and the traditional subordination of women
to menial tasks; yet with these handicaps women have achieved much. An
example of this is afforded by the special commemorative stamps issued
by the Turkish Government in connection with the Istanbul Conference.
Six of these stamps are of six women to whom the Nobel Prize had been
awarded: Marie Curie (Science), Grazia Deledda, Selma Lagerlöf and
Sigrid Undset (Literature) and Jane Addams and Bertha von Sutter
(Peace). In addition there was a stamp for Carrie Chapman Catt. Since
that time the achievement of women in most activities has been considerable, and in one creative field, the literature of the novel, at least equal
to that of men.

In the latter part of her address, Margery Corbett Ashby gave an indi-

cation of some of the salient features in the progress made towards equality
and the status of women, and also regrettably of some of the setbacks. As
it marks to some extent the stage of advance by 1935 it is useful to give
a copious extract:

"It is difficult", she said, "to balance the tale of our gains and losses;
since the Berlin Congress we have won equal suffrage in Turkey, our
hostess country, in Spain, in the great Republic of Brazil and Uruguay,
in South Africa, in Ceylon, Siam, and a measure of suffrage in Portugal
and in the Province of British India, Behar. Municipal suffrage has been
won in Chile, Greece, Peru, Roumania and eligibility in Jamaica. Women
have been elected MPs for the first time in Belgium, Brazil, Ceylon, New-
foundland, Norway, New Zealand and South Africa. In 1929 at the date
of our last Congress, Germany had 39 women MPs, Great Britain 15,
Finland 14, and Denmark 4.

"Women have been elected senators in Burma and Canada. A woman has
been president of the upper chamber in Austria, and Sweden has had
women in the senate.

"The Irish Free State, Spain, Brazil and Ecuador have proclaimed equal
rights for men and women. Austria gave equal rights before the law,
Romania has improved women's civil status, the Province of Quebec
in Canada has given married women the right of tutrix and to dispose of
their own earnings.

"Chile, Finland and USA have admitted women to posts in the consular
and diplomatic services. India has raised the age of marriage to 14 for
girls and 16 for boys. New Zealand to 16 for both, Iran to 16 and 18.

"Poland has appointed a second woman judge, Denmark the first, and
in the USA for the first time a woman has been appointed a member of
the cabinet; another, assistant secretary of the treasury, and a woman
director of the mint.

"Women can now be lawyers in Ceylon, Egypt, Japan, Ireland and New
Zealand; Peru and the USA have given women improved or equal nationality laws, a great advance on the Hague international standard. In Spain
a women during a short period was director of prisons and another was
director of public assistance and social welfare.

"In the fight for an equal moral standard between men and women we
won an amazing victory when the League of Nations condemned regulation of vice, licensed houses of ill fame, registration of prostitutes, and
compulsory medical examination as an exceptional measure against women.
Each nation allowing any of these methods is definitely retrograde and
sacrifices the health of the race to an obsolete medical theory, to police
convenience and to the sexual irresponsibility of men.

"So much for our gains, what of our losses? The attack on democracy
is a definite setback to women. In some countries where the responsible

cooperation of women in parliament seemed fully established the woman MP has entirely disappeared or their number has dwindled. Moreover women have lost their places in local governments, municipalities, boards of various kinds as well as in ministries.

"If you destroy the ideal of equal personal responsibility for good government, and arrange fancy categories of responsibility, women are relegated to a lower place. Their place in society is dictated to them by men, not evolved to suit their own needs.

"In the break-down of international trade, monetary fluctuations, quotas and restrictions, and fall of prices, unemployment has become an overwhelming menace to the economic stability of states. Women everywhere have been victims of discriminatory legislation. In Germany and Italy such attack on the right of the adult individual to work has been decked out as a principle. In most countries governments have not been so cynical but have frankly ousted women to make room for men. Chaos is the result. In Great Britain for instance, the latest figures show that out of five women four are wage earners at some time of their lives. To oust them would be to disorganise modern industry, so they are retained, for the most part in lower grade work at wages which menace the standard of life of men workers and their families."

Twenty resolutions were adopted at the Istanbul Congress. The first was a general declaration of principles. It states that the Alliance reaffirms its adherence to the principles which have actuated its aims and work since its inception, and that these have not been, and cannot be, affected by changes in the political or economic structure of the world. The re-formulation of these principles at Istanbul were:

"1. Political Rights. That in all states, whatever their system of government, women should possess full, free and identical rights of citizenship with men.
"2. Economic Rights. That the right to work of all women be recognised and no obstacles placed in the way of married women who desire to work; that all avenues of work should be open to women and that education for professions and trades should be available for women on the same terms as for men; that all professions and posts in the public service should be open to men and women, with equal opportunities for advancement; that women should receive the same pay as men for the same work."

Considering the reluctance in many states to accord equality of citizenship among men and women and the persistence of ideas of social and economic relationship based on tradition and custom, these principles were very advanced for 1935, and it is possible that even in 1979 there are many men and indeed a fair number of women who would consider them too revolutionary for adoption. This is particularly the case with regard to the second principle on economic rights. Even in 1979 there are many branches of economic life where the principle is neither accepted nor operative, largely because of prejudice based on traditional thinking, although other reasons may be given.

The resolutions covered a wide variety of subjects, and almost all mark a considerable step forward. The second was concerned with East and West cooperation, which the Alliance itself increasingly embarked on as subsequent stages in this history will show. In the third resolution on child marriage its dangers to health and its injury to the vitality of the race was stated, and the governments of the countries where it existed, were urged to introduce legislation vigorously enforced to suppress it. Some of the resolutions were reiterations in different wording of resolutions at previous Congresses. Among those which introduced new factors because of recent developments was the fifth resolution on economic conditions which was particularly opportune at this period of world economic depression. Its soundness makes it applicable not only to 1935, but to any period of economic difficulties.

"This Congress", it says, "representing many millions of women throughout the Eastern and Western World, and voicing the views of that section of the community most closely associated with the personal distribution of the means of life to the family, records its conviction that destruction of urgently needed necessities cannot improve the condition of the world, and is fundamentally unsound and wrong in principle.

"The Congress called upon all governments to consider how purchasing power can be made available for those whose paid work is temporarily or permanently not required by the community and, further, to consider what effective action can be taken whereby the productivity of the earth and of industry can be distributed for the benefit of peoples of the world. It urged affiliated societies to study seriously practical means for remedying some of the economic evils of today by measures such as shorter hours of work, the creation of new industries, facilities for low interest credits, adjustment of currency to correspond with increase of population and with the modern requirements of life, by raising of standards of living all over the world, and stabilization of prices of commodities."

The lengthy eighth resolution was concerned with peace and emanated largely from the International Committee for Peace and the League of Nations. Women's work for peace is covered in the preceding Chapter (10).

The Nationality of Married Women

The ninth resolution on nationality was a subject on which the Alliance had done a considerably amount of work in collaboration with the League of Nations. As it sums up and contains the substance of resolutions on the subject at previous congresses and represents for the time rather advanced thinking it is worth giving in full. The conception of nationality is based on equality. The resolution which emanated from the committee on the civil status of women asked for the adoption of an international convention to make provisions in matters of nationality:

"That husband and wife should each enjoy independently their own personal nationality; that a women whether married or unmarried should have the same right as a man to retain or to change her nationality, and that in every respect there should be equality of the sexes and such as to include the following:

"1. *Retention of Nationality*
   (1) A woman shall not lose her nationality by reason (*a*) that she married a foreigner, or (*b*) that during her marriage her husband loses his nationality by naturalisation in another country or otherwise.
   (2) Where before the coming into force of legislation based on this convention a woman has lost her nationality by reason of the fact that she married a foreigner or that her husband had lost his nationality by naturalisation or otherwise, she shall on her own application re-acquire her nationality.

"2. *Acquisition of Nationality*
   (1) A foreign women shall not by reason of marriage acquire the nationality of her husband.
   (2) Naturalisation of the husband during marriage shall not involve naturalisation of the wife.
   (3) A married woman shall be naturalised under the same conditions as a man.
   (4) Special facilities shall be given for one spouse to acquire the nationality of the other.
   (5) Where before the coming into force of legislation based on this convention a woman by marriage or by the naturalisation of her husband acquires his nationality she shall retain it unless she makes a formal declaration of alienage.
"3. With respect to derivation of nationality from a parent, the nationality of one parent shall be given no preference over that of the other."

The tenth resolution was mainly a representation to the League of Nations to continue its work on equal moral standards.

Like conditions of work for men and women was another resolution (eleventh) resulting largely from the work of an international committee on the subject and combining resolutions at previous Congresses. A petition on the right to earn of the woman, married or unmarried, was drafted and later sent to the International Labour Conference in June, 1935. Among the points made in this petition are:

"That the essential rights of human personality are the same for a woman as for a man and are the same whether she is married or unmarried.

"That to deny a woman's right to earn because of marriage is to deny her one of the essential rights of human personality.

"That to prohibit women workers undertaking labour previously undertaken by male workers is to deny women one of the essential rights of human personality and to make such labour a male monopoly.

"That work itself suffers when employment is given on account of sex rather than capacity."

The last resolution for which one of the committees was responsible was the twelfth on the civil status of women and was concerned mainly with the rights of married women under the law.

Among other subjects of resolutions were Slavery (13), Refugees (15) and Racial Discrimination (20).

All the resolutions adopted at the Istanbul Congress were sent to the League of Nations, and to the various governments of the world through the Alliance auxiliaries.

A little before the Congress the Alliance received a proposal from the International Council of Women for the fusion of the two organisations. Resolution 14 referred the matter to the new board to consider whether it was in favour of co-operation or fusion. The board met at Geneva in September 1935 and decided to submit the question to the Alliance auxiliaries with a recommendation that it should be co-operation rather than fusion. This was accepted.

One regrettable aftermath of the Istanbul Conference was the attitude of the Turkish Government that now women had the franchise on equal terms with men, the existence of the Union of Turkish Women, the society affiliated to the Alliance and whose president acted as host at the Congress, was no longer necessary and it was disbanded. This meant that Mme Latife Bekir had to resign from the board. Considering the services she had so recently rendered to the Alliance and to the cause of equality it was a sad occasion.

CHAPTER TWELVE

1936–1939

The status of women. The work of the Alliance and the League of Nations

One of the most important matters to which the International Alliance of Women, and several other International Women's Organisations devoted much of their activities during the period from 1936 to the outbreak of war in 1939, was the status of women throughout the world, partly because the League of Nations decided to act in the matter.

The twelfth resolution of the Istanbul Congress, besides being concerned particularly with a married woman's freedom to dispose of her earnings, and with the legal requirements in the matter of the payment of alimony in the case of separation or divorce, also directed attention to equality of the sexes in all departments of life. It was stated in this resolution that all women's efforts should be devoted to this. The Alliance decided "to support by all the means in its power the principle embodied in Article I of the treaty signed at Montevideo in December 1933", the text of which is as follows:

> "The contracting states agree that upon the ratification of this treaty men and women shall have equal rights throughout the territory subject to their respective jurisdictions."

The board of the Alliance met in Amsterdam in May 1936, and devoted much of its time to the question of the status of women and the prospective action by the League of Nations. This discussion was continued at a further board meeting in Brussels in the following September. At the Amsterdam meeting the board issued an appeal to the women of the world prompted by growing totalitarianism in Europe and the threats to freedom, democracy and peace. The similarity and integration of aims of democracy, peace and the women's movements was stressed in this message, and it was stated that: "In 1937 we shall know what is the civil and political status of women in all countries, through an inquiry by the League. It is the first time in human history that a world assembly has wanted to get a clear picture of the rights and disabilities, the triumphs and the defeats of women. What that picture is going to be we do not yet know, but if it is good it will encourage us to use our power for the solution of the appalling problems of the present time."

In the mid-thirties the darkening shadow of the totalitarian state that was falling across the world, obliterating respect for the individual, putting might before justice, and blind obedience before free accepted discipline, made work in the cause of the women's movement especially difficult at this time, but the work of the women's international organisations continued bravely and untiringly, rather spurred by these obstacles than deterred by them. A further message from the board meeting in Brussels of September 1936 claimed that "The woman's movement now is in the van of those who are working to prevent the world slipping back into despotism. If we insist on our rights as human beings we are fighting the battle of every man who suffers for his race, his creed or his opinions. Men are impatiently throwing away their liberties because they would not use them wisely for the well-being of all mankind without distinction of nationality or sex. Women, even where they have won political freedom, are too near the fight to undervalue this great possession."

In the autumn of 1936 the League of Nations published the communications it had received from seventeen governments and eight women's organisations on the status of women. In a few of the communications from governments it was pointed out that the question of the status of women is one of internal national policy, unsuitable for international regulation. In these communications Governments seemed desirous of proving that women in their countries have a status which, if not yet equal to that of men, is yet a high one and is steadily improving. Yet when these claims were examined it was seen that they were not always well founded, and that there was evidence in several of these countries of women's subjection. In its issue for November 1936, the *International Women's News* gives two examples—Brazil and Turkey—where it was claimed by the government that women have equal rights, where in fact there was a degree of subjection. To quote, "In Brazil, for instance, where the new constitution lays down that no privileges shall be granted and no distinction made on the ground of birth, sex, race, the occupation followed by the person concerned or his parents, social class, wealth, religious beliefs or political ideas, the long extracts from the civil and criminal codes reveal some startling facts. For instance, it appears that it is still necessary for a wife to obtain her husband's consent to engage in an occupation; certain restrictions on female labour are provided with a view to the protection of the race; and most striking of all, adultery on the part of a married woman is punishable with a term of imprisonment of from one to three years, while the husband is only to be punished if he keeps a concubine.

"In Turkey: 'The right to represent the conjugal union is given to the husband; in the absence of agreement in regard to the joint exercise of paternal power, the father's decision is effective; the domicile of a married woman is deemed to be the same as that of her husband; a married woman cannot carry on any trade or profession without the consent, either expressed or implied, of her husband.' It is true that this information is followed by a statement that 'All this does not confer on the husband any kind of marital guardianship'. Well, well, it certainly does confer on him some very special rights."

Among the communications from women's organisations was one from the Pan Pacific Women's Association suggesting that governments be asked to send summaries "of the laws affecting women in colonies, protectorates and mandated areas, together with information on native customs affecting women in regard to marriage, sales or arbitrary disposal of the persons of women or their property". This proposal was supported by the Alliance.

A liason committee had been formed at Geneva to collate the memoranda of the women's organisations on the status of women so that a united front could be presented to the League of Nations. This "First Committee", as it was called, prepared a resolution for the Assembly of the League of Nations. In this reference was made to the Assembly resolution adopted on 27th September 1935, and to its ruling that "conditions of employ- ment, whether of men or women is a matter which properly falls within the sphere of the International Labour Organisation". The hope was expressed by the first committee, therefore, that the ILO "will, in accordance with its normal procedure undertake an examination of those aspects of the problem within its competence, namely, the question of equality under labour legislation, and that it will, in the first place, examine the question of legislation which effects discriminations, some of which may be detrimental to women's right to work".

The resolution of the first committee asked the Council of the League of Nations[1] to appoint a committee of experts of both sexes to study the many questions relating to the status of women, and asks that this committee should seek the advice and co-operation of competent scientific institutions, and that "it should have power to consult women's international organisations and invite their co-operation in any form which it thinks advisable".

In October 1937 financial provision was made by the League for a committee of experts. This was encouraging to the liaison committee of women's international organisations and it worked for the maximum publicity and education among women's organisations in all countries. Two specific recommendations were made: "That study groups should be formed to study material on the status of women in their own and in other countries, and to make proposals as to the changes necessary if that status is to be improved; and panels of men and women lawyers should also be formed to advise concerning the application of existing legislation affecting women, and to watch proposals for new laws and for amendment in existing laws."

In order that this national work should be collated for international use reports were requested by the liaison committee on what had been done. The committee also made suggestions to the League of the names of persons who might serve on the forthcoming committee of experts. This committee was appointed early in 1938 and consisted of seven members, four women! Miss Hesselgren (Sweden), Mme Bastid-Basdevant (France), Dr Godjevac (Yugoslavia) and Dorothy Kenyon (USA), and three men; Professor H. C. Gutteridge (Great Britain), M. de Ruelle (Belgium) and M. Paul Sebestyen (Hungary). This was the first time that a committee of the League of Nations had more women than men. Professor Gutteridge, who was Professor of Comparative Law at Cambridge University, was elected chairman. Its first meeting took place in April 1938. Its appointment was a considerable step forward towards the equality of the sexes in civic, social and economic life, and it was celebrated in many countries by Woman's Day, which in Great Britain, Argentine and Brazil, took place on 14th May 1938, and on near dates in a few other countries. In France it was celebrated on 20th May.

In Great Britain the main centre for the celebration was University College, London, where an all day conference was held, when the twelve points formulated by women's organisations as their demand for equal status were discussed. This demand was submitted to the British Government at the same time as the submission to the women's liaison committee in Geneva. Among the points were equal conditions and equal pay in all public services, equal minimum wage under trade board decisions, removal of the marriage bar, admission of women to the House of Lords, abolition of the special laws against prostitutes, and independent nationality rights. A public session was held in the afternoon which was addressed by Professor Gutteridge. Celebratory meetings on the same day were held at many provincial cities and towns, including Birmingham, Liverpool, Glasgow, Bradford, Newcastle, Nottingham, Preston and Portsmouth.

Meanwhile at its first meeting the League of Nations committee of experts produced a scheme of work following consultation with the Institutes of Private Law in Rome and Paris. Representatives of women's organisations were invited to meet the committee and comment on this first stage of the work. Considerable difficulties confronted the committee, among them were (1) to determine the geographical scope of the enquiry; (2) the division of work in accordance with the Assembly resolution; and (3) the application of laws in these matters.

In the first category it was found that there were so many systems of law and different religious influences that it would be necessary to make the enquiry in stages. Initially, therefore, it was decided to study the status of women under European systems of law and systems derived from them, which would embrace not only Europe but America, Australasia and South Africa, and would also possibly include the status of women under Moslem law which is well codified, and also possibly the status of women in China and Siam, where the modern codes were influenced by German law. But to comprehend the status of women in countries strongly influenced by oriental religious customs as in India, or by tribal customs as in many parts of Africa, would complicate and delay the enquiry possibly for years. It was therefore decided to concentrate on the status of women under European and kindred systems of law.

In the second category it was necessary to decide what part of the enquiry was strictly the province of the International Labour Organisation and of the expert committee. Obviously the conditions of work for women was a matter for the ILO, which had produced a report on the subject due to be published in July 1938, but until members of the Expert Committee could study this they were hardly in a position to determine the scope of approach of its own enquiry where it touched the employment of women. Co-operation with the ILO was proceeding.

With regard to the application of laws the committee secured the very ready co-operation of the women's organisations in ascertaining the facts. It was one thing to have a law and another to experience its full implementation, which so often depended on a sympathetic and progressive public, especially where prejudice and custom are powerfully against an improved status of women.

Nine months later on 7th January 1939, the committee of experts on the status of women, invited representatives of the women's international organisations to a conference to discuss the progress of the enquiry. The statement made by Professor Gutteridge was in part a repetition of what had been decided nine months earlier with some modifications. For example it was found possible to comprehend with the European systems of law, in addition to the Muslim system, that of Hindu law as it had an extensive literature and was highly developed.

The main purpose of the conference, however, was to enlist the further help of women's organisations in ascertaining the application of laws, so that the information collected could be transmitted to the scientific institutes. Specifically the information required was: (a) case law, jurisprudence and decisions of the courts; (b) administrative decisions; (c) pre-existing or subsequent laws which have the effect of nullifying the provisions of laws effecting an improvement in the status of women; (d) concerted refusal to give effect to laws; together with the sources and dates of the information which should be as full as possible.

This information was required by 1st January 1940, but, alas, by that time the second world war had been in progress for four months. The committee of experts could hardly be expected to complete its work and issue a final comprehensive report in the difficult conditions of war. With the general curtailment of the activities of the League of Nations the committee was disbanded, but the work on the status of women was continued, somewhat differently under the United Nations Organisation several years later, and this is considered in later chapters.

REFERENCE

1   The Council of the League of Nations was really the executive committee of the League. It met every third month, and reported to the Assembly (representatives of all member states) which met every year.

CHAPTER THIRTEEN

1937–1939

European unrest and the threat of war. The Zürich Study
Conference and the Copenhagen Congress

Among its major activities between Congresses, the Alliance often
arranged study conferences, which not only meant the study of matters
of current importance for the woman's movement on an international
basis, but a periodic coming together of delegates from affiliates all over
the world. The reader will have been aware of a few such study conferences up to about 1930.[1] The economic depression in the early thirties and
the uncertain political situation and threat of war in the late thirties,
made it difficult for the Alliance to plan and hold such conferences which
it was very keen to do. Three were planned in the late thirties: one at
Zürich from 25th February to 1st March 1937, at Warsaw in September
1937, and at Stockholm in October 1938, but only the first named actually
took place, the others were cancelled because of the uncertain situation
in Europe.

The first session of the Zürich conference was a round table discussion
on the question, "How can nations ensure their freedom and independence today?", a subject obviously prompted by the aggressive and despotic
action of Fascist Italy with its invasion and domination of Abyssinia in
1936, and with the similar action of Nazi Germany with its threatened
invasion and domination of Austria and Czecoslovakia which subsequently
took place in 1938 and 1939.

The other sessions were devoted to what had become for the Alliance
the familiar, traditional subjects of, "why the vote must be won", "democracy and women's suffrage", and the topical one, again resulting from the
effects of the depression, of "women's work and unemployment".

The discussion at the first session on the freedom and independence
of nations was divided into five questions: "(a) Can treaty obligations be
regarded as inviolable unless there is effective machinery available for
peaceful change? (b) How can profit be eliminated from the manufacture
and traffic in arms? (c) How can the organisation of collective security and
mutual assistance be strengthened? (d) Should we favour the re-summon-
ing of the Disarmament Conference to attempt the achievement of a

limited convention. (e) How can we establish within the framework of the League of Nations effective machinery for remedying international conditions which might lead to war?"

"The suffrage session dealt with two aspects, (1) How the vote was won. What the vote has done" with speakers from enfranchised countries; and (2) "Our best methods of propaganda; Our chances of success", with speakers from unenfranchised countries.

The round table discussion on "Women's work and employment" was divided into sections with the following significant titles: (a) "the economic consequences of sex distinctions in the labour market"; (b) "the married woman worker"; (c) "women and trade union and professional organisation"; (d) "How to secure equal opportunities for training"; "equal pay"; (f) "Women workers and family responsibilities".

Judging from the numbers who attended the Conference it could be regarded as a success. An attendance of about 150 was expected, but instead there were some 350, which although contributing to making it a successful conference meant difficulties in organisation.

Several resolutions were formulated and agreed for each subject. The resolutions on peace gave great support to the League of Nations which was regarded as the main instrument towards this goal. The League was reminded that although it had achieved some progress towards the maintenance of peace it had not gained a victory over national egoism, and that a further effort was required. One of the political phenomenon of the thirties was the growth and intensification of nationalism in almost every country, stimulated in the first place by such trends in Germany and Italy, which produced a movement in the democratic countries towards an opposing nationalism, and thus the give and take of international collaboration was becoming less. These circumstances made the work of the League of Nations more difficult, and one of the resolutions was that nothing must entail the abandonment nor the weakening of the mechanism of the League of Nations.

The resolutions concerned with women's work were based on the assumption that "every woman, married or not, has an indefeasible right to the same educational facilities, and the same access to professional work as a man under the same conditions". After an explanatory preamble based on the defects of present customs and systems the conference made a declaration of requirements. This represents advanced thinking in 1937, and even in 1979 it could not be said that in European countries all these requirements had been implemented; in some perhaps, but not all.

Briefly the conference declares that:

1. All educational establishments should be open to women on the same terms as to men, with an equal right to employment on the teaching

staff for both sexes, and the same diplomas for both sexes.
Professional and Vocational training for both sexes should be developed, and should be available under the same conditions and with the same examinations for men and women.

2. All forms of work, shall be open to women, married or not, under the same conditions of salary and promotion as for men.

3. All women engaged in paid work should belong to professional organisations and should work within them for the common interests of the members of their profession, with equal rights and responsibilities as men.

At the board meeting of the Alliance held at Geneva in September 1937, Winnifred Kydd of Canada resigned from the board because of the pressure of her professional work and because of the distance of her country from Europe where most of the meetings of the Alliance were held. She was replaced by Anni Voipio of Finland.

The resignation of Winnifred Kydd was regrettable not only because she was a valuable member of the board, but because it severed a very important link with North America. It was felt by many members of the Alliance that for an organisation that aimed to be world-wide it was perhaps too much concentrated in Europe. At the time of Winnifred Kydd's resignation there were 21 members of the board, including the president and vice-presidents, and of these 15 were from Europe and 6 from the rest of the world, of which only one other was from North America, namely Josephine Schain from USA. There were constant endeavours to make the representation on the board more broadly based, and it is therefore a little surprising that Winnifred Kydd was replaced by a European. Instead efforts should have been made to continue the Canadian representation. By the time of the Copenhagen Congress there was no member of the board from North America as Josephine Schain had resigned.

Copenhagen Congress 1939

In the early years of the Alliance a Congress was held every two years, with the exception of that in London in 1909 when it was held after a year. Since the first world war it was generally the aim, in accordance with the constitution of the Alliance to hold a Congress every three years. This had been achieved except for the time of the acute economic depression in the early thirties when the projected Athens Congress for 1932 was cancelled. The next Congress after Istanbul was due in 1938 but as the International Council of Women was celebrating its jubilee in that year, it was decided to postpone the thirteenth[2] Congress for a year. It was held in Copenhagen from the 8th to 13th July 1939.

The Congress was pervaded by the general consciousness of the darkening clouds of war and the impending storm, but everybody tried to put a brave optimistic face on circumstance, led by the indomitable president, Margery Corbett Ashby. It was inevitable that the attendance was not as good as at former Congresses in view of the uncertainties at this time, and thus some countries were not represented, while others sent restricted delegations. Yet in spite of all this the goodly number of 200 from 20 countries attended.

The Congress opened in the magnificent City Hall, with a speech of welcome by Mr Stauning, the Prime Minister of Denmark, a speech full of apprehension about the grave tension of international affairs. "We hope", he said, "for the maintenance of peace and we tremble for the sake of humanity and for the civilisation which has been built up, we dread the war which is always threatening". He spoke of the policy of peace and neutrality that is established in Scandinavia—Sweden, Norway, Iceland, Finland and Denmark. "There are", he said "other countries than those, where the same will to preserve neutrality prevails, and we entertain a fervent wish to see this circle extended", and added, perhaps regretfully, that, "we exercise no influence on world-politics". At the same time he spoke of the measures that Denmark had taken towards the enfranchisement of women, and he was able to say that, "30 years ago women obtained municipal vote and eligibility; and 25 years ago women obtained political suffrage and eligibility. Freedom of speech, right of public meetings, a free press, religious liberty and the right of determination have been ensured to all men and women, and the great majority of the people feel sincerely attached to the system of democracy and want to safeguard the liberty granted to the people."

In her presidential address, Margery Corbett Ashby, made some pertinent remarks about the common traditional attitude of men towards women's place in society based largely on customs forming prejudice. She spoke of men's theories about woman's place in the world, summed up in the phrase, "children and kitchen or a plaything for his leisure" which she typified as "brutal and narrow".

"In a democracy", she continued, "men have no theory about women's place but accept them as an intrusion into 'man's sphere' with philosophic or annoyed patience. They make room for us by their side and yet do not elaborate a counter theory to that of fascism and say to the young woman 'What kind of world do you women want, what form of society suits you, what handicaps do you want to be free from? I have my ideas and you can help or hinder me, but if we can pool our ideas and work for our common ideal no force can withstand us'.

"Democracies can only survive if their theories of equality are logically carried out and women's needs and women's gifts are felt by men to be an intrinsic part of the community.

"A community which, instead of sex rivalry or sex subordination, substituted a working partnership of sex collaboration would be immeasurably strong in vitality and purpose."

She gave a summary of progress since the Istanbul Congress in 1935. "We can", she said, "congratulate the women of Bulgaria on obtaining the municipal and parliamentary vote, though not the right to sit in Parliament. In Romania women have won the vote and our congratulations to the new women senator, Marie Pop, are mixed with regrets that her duties prevent her from coming here. In south-west Africa women of European races have the vote. In India over fifty women sit in the provincial parliaments and several women are ministers."

Reference was made to the attitude of totalitarian states to the position of women. "In some countries", she said, "we see a deliberately organised reaction under a theory that lays down that the state is best served by driving woman out of her newly acquired position, by limiting her education and her chances to work to cooking and the cleaning of the home, the breeding of children and for a select few the organising of social work directed to this end. The state is therefore increasingly interested in the physical well-being of its mothers, but not in their intellectual acquirements or in their personality.

"The unparalleled and intensive war preparations have however had a notable and similar influence on all states. In the democratic countries this involves no change in mental attitude. It is merely an extension of the opportunities for women. They are needed for the new war industries, for civilian defence, evacuation schemes and so on. Their work is voluntary and propaganda must make it attractive and conditions must satisfy. There has been an outcry in England where difficult and dangerous war work for women is still paid two-thirds that of men—lorry drivers in gas masks at night. Thanks to our efforts, in case of death, pensions for dependants will be equal.

"In other countries women have been recalled to the work from which they were driven. The pressure on men to enter the army, the secret police, the growing bureaucracy makes the readmission of women to offices, agriculture, and factories necessary. But just as the state for its own ends threw them out, so for its own ends it drives them back. In neither case are they free or consulted. The state has changed its practice but not its theory —the subservience of women. But can this last? Under the first condition of home life women were isolated and lacked the stimulus and strength that comes from association. Today working in masses together, will there not inevitably grow up in spite of all state propaganda, a burning desire to have some say, some responsibility in the ordering of their own lives, the conditions of their employment, the object of the intensive work? Where theory and practice are so divorced will not the strain be too great to bear and may we not hope to see among the women of those countries a new and hopeful movement for liberty of expression?"

Fifteen resolutions were adopted at the Congress. The first was a general declaration of principles, in which the influence of the European political climate is apparent. "The sacredness of human personality", it is asserted, "has always been the keystone of the woman's movement, which rebelled against an imposed standard of faith, behaviour and economic status. Our great pioneers fought for freedom of conscience and personality, for the right to choose their own careers, to participate in national and political life, and to help to shape the destiny of the nation.

"Their fight was essentially a part of the great struggle against oppression of creed, race, class, and sex. It was in favour of the right to education, and economic freedom as well as of preparation for the task of citizenship."

International Committees

Many of the resolutions of each Congress emanated from the work of the international committees, which together formed much of the major work of the Alliance, and it is important, therefore, to follow the changes that took place in them. After the Paris Congress in 1926 the following committees were appointed:

1. Equal moral standard and against the traffic in women—chairman: Dr Paulina Luisi.
2. Like conditions of work for men and women—chairman. Fru Arenholt.
3. Nationality of married women—chairman: Chrystal Macmillan.
4. Family allowances—chairman: Eleanor Rathbone.
5. Unmarried mother and her child—chairman: Frau Adele Schreiber.
6. Work in the enfranchised countries—chairman: Mme Plaminkova.
7. Peace and the League of Nations—chairman: Ruth Morgan.
8. Women police—chairman: Rosa Manus.
9. Equality of women under the law—chairman: Mme Grinberg-Aupourrain.

The first six had existed previous to the Paris Congress, the last three were new.

After the Istanbul Congress the number was reduced to five, numbers 1, 2, 7 being retained, 3 being combined with a committee on the civil status of women, and 9 with a committee on suffrage.

The five were:

1. Suffrage and equal citizenship—chairman: Senator F. F. Plaminkova.

2. Equal moral standard—chairman: Alison Neilans.
3. Like conditions of work for men and women—chairman: Froken Ingeborg Walin.
4. The civil status of woman—chairman: Milena Atanatskovitch. Rapporteur on nationality—Chrystal Macmillan.
5. Peace and the League of Nations—chairman: Josephine Schain.

At the Copenhagen Congress the first three committees remained the same, but with Mme Halina Siemienska becoming chairman of the first, and Mme Plaminkova of the third; the fourth changed its title to "The legal status of women, including nationality" with Mme Andree Lehmann as chairman; while Mme Malaterre-Sellier became chairman of the peace committee.

Two committees were added:

6. The protection of maternity, with Mme Ivanova as chairman, the appointment of which was the subject of the third resolution of the Congress.
7. A youth committee with joint chairmen: Marie Ginsberg, Milena Atanatskovitch and Froken Margot Petersen.

The fourth resolution on suffrage, sponsored by the appropriate committee, was addressed to countries where it had not yet been granted to women, and specific action in the case of Argentina was agreed. A petition was to be presented to the president, asking him to support the claim to suffrage of Argentine women, whose high standard of culture is recognised throughout the world.

Resolution five on nationality and seven on the legal status of women emanated from the civil status of women committee, which as noted changed its title. In view of impending war the subject of nationality had some degree of urgency. The proposals made on the subject were a repetition of those made at the Istanbul Congress given in the previous chapter. They were rational and progressive on the simple basis of sex equality, yet in the light of custom they appeared almost revolutionary.

In the matter of the legal status of women it was pointed out that legislation in many countries still puts obstacles in the way of civil equality, economic independence and advancement in professional life for the married woman, and that marriage guarantees less and less economic security for a woman and her children. Among its recommendations were: (1) that efforts to realise the principle of complete civil equality between men and women be intensified; (2) that laws which treat unequally married and unmarried women in regard to their legal capacity shall be abolished; and (3) that all limitations on the entry and advancement of women in professional life be abolished.

It was also recommended that as divorce is becoming more frequent the support of children in such cases should be strongly insisted upon and that penalties should be imposed equally on a husband or wife who do not fulfil their obligations.

In the tenth resolution, also concerned with the status of women, the Congress expressed satisfaction with the appointment by the League of Nations of an expert committee, and counts on the co-operation of the societies affiliated to the Alliance to supply information on the position of women by 1st January 1940. Hopes were expressed that when the results of the studies are available the societies should use them as a basis for a campaign for equality of status. The request was also made that an international convention for equal rights of men and women should be drawn up by the League of Nations. It also requested that the League should appoint a committee to consider the status of women of primitive peoples. This, it will be remembered was excluded from the work of the committee of experts as requiring separate and prolonged investigations which would seriously delay the work of the committee (see Chapter 12).

The work of the committee for "Like conditions of work for men and women" is closely related to that concerned with status. The ninth resolution devoted to this is fairly long and detailed, but it is important and represents such well thought-out logical and advanced thinking that the essentials must be quoted. To many influenced by traditional custom, and thus prejudiced, many of the demands must appear revolutionary, and in many countries and sections of the population must appear so even in 1979, although the demands in many countries have been largely acknowledged in principle and implemented by legislation.

Women in Public Services

The Congress demanded "that all government and public authorities open their services to women, married or unmarried, on equal terms with men in every respect: training, pay and promotion". This was followed by a request that affiliates to the Alliance should support professional organisations of women in these services in their efforts to obtain better conditions, and that where no such professional organisations exist, the affiliated societies shall endeavour to encourage their formation.

"This Congress is convinced that women will never make their full influence felt in national and international affairs until they have an adequate share in the framing of policy, and for this purpose they must have equal opportunity with men to serve in all government positions at home and abroad, in the diplomatic, consular, colonial and dominions services, and on all committees and commissions, both national and international to which the various governments make appointments". All governments were called upon "to give women equal access with men to all key positions where policy is framed and an equal chance with men to hold these positions".

It also called upon governments concerned to withdraw all restrictions hampering the freedom of women to work.

Study of the status of women by the International Labour Organisation

The Congress appreciated the valuable study of the existing legal status of women workers contributed by the ILO as part of the general examination of the status of women being made by the League of Nations. As the next step would be to formulate demands for reforms for the equality of status between men and women the Congress suggested a formulation the main points of which were:

1. That regulations dealing with hours of work, night work, dangerous or unhealthy work shall be based upon the nature of the work and designed for the adequate and scientific protection of all workers, irrespective of their sex.[3]
2. That to facilitate the task of the woman worker with children, public authorities shall establish, or where they exist increase crèches and nursery schools, and provide other facilities, and up-to-date living accommodation to eliminate much unnecessary housework.
3. The curricula of schools should include some training in domestic work for the children of both sexes, and public opinion should be educated to understand that there should be mutual responsibility in the home, and that where the woman contributes financial support through her paid work the man should take a fair share in the domestic tasks and in the care of the children.
4. Where employment is considered to involve risk to the morals of those employed, measures of protection or of prohibition shall follow the same principle for adolescents of either sex, while other measures should ensure that all establishments are run with due regard to public decency.
5. That women should be encouraged to join the appropriate independent trade unions and professional organisations to secure improvements in wages and conditions, and a policy of complete sex equality; and where the question of wages is dealt with by law, no minimum wage regulation shall discriminate between men and women, either by fixing a lower minimum wage for women, or by classifying women in the lower paid grades or processes.
6. That all forms of social insurance shall be based on the principle of equality of the sexes, with equality of contribution and of benefit for men and women.

The following resolutions were recommended for study with a view to further consideration by the next Congress, or by a special Conference.

(a) Family Allowances
The acceptance of the principle of further economic provision by the community for dependent children, including family allowances, because it is (1) a contribution towards alleviating poverty and malnutrition; (2) it raises the status of the mother; and (3) facilitates the adoption of Equal Pay for Equal Work between men and women.

(b) Equal Pay
Whereas it is essential for the freedom of women that they shall have the right to earn their livelihood on the same terms as men, the present limitation of economic opportunities and low wages is both one of the main causes of prostitution and of the continued dependence of women. One of the great obstacles to the admission of women to all branches of paid work on the same terms as men is the illogical and unsound method by which the existing wage-system includes the cost of rearing children in the wages paid to men but not to women; it was declared that:

"1. The wage-system must be altered by deducting from wages the 'family-factor' contained in all wages of a certain level, this family factor being given to parents only. This deduction should be operated by the following method:

Every wage-earner, man or woman, earning more than a minimum living wage for a single person shall by law be obliged to pay a certain percentage of this wage to a children's insurance fund, which shall be used to re-distribute to those of the contributors with children under a certain age a family supplement based on the percentage paid in by every one.

"2. This scheme would ensure that only those male or female wage-earners who have children obtain the family rate of pay. The principle of equal pay for equal work could then be established without prejudicing the interests of children. There would be no further excuse for giving unequal pay for equal work, the argument of the greater family liability of the male worker being invalidated.

"3. This scheme will further free access to all forms of work for women, married or unmarried, the argument of men's privilege or monopoly as breadwinner for the whole family being equally invalid.

"4. All societies affiliated to the Alliance should work in their respective countries to secure such legislation.

"5. The International Labour Office shall be asked to put the question of equal pay by means of the deduction of the 'family-factor' from wages on the agenda of its next conference."

There was a concluding paragraph on women's status in regard to schemes of national social insurance adopted in many countries, requesting that new legislation in this field should be on the basis of equality, irrespective of sex.

The sixth resolution by the equal moral standard committee was concerned largely with prostitution, a matter it contended which concerned the individual conscience and should not be regarded as a legal offence, but methods of exploiting for profit the prostitution of others is a matter of concern. Women's organisations in all countries were urged to investigate conditions in their cities and to press upon their governments the need for reviewing and strengthening the laws relating to prostitution, especially where those who use the prostitution of others for financial gain are able under existing laws to evade punishment.

The concluding resolutions were concerned with "Forced marriages" (11), "Refugees" (12), "Children's courts" (13), "Provision of recreation for soldiers" (14), and "Propaganda campaigns" (15).

As in all conferences resolutions were not agreed without differences of opinion, indeed without some degree of conflict, but as in all democratic organisations the will of the majority prevailed. Sometimes the debates and the occasional disharmony betwen delegates proved difficult and tiring. To peep behind the scenes for a moment—Margery Corbett Ashby in a letter to her husband during the Congress mentions some of the discords: "This is pure H——", she writes, "yesterday we were told that if the Czech flag were carried by the page introducing Madam Plaminkova the Prime Minister wouldn't come. The flag is still flying in Prague but is apparently not allowed for export! So we had a row with the Danish ladies and insisted that we would have no flags at all, and of course there will be none. Charaoui has resigned and withdrawn her Egyptian delegation because we refused to send a letter saying we stood for the immediate cessation of all Jewish immigration into Palestine.

"The French Mme Brunschvieg is absolutely furious because the anti-restrictionists are in a majority on the equal conditions of work committee, and a resolution presented by them was voted. I pointed out that the restrictionists presented no resolution of any kind at all and that if it had been left to them nothing at all would have been ready for discussion. Indeed this morning I feel absolutely sick mentally and physically!" She signs the letter "Your distraught wife". That was written on the 8th July. A letter three days later began, "Today I am rather more cheerful", for many differences were resolved.

Margery Corbett Ashby who had been the main guiding spirit of the Alliance since she became president sixteen years earlier, in 1923, had reason to be pleased at what the Alliance had accomplished, especially during the difficult years of the thirties. An indomitable purpose to continue and go ahead at all costs in a sacred cause was always strongly apparent.

The threat of war by Nazi Germany had overshadowed the Congress. An unpleasant incident proved to be a foreboding of coming events. After the farewell dinner the officers and delegates went to their rooms. A little later Rosa Manus, very disturbed, knocked at Kathleen Bompas' (the Secretary) door and said: "I think my room has been searched." They both went to her room and found that a number of papers had disappeared. The rooms of other officers of the Alliance had not been disturbed. Margery Corbett Ashby and Kathleen Bompas tried to persuade Rosa Manus to return to England with them but she had to refuse in loyalty to her own country. Her sad fate at the hands of the Nazis is recorded in the next chapter.

This was the last Congress of the inter-war years and concludes the second long period of the persistent endeavours of the Alliance to secure political, economic, legal and social equality of women with men in all communities throughout the world. Each period is divided by a world war, with its tremendous effects on social values, prompting their widespread re-examination.

Much of the most important work of the Alliance has been centred in the international committees or commissions. This was increasingly the case in the inter-war period when its work was gradually settling down to a definite routine. In each triennial period the committees had a programme of work and prepared the main resolutions which were debated and generally agreed often unanimously, sometimes with amendments, occasionally by a majority vote, but rarely rejected.

After each Congress the delegates from the affiliated societies in various countries submitted the resolutions to their governments, while the headquarters sent them to the League of Nations and its committees most concerned, and to other international bodies.

Similar resolutions were inevitably presented and agreed at successive congresses, as the cause is a lasting and consistent one, minor changes being made as conditions were affected by events, while new aspects sometimes changed the approach to a subject. As the history of any cause will demonstrate it is only by constant reiteration of the arguments over the years that they will gradually penetrate the public consciousness and the heads of government.

Much improvement in the position of women in many countries had occurred by 1939 since the beginning of the century. How much this was due to the propaganda and the untiring efforts of the International Alliance of Women it is, of course, impossible to say. But it can be said that no international organisation had done so much in the century for the cause of political, legal, economic and social equality of men and women as the Alliance. The sum of achievements from 1902 to 1939 is manifold and, I think, impressive. A few of the significant are that the parliamentary vote on equal terms with men had been obtained in many countries throughout the world, thirty-three compared with two in 1902, when the Alliance was formed. Women had become members of parliament and of local governments in many countries, although admittedly such membership was proportionately small. At the beginning of the century only a very few universities were open to women, in 1939 those of the western world were nearly all accessible to women. In 1902 a small minority of professions were open to women, by 1939 this had changed to a majority. Much had been done for the status of married woman and her property. An indication of what had been achieved is given in Appendix 6.

Although much had been accomplished there was still a long way to go. The IAW wisely realised that the first step was to get principles of equality accepted by international bodies and governments and then in the second stage to secure their implementation. Thus it was always the policy of the Alliance to work as closely as possible with the League of Nations and to influence it to accept these principles and recommend them to governments. At the same time the IAW by means of its affiliated societies in countries throughout the world presented the same principles in the form of resolutions to their governments. Further, by collecting world-wide information through its affiliates it greatly assisted the League of Nations, own research, preliminary to its own formulation of principles.

The essential pattern of work and collaboration evolved in the inter-war period was to continue to an even greater extent with the United Nations and will be described in later chapters.

REFERENCES

1   The Peace Study Conference was an example (See chapter 8).
2   It is called the thirteenth on the basis that Washington in 1902 was the first, although for strict accuracy Berlin in 1904 was the first, when the Alliance was actually formed.
3   This was a majority decision. The delegations from Brazil, Bulgaria, USA, France, The Netherlands, Poland and Yugoslavia opposed because the working women of their countries had not been consulted.

CHAPTER FOURTEEN

1939—1945

Continuing the work of the Alliance in the second world war

Two urgent matters for the Alliance to decide at the outbreak of war on 3rd September 1939 were its attitude to the war, and the best methods of maintaining links with various members throughout the world, so as to be in a good position for revival. The president of the Alliance affirmed, on behalf of the board, a policy of absolute neutrality as required by the constitution. This policy can be appreciated and understood in the case of an international association, but it puts members in an ambiguous position, for as citizens of a country they are dedicated to the cause in which their country fights, yet as members of an international body they are neutral. This attitude of neutrality was reiterated in the Alliance journal for December 1939, and it was pointed out that such neutrality is the only possible attitude for a truly international organisation, although it is recognised that individuals must take sides if they belong to a belligerent country. Yet if the international organisation has among its chief objects the support of certain principles and systems, then it is surely logical and realistic for the organisation to support those belligerents who are fighting partly for its own causes. This was certainly the case in the second world war and the Alliance seems to have recognised this, for it is stated in the article already cited (December 1939) that "the present war is being waged by two democratic states against a state which has definitely abandoned the system of democratic government". "Can the Alliance", it asks, "therefore remain neutral?" The question is obviously asked because the Alliance was always a great supporter of democracy and democratic government, and was strenuously opposed to all forms of totalitarianism. In spite of its constitution it was thus really impossible for the Alliance to remain neutral.

One of the main efforts of those at the headquarters of the Alliance was to continue functioning with a necessarily reduced income and to maintain as many contacts as possible with members and affiliates throughout the world, so as to ensure survival. At the outbreak of war the headquarters office was at 12 Buckingham Palace Road, London, but this had to be abandoned for economic reasons, and from 1st October the head-quarters secretary, Mrs Bompas, carried on the secretarial work and also editing the journal from her home at Ashford in Kent. The important historical records were stored in the president's house at Horsted Keynes in Sussex.

It will be remembered that in the first month of war, in September, the German armies overran and occupied a large part of Poland. On 17th September the USSR moved to a frontier well inside Poland as a protective measure. Then the war, except for occasional bombings and the conflict in the north between Russia and Finland from November 1939 to March 1940, was mainly stationary until Germany invaded Denmark and Norway in April 1940. This stationary period provided some opportunity for the Alliance to continue its activities. Perhaps the most important event was a board meeting in Paris from 6th to 8th March 1940, at which there was a very full attendance from eight countries including some members of the peace committee who were especially invited to attend. It was decided at this meeting to hold a conference at Geneva on postwar international organisation, on 31st May and 1st June, for the Alliance international committee, members of the board and presidents, attended by one other representative, of each affiliated society. The main purpose of the conference, as implied, was to discuss the policy of the Alliance towards reconstruction on the conclusion of the war, and to give special consideration to the problems which particularly confronted women at that time and in the after-war period.

If conditions had remained in Europe very much as they had been from October 1939 to March 1940, then the Alliance would certainly have held this conference at the end of May, but the war moved rapidly from April until the late summer. Following Germany's invasion of Denmark and Norway in May 1940 her armies swept across the Netherlands and Belgium and invaded and occupied the whole of France. British troops carried out a memorable evacuation at Dunkirk, and the summer of 1940 was the period of the Battle of Britain, probably, as subsequent events showed, one of the decisive battles of the war. It was, therefore, impossible to hold the Alliance meeting in Geneva as arranged and it was inevitably postponed. Also, in the light of the devastating invasions of the German army, it was becoming increasingly difficult to maintain links with the world-wide members of the Alliance, and arrangements were made in case the headquarters of the Alliance and the home of the president were temporarily cut off from communication with other countries, especially in the event of an invasion of Britain. The office of the Alliance would therefore be transferred to Mlle Emile Gourd at Geneva, while Carrie Chapman Catt at New Rochelle, New York, would, if necessary, act as president.

It was difficult for the IAW to continue publication of *The International*

Women's News, as it depended on world-wide subscriptions. It was, however, fortunate in being able to secure through the generosity of Mrs Rebecca Sieff, its continuation by the Women's Publicity Planning Association, which maintained publication from October 1940 to December 1945. In January 1946 it reverted to the Alliance. During the period when it was produced by the Women's Publicity Planning Association it changed in character, giving some news of the Alliance, but becoming much more general with articles by well known people not always on the women's movement. The prominent women of the Alliance figured only occasionally. Its format was heavier and less attractive, it became much more commercial and moved in character towards the popular newspaper, Yet the Alliance had cause to be grateful to the Women's Publicity Planning Association and to Mrs Rebecca Sieff for, by their action, the journal was kept alive and maintained a measure of contact among members, and it was very much easier, therefore, for the Alliance to restart its own journal than if publication had ceased entirely. Miss Hamilton Smith became the new honorary editor with the issue for January 1946.

In nearly all European countries there was a much greater utilisation of the contribution that women could make to the war effort than there had been in the first world war. In Great Britain, for example, women were subject to the same direction to employment of national importance as were men. In addition to the traditional activities such as nursing, there was a proportion of women doctors. Work in munition factories was greatly extended following the experience of the first world war, and women provided auxiliary services for the Royal Navy (WRNS), the Army (ATS) and the Royal Air Force (WAAFS.) Women not only completely manned searchlight sites, but took part in anti-aircraft operations. Women from the professions, public life and politics were also employed in diplomatic and propaganda services, among them several prominent members of the Alliance. The president, Margery Corbett Ashby, for example, went on a government propaganda mission to Sweden during March and April 1942. Its purpose was to explain the British point of view to as many and as varied audiences as possible of neutral Sweden. Being a gifted and eloquent speaker, with some knowledge of Swedish, and one who easily made social contacts, with a sense of what was diplomatic, Margery's visit was probably of considerable benefit to the British cause in Sweden. The many audiences she addressed were by invitation, because it was important that they should not be known as public meetings, for German women would then agitate for public meetings in German interests. She spoke to various women's and social organisations, to the League of Nations Union, the co-operative societies, trade unions and to groups of university students. She met the Crown Princess of Sweden with whom she had an hour's conversation, "in a quite fantastically gilded drawing room" as she described it in a letter to her husband. She spent three days with the former Swedish foreign minister, Mr Sameller, and his wife, in a vast sixteenth-century castle overlooking the port of Gaule. Several audiences were invited to the castle to hear her give the British point of view.

In this visit she not only did some useful propaganda work for Britain, but she gained several valuable impressions of a neutral country hemmed round with belligerents. Difficulties over food were as great as in Britain, for Sweden was dependent on imports for much of her food, and rationing was severe. Margery Corbett Ashby found sympathies with both sides in the conflict, and the recent course of events affected these sympathies. "German brutalities in Norway deeply shocked the people and greatly reduced the small numbers of Nazi-inclined folk." Yet fear of Germany was new, but fear of Russia was very old, a fear greatly aggravated by the recent Russian domination of Finland, resulting from the Russian-Finnish war in the winter of 1939–40. This great traditional fear of Russia was perhaps more widespread than any disgust of Germany, and the circumstance that friendly Britain and Russia were now allies fighting Germany made the international picture a very complex one for Sweden.

During the war the Alliance suffered casualties to its members, three of which were in tragic circumstances. Frantiska Plaminkova of Czechoslovakia, who was the second vice-president of the Alliance, was executed by the Nazi invader; Rosa Manus of the Netherlands, who was third vice-president, was interned and died probably on the way from the concentration camp at Ravensbruck to Auswitz;[1] and Halina Siemienska of Poland, a board member, was killed by the Nazis while she was helping her daughter to escape after witnessing the murder of her husband.

These three women had worked hard, both in their own countries and internationally, for the equal status of men and women, and they were among the most valuable members of the Alliance. Frantiska Plaminkova was the first woman senator in the Czech Parliament, and she presented the yearly budget to the Senate. She knew full well the dangers she was running under Nazi occupation, but she declined all offers of hospitality in other countries declaring she must stand by her people. As chairman of the Enfranchised Woman Commission she was determined to channel women's new responsibilities into good social reforms. She returned from her last Congress at Copenhagen to die at Nazi hands.

Rosa Manus, who was one of the most vivid figures of the Alliance, had attended every Congress since that at Amsterdam in 1908, and for the following thirty odd years she was a tireless worker. She was not only an excellent speaker but a splendid organiser. At the Amsterdam Congress she initiated and organised an impressive exhibition devoted entirely to women's work (allegedly the first of its kind) which comprehended education, social services, agriculture, scientific research, crafts, industry and the visual arts. In the early years she often accompanied the first president, Carrie Chapman Catt, on several of her propaganda missions, including a long tour of South America. It was Rosa Manus who organised the Alliance peace conferences at Amsterdam and Dresden. She had a magnetic attraction for youth, and it was due to her influence that many young people joined in the work for sex equality.

Many other prominent women workers in the women's movement died during the war years, among them Charlotte Despard who died at Antrim, Northern Ireland, in the autumn of 1939 at the age of 95. She was for many years president of the Women's Freedom League,[2] and was an ardent worker for the women's movement and the Alliance. Selma Lagerlöf, one of the greatest Swedish writers of her time, died early in 1940. She received the Nobel Prize for Literature in 1909, and was regarded with particular affection by the Alliance, for she wrote her pamphlet "Home and State" especially for its Congress in Stockholm in 1911. Also in 1940, Ray Strachey (Mrs Oliver Strachey) died, the author of *The Cause*, published in 1928, which survives as one of the best histories of the Women's Movement. Ray Strachey was a notable figure at the Istanbul Congress which she attended with Lady Astor.

Another valuable member of the Alliance who died towards the latter part of the war was Alison Neilans, a member of the board, who had done useful work as chairman of the international committee for an equal moral standard and against traffic in women, and who, in her work, perpetuated much of the spirit of Josephine Butler.

REFERENCES

1   See article in *International Women's News*, February 1946 (Vol. 40, No. 5, p. 50).
2   The Women's Freedom League was founded by Mrs Despard in 1907 as a breakaway group from the Women's Social and Political Union. It contributed to many of the suffragette activities although its militancy was never of the destructive type. One of its most spectacular militant actions was when Muriel Matters chained herself to the secluding purdah-like iron grille of the Ladies Gallery of the House of Commons, an action which concluded with the removal of the iron grille together with Muriel. This was significantly the final removal of the grille. The headquarters of the League was at the well-known Minerva Club. The League was disbanded at the end of 1961 (see article by Sylvia Hayman in *IWN* February 1962).

CHAPTER FIFTEEN

1945–1947

*Revival of the Alliance. Status of women's progress. Congress at
Interlaken*

The war in Europe ended on 8th May 1945, the street lights went up and
there was jubilation, quiet joy. and relief mingled with sadness according
to individual circumstances and temperament. There were, however, to be
several years of enforced restraint and "making do" before a return to
conditions which would give a satisfactory standard of living for the
majority. Food continued to be rationed for several years, and relaxation
was very gradual. There was an immense housing shortage amounting to
over 30 million dwellings in Europe, caused not only by war devastation,
but by the severe reduction of house building during the six years of war.
Transport and various forms of communication and other services took
several years to recover even to pre-war standards, and it was not until
the early fifties that it could be said that reconstruction was well on its
way.

Since the first world war the Alliance worked very closely with the
League of Nations as one of the chief means of furthering some of its
objects, especially the improvement in the status of women throughout
the world, and the Alliance had an office in Geneva largely for liaison with
the League. After the second world war the League of Nations became the
United Nations, essentially a continuation with a change of name, carrying
on similar work but with a more complete membership and a more widespread influence. The Alliance worked with the United Nations organisations as it had done with various committees of the League, and this
represented one of the fundamental activities of the Alliance.

As mentioned in Chapter 12, in the late thirties work on the status of
women occupied much of the time of the international women's organisations in collaboration with the League of Nations, and its Expert Committee for study of the subject. Also the International Labour Organisation
published a report in 1939 on *The Law and Women's Work: A Contribution to the Study of the Status of Women* first in French and later in English translation (see Chapter 14). Meanwhile the IAW, with other women's
organisations, had asked its affiliates to collect information for the use

of the Expert Committee of the League. Numerous replies to the questionnaire were received from affiliates in many countries and summaries of
these were published in *International Women's News* from January to
May 1946. To continue the work of the League's Expert Committee on the
Status of Women a Sub-commission to the Commission on Human Rights
of the Economic and Social Council of the United Nations (ECOSOC) was
established and held its first meeting in April 1946, submitting its report
to the Commission on Human Rights. The report stated that the aim of
the Sub-commission is "to raise the status of women to equality with men
in all fields of human enterprise", and to undertake a world-wide survey
of the status of women, and thus continue the work begun by women's
organisations and the Expert Committee of the League. The Sub-commission asked ECOSOC to take immediate action in the matters of education
and political rights, and to ask all governments of countries where women
have not yet the franchise to take action immediately to grant this right
to women. In addition to education and political rights the report covered
civil rights, which includes equal rights in marriage, property, guardianship of children, and independent nationality. Social and Economic rights
were outlined as including prevention of discrimination against women in
social and economic status and customs and the abolition of traffic in
women. Later in 1946 this Sub-commission became a Commission reporting direct to ECOSOC.

In April 1945, a little before the war ended, a board meeting of preparation for the renewal of activities was held at the president's home in Horsted Keynes in Sussex. Thus in spite of difficult conditions following cessation of hostilities prominent members of the IAW were quick in making
contacts and restoring the partially severed links. The president was particularly active in doing this and she visited, among other countries,
Czechoslovakia, Poland and Norway.

A meeting of the International Committee (board and presidents of
affiliated societies) of the Alliance was held in Geneva at the end of
October 1945. It was regrettable that Margery Corbett Ashby was unable
to be present as her husband was then seriously ill. Affiliates from Australia, Egypt, France, Great Britain, Iceland, India, Sweden and Switzerland were represented.

Amy Bush, who attended, recalls that the meeting was a very moving
occasion. Women who had survived the ordeals of invasion, the concentration camp and the horrors of war wept when meeting their fellow members after six years. The meeting, alas, was the last one to be attended by
Mrs Asmundssen of Iceland, who died in Paris on her way home. Mme
Brunchvicq of France who also attended died before the Congress in the
following year. All the arrangements for the meeting were made by Emilie
Gourd of Switzerland, the Hon Secretary from her sick bed. She too, died

shortly afterwards. She had been a very valuable member of the Alliance. For over twenty years she had been the Corresponding Secretary of the Alliance in Geneva, acting as liaison officer with the League of Nations and the ILO, greatly facilitating the collaboration of the Alliance with both. It was the unanimous opinion that the work of the Alliance must continue, for there was still much to be done before equality of the sexes in all spheres could be said to be achieved. It was felt that an early Congress was essential, as "only a Congress can really take the final decisions on policy and programme". It was also agreed that there should be a further change in the name of the Alliance from "International Alliance of Women for Suffrage and Equal Citizenship" to "International Alliance of Women. Equal Rights. Equal Responsibilities".[1] These decisions adumbrated a brief for the board which met in London in March 1946. It was then agreed that the Congress should take place from 10th to 17th August that year at Interlaken in the lovely Bernese Oberland.

At the time of the Congress there were affiliates of twenty-five countries of whom sixteen were represented, another five countries had national representations, making representatives of twenty-one countries who attended which was no mean achievement just over a year from the end of the war with the difficulties of organisation and re-establishment of normal communications.

In her presidential address Margery Corbett Ashby stated that since the last Congress women had obtained the suffrage in France, Italy, Albania, Yugoslavia and Japan. She referred rather bitterly to the circumstances that in their host country, Switzerland, women had not yet the vote. She spoke of the magnificent work of the Swiss women's voluntary service and the work for refugees and remarked that "our pleasure in coming to this lovely, hospitable country and town is only marred by our surprise and resentment that our hostesses, the women of so-called democratic Switzerland, are in the same category as the women of unhappy fascist-ridden Spain. How is it possible that Switzerland should lead the world in engineering and use of electricity and be a 'museum piece' in its attitude to women."

She gave an assessment of progress since the last Congress:

On the credit side:

1. Women in most countries have lost their sense of inferiority and acquired political equality.
2. The United Nations have proclaimed sex equality as a fundamental human right necessary for the attainment of peace, liberty and economic security and have asked for our co-operation.

On the debit side we must, however, say this:

1. In most countries women are still paid less for equal work or work requiring equal skill.
2. In practice, posts or responsibility in industry, professions and government are not given to women.
3. The legal and economic position of the married woman is profoundly unsatisfactory. It is our largest unsolved problem.

Understandably the first resolution adopted at the Congress was on "Peace". After expressing sorrow and sympathy with the sufferings caused by the war and realising that international organisation is essential to prevent its recurrence, it was claimed that this must be based on equal rights for men and women and on fundamental freedom for all without distinction of race, sex, language and religion, and it was noted with satisfaction that the Charter of the United Nations is based on such principles. The resolution emphasised that only where women possess equal citizenship can they exercise to the full their influence for international co-operation and peace, and it was urged that full use be made of articles 57, 63 and 71 of the Charter[2] in order to secure the best possible co-operation between countries and with the specialised organs of the United Nations. It also urged that the sources, scientific development, manufacture and use of atomic energy for all purposes be under the control of the United Nations. Although sensible and sound, as subsequent events have shown, it is too idealistic for realisation in the twentieth century, yet it would be a strong factor in preventing atomic warfare.

The second resolution was entitled "Democracy", and although this was one political basis for all the recommendations of the Alliance, and was part of its philosophy, it had not before been separately the subject of a resolution. It was inspired, of course, by the belief that the second world war was in part a war of democratic countries against the despotism and totalitarianism of Nazi Germany and Fascist Italy. For the Alliance the conception of democracy means a system "in which the supreme control of government, carried on through parliament, executive and judiciary rests, in the last analysis, with the people: (a) In which no individual or institution is above the law, where impartial justice protects the individual against arbitrary action by any public or private institution and against injustice by any other individual; (b) Which arrives at its conclusion by free discussion, without an artificial unity based on suppression of opinion; (c) Which gives equal rights to all citizens whatever their differences of religious or political opinion or their racial origin, and protects individuals and groups in their fundamental human rights; (d) Where there is a free press, freedom of speech and association, universal and free education, free choice of a career and the use of leisure and opportunity for employment and social security."

This is possibly one of the best definitions of democracy that has been given. Section (c) concerned with equality includes that of man and woman and is amplified in another part of the resolution that woman's battle is the battle of all mankind, and there can be no freedom for women where freedom is no longer a recognised right of every individual. It is remarked that "whilst no existing democracy is perfect, it can and will be perfected by the steady growth of civil responsibility which it fosters among men and women".

Although most countries aimed to move towards a realisation of the principles expressed in this resolution, (and in many they were much nearer to this realisation in 1979 than in 1946), in none could it be said that they are completely realised. The term democracy has often been improperly used, and many states are called democratic that are not in the least so according to the principles stated.

The third resolution under the heading of "Political Rights" was concerned with woman suffrage. Although it was possible to state that equal suffrage had been granted in most countries there were still some which had not taken this step, and it was implied that until they do it would not be consistent with their membership of the United Nations. The call was also made to governments to appoint women on equal terms with men to all posts in the governing and administrative organs of their countries.

The fourth resolution was on "Economic Rights", and was partly a repetition of the claims for equal pay and conditions of work for men and women, and also for training made at former Congresses. The theme of the conditions of work with the equitable economic conditions in the home was continued in the next resolution (5) with the new title of "Housewife and Worker". This resolution arose from the extended employment of women during the war in a wide range of new activities. It involved the economic status of women and posed the conditions whereby the combined functions of home-maker, wage earner and member of society can be possible to the married woman without laying upon her an intolerable burden. Among the measures proposed were "The sharing of responsibility for the training and care of the children between both parents, so that while the special function of the mother is recognised, she shall be free to take part in the social and civic life of the community and, if she so desires, in employment outside the home; and the provision of opportunities for part-time work at the proper standard rate of wages, available for workers of both sexes."

The sixth and seventh resolutions followed logically on this. The former was concerned with the circumstance of a woman being deprived of rights when entering the state of marriage and demanded therefore that a married woman should retain the rights that she enjoyed before marriage, especially the right to: "(1) Bear her own name; (2) Retain her independent nationality; (3) Share in the choice of the common domicile, or choose her own domicile where circumstances require it; (4) Exercise any activity or profession she may choose; (5) Exercise all rights over the property she possessed before marriage or as acquired in the course of marriage; (6) Have the same rights as her husband over property held in common; (7) Enter into any contract with her husband authorised by the law as between unmarried persons; (8) Exercise equal rights with her husband over the children born of their marriage."

Dr Bertha Lutz, for several years president of the Brazilian Federation for the Advancement of Women. A very active member of the IAW and vice-president 1952–1958.

The eighth resolution concerned with an equal moral standard and traffic in women repeated the essential principles given in resolutions at former Congresses. It pointed out, however, that the war and post-war conditions increased the commercial exploitation of prostitution which constitutes the offence indicated in the Fifth Convention against Traffic in Women drafted by the League of Nations in 1937. It demanded that the United Nations should take steps to secure the signatures and ratification of State Members to this Convention and that a clause be inserted in the Peace Treaties that all the signatories to these treaties shall be bound by previous Conventions against Traffic in Women of 1904, 1910, 1921 and 1933, and the measures proposed in that of 1937 be inserted in the treaties.

The tenth, eleventh and twelfth resolutions were concerned with refugees, desplaced persons and migration, all matters prompted by the war and its aftermath. Mention was made of the millions or refugees, stateless and displaced persons that "are today without a home, without work and without hope whose tragic state shows no improvement". The Alliance said that these sufferings called for large scale schemes of migration by governments and the settlement of refugees in suitable regions; the provision of transport thither with their families; for help in taking their place in their new country and by degrees to give them full citizen rights. The Alliance also proposed that those countries with wide and rich territories not yet fully exploited or populated should extend a welcome to the largest possible number of refugees, consistent with the willingness to receive immigrants of the inhabitants of each country.

"The Jewish Refugees in Concentration Camps" was the subject of the last resolution (12). It began by reminding us of the atrocities perpetrated against the Jewish people by the Hitler regime, resulting in the slaughter of six million of its peaceful members, and stated "that hundreds of thousands of innocent Jewish refugees are still detained today, one-and-a-half-years after the end of the war, in the concentration camps to which they were sent, for no other crime than that they have survived the atrocities inflicted on them . . . which is in contradiction to the elementary human rights laid down in the Charter of the United Nations, and demands that the UN take steps to secure their immediate liberation".

Many of these resolutions needed the emphatic statements in which they were given, and one feels that the IAW rendered a service to humanity by so doing.

Many changes took place at the Interlaken Congress in the officers of the Alliance. First, Margery Corbett Ashby did not wish to be nominated again as president. She felt that because of the contributions of women to war work and the more active roles that they were likely to perform in society, and having reached the age of 64, she should make way for a younger woman. As subsequent events showed, it was a rather premature decision, for Margery was destined to give very many more years of first rate service to the Alliance. She had proved herself a very worthy successor to Carrie Chapman Catt. During the twenty-three years of her presidency the Alliance had increased in strength and influence and embarked on an ever widening field of activities, she had seen it through the difficult period of the world economic depression in the early thirties, and had done the major work in securing its revival after the second world war. The Alliance was fortunate in having so gifted a person—orator, linguist, diplomat in the best sense, with a wide political knowledge, kindly and imaginative— as its leader for so long a period. She was succeeded by Dr Hanna Rydh of Stockholm, whom Margery first met at the Stockholm Congress of 1911, which was the beginning of a lifelong friendship. Margery confessed to the joyful relief when Hanna Rydh agreed to become president. Dr Rydh was a well-known archaeologist, scholar and author, she was one of the leaders of the woman's movement in Sweden and the wife of the Governor of a Swedish province which gave her a valuable passport on her subsequent journeys.

Margery Corbett Ashby became the second honorary president with a seat and vote on the board. Mrs Adele Schreiber became an honorary vice-president, and the five vice-presidents elected were all new to the office, two—Hoda Charaoui Pacha and Marie Ginsberg—having been members of the board. Elisabeth Vischer-Alioth of Switzerland succeeded Emilie Gourd in the important position of corresponding secretary, and Mrs Nina Spiller, who had succeeded Mej. E. H. Piepers at the Copenhagen Congress of 1939 as treasurer, continued as such at Interlaken. Most of the other members of the board were new with the exception of Margarete Bonnevie of Norway and Marguerite Boyer of France. Among the new members of the board destined to play a very important part in its future activities was Andrée Lehmann of France.

Seven committees had been appointed at the Copenhagen Congress (1939), and these were responsible for most of the resolutions at the Interlaken Congress. At this Congress five committees were appointed for Peace; Equal Civil and Political Rights; Economic Rights; Equal Moral Standard and Finance. As the subjects had become traditional to the Alliance the work of such committees was largely revisionary in the light of contemporary events.

In October that year, shortly after the Interlaken Congress, Dr Hanna Rydh and Margery Corbett Ashby and others of the Alliance, attended the ten day Conference of the International Assembly of Women in the Catskill Mountains, USA. They found it stimulating to meet so many women from diverse quarters of the globe, and discuss questions with them at nine round-table study groups, but it prompted the criticism of indefiniteness, and one wonders whether the value of such occasions is not mainly the social one of kameraderie of intellectuals rather than that of any conclusions reached. Margery Corbett Ashby took the opportunity while there of visiting Carrie Chapman Catt. Margery records that as ever Mrs Catt "radiates inspiration and courage. How wonderful when nearing 88 to have so shrewd a grasp of modern problems, to keep one's faith in progress, never to lose heart." This was the last time Margery was to see her old leader, for three months later Carrie Chapman Catt died on 9th March 1947. She was buried in Woodlawn Cemetery by the side of her friend, Mary Garrett May. On a memorial stone is inscribed, "Here lie two friends united in friendship for 38 years in service to a great cause". Her great mission in life had been to secure for women their enfranchisement throughout the world. When she began her work in 1902 only two sovereign states in the world had given parliamentary votes to women, New Zealand and Australia, when she died 53 countries constituting the majority had given

Hanna Rydh, a noted Swedish archaeologist, president of the IAW 1946–
1952. She travelled widely and through
her efforts the Ethiopian women were
affiliated to the IAW.

the vote to women. In 1979 all but Lichtenstein had done so.

There were many tributes to her work throughout the world. Margery Corbett Ashby said at the conclusion of an eloquent article in *International Women's News* (April 1947) that, "when a social history of our times come to be written Carrie Chapman Catt will take her place as one of the few human beings who really shaped history. When democracy began to be challenged she gave it new strength by forcing men to re-argue its first principles and to include women, half the human race, within its machinery."

In the *IWN* for April 1947 there appeared an article from Margery Corbett Ashby entitled, "Discrimination, Flagrant and Unjust", which vigorously criticised the section of the Draft Convention prepared by the International Labour Organisation on the protection of workers in "non-Metropolitan territories" (colonial and mandated) concerned with the prohibition by law of discriminations against workers based on race, colour, religion and tribal association, but discrimination on grounds of sex was excluded because regulations prohibiting the work of women underground, or similar measures, would be impossible. Margery contended that this pretext for leaving women outside the law was inadmissible, and that the Draft Convention was at variance with the principle of the equality of the sexes stated in the preamble of the Charter of the United Nations. Several details of the discrimination were discussed. The Alliance sent its protest to the ILO and wrote to the Secretary General of the United Nations asking if the ILO working with the UN can disregard the basic equality of the sexes as laid down in the Charter of UN. It was with some satisfaction that *IWN* was able to record a few months later in August 1947 that the Article on non-discrimination of the Draft Convention had been revised and the word sex had been inserted between 'colour' and 'belief'. This is an interesting example of the watchfulness in the interests of women by members of the Alliance of the deliberations of the UN, the ILO and other international bodies.

It will be remembered (Chapter 4) that Carrie Chapman Catt made a memorable tour in the Far East with the purpose of stimulating interest among the women of Asia in the women's movement, and to encourage them to form societies for the promotion of woman suffrage. Dr Hanna Rydh, accompanied by the treasurer, Mrs Nina Spiller made a similar tour of the near east, Egypt, Iraq, Iran, Mesopotamia and Ethiopia to interest the women of these countries in the work of the Alliance and to get them to join in its activities. One of the results of this propaganda mission was that among the additional affiliates to the Alliance admitted at the next Congress, that at Amsterdam in 1949, were Ethiopia, Iraq and Iran. A special number of the *IWN* (September 1947) was devoted to Dr Rydh's visit to these countries in which she gave interesting accounts of her discussions with the women of these countries. For example, in the article on Iraq she noted that "the efforts among the women themselves have been less directed towards obtaining political rights, than to education and charity. With the affiliation, however, of the Women's Union to the Alliance the work for civil rights will be more active. That there are also young women excellently fit for politics and the diplomatic service, was clear. But first women must help their sisters out of the veil. It can never be repeated too often that the veil is no mere fashion, it is a wall which materially and spiritually is debarring its bearer from co-operation with men in a world crying for co-operation".

REFERENCES

1 The first change of title was made at the Paris Congress in 1926, when the original title of "The International Woman Suffrage Alliance" was changed to "The International Alliance of Women for Suffrage and Equal Citizenship."

2 Articles 57, 63 and 71 of the Charter of the United Nations are:
Article 57: (1) The various specialised agencies, established by inter-governmental agreement and having wide international responsibilities, as defined in their basic instruments, in economic, social, cultural, educational, health and related fields, shall be brought into relationship with the United Nations in accordance with the provisions of Article 63.

(2) Such agencies thus brought into relationship with the United Nations are hereinafter referred to as specialised agencies.

Article 63: (1) The Economic and Social Council may enter into agreements with any of the agencies referred to in Article 57, defining the terms on which the agency concerned shall be brought into relationship with the United Nations. Such agreements shall be subject to approval by the General Assembly.

(2) It may co-ordinate the activities of the specialised agencies through consultation with and recommendations to such agencies and through recommendations to the General Assembly and to the Members of the United Nations.

Article 71: The Economic and Social Council may make suitable arrangements for consultation with non-governmental organisations which are concerned with matters within its competence. Such arrangements may be made with international organisations, and where appropriate, with national organisations after consultation with the Member of the United Nations concerned.

CHAPTER SIXTEEN

1948–1952

Declaration of Human Rights. The Amsterdam and Naples
Congresses

As we have seen, the Alliance had worked as closely as possible with the League of Nations on the Status of Women, equal with that of men in all fields of political, social and economic life. It continued to work in the same active manner with the League's successor, the United Nations. Early in 1948 the Alliance was granted consultative status in Category B, which was a considerable recognition of its value in its special fields of study.

It should be explained that the Charter of the United Nations empowers the Economic and Social Council to consult with international non-governmental organisations on matters in which they have special knowledge and competence. In 1948 there were nearly a thousand non-governmental organisations in world affairs of which 83 were accorded consultative status in the Economic and Social Council and its functional commissions. Nine of these were given this status in Category A which means that they have interest in most of the activities of ECOSOC. Seventy organisations were given status in Category B which includes those organisations with special competence in a few of the activities of ECOSOC, while Category C is for those organisations concerned with creating public opinion and disseminating information. Associations with consultative status send their representatives, called consultants, to the meetings of the Council and its Commission, who are given freedom to participate in the activities of the Council and Commissions. Generally only international organisations are given this consultative status. National bodies are expected to make their representations to their governments and to international associations. What this consultative status meant for the International Alliance of Women was that it could have a representative at UN headquarters to attend meetings of ECOSOC, its Commissions and Committees whose work was of concern to the Alliance such as the Status of Women, Human Rights and Social Commissions. Mrs Burnett Mahon of the United States League of Women Voters was the first consultant for the Alliance, later assisted by Mrs Baker van den Berg and Mrs Burgess.

The International Committee of the Alliance met occasionally between Congresses. It consisted of the board and presidents of affiliated societies. It met in Rome at the end of May 1948, with the addition of some of the members of the special commissions who took the opportunity for discussion and making recommendations. The Peace Commission under the chairmanship of Margery Corbett Ashby made several recommendations for consideration at the next Congress, among them one on the migration and accommodation of refugees. The Commission reiterated the tenth resolution of the Interlaken Congress on the matter and proposed "that those countries with wide and rich territories not yet fully exploited or populated should extend a welcome to the largest possible number". It noted "with satisfaction that some of the countries of South America (Chile, Venezuela) are opening their doors to emigrants from all countries who wish to settle there and are offering facilities for such settlement". The proviso was added as before that no country should be forced to take immigrants against the will of its inhabitants.

The liaison committee between the League of Nations and women's international organisations whose function and work was described in Chapter 12 continued to represent women's organisations with consultative status to the United Nations. The liaison committee made several representations to meetings of the Human Rights Commission at Lake Success held in June 1948. Consideration was given to several amendments proposed by the committee which were accepted in whole or part. In the matter of equal pay the points emphasised by the liaison committee were accepted but phrased a little differently. At these international gatherings of many sovereign states there was inevitably considerable discussion on wording, the use of the best terms and the avoidance of ambiguities. For example, Mrs Eleanor Roosevelt and Mrs Mehta asked for the deletion of the word "women" as "everyone" includes women and the mention specifically of "women" in any part might by inference mean their exclusion where it is not mentioned.

The Universal Declaration of Human Rights, which was adopted by the United Nations on 10th December 1948, was welcomed by the women's organisations because it was based on equality of all persons and was opposed to all forms of discrimination. To summarise its provisions: Articles 1–5 set forth the fundamentals of human rights; Articles 6–12 are concerned with legal rights and protection; Articles 13–16 with movement and domicile and rights of nationality, marriage and religion; 17 with property; 18 and 19 freedom of opinion and expression; 20 and 21 freedom of assembly and participation in government; 22–25 with social and economic rights; 26–27 with rights to education and cultural life; 28 with social and international order, while 29 covers individual obligations to the community. The rights throughout apply to "everyone" and to a "person", and mention is made of "man" or "woman" only in Article 16 dealing with marriage.

Following the Declaration of Human Rights the Status of Women Commission held its second session in Beirut in March 1949, and at the same time the IAW held a conference there. The Commission discussed educational opportunities for women, application of the penal law to women, conflict of laws pertaining to nationality, domicile, marriage and divorce; the property rights of married women, and equal pay. The Commission pointed out that although Article 8 of the UN Charter states that the UN shall place no restrictions on the eligibility of men and women to participate in any capacity and under conditions of equality in its principal and subsidiary organs only a small number of women had been appointed to high posts in the Secretariat of UN, and the majority occupied minor positions. A request was made to the Secretary-General to report on the matter and also on the extent to which member governments included women in their delegations to organs and agencies of the UN. Although the principle of equality was accepted in the UN Charter and in the Declaration of Rights, implementation is a different matter, for traditional thinking, customs, habits and prejudices die very slowly.

Because of the different laws in the member states of the UN the application of both the Charter and the Declaration of Human Rights, is fraught with difficulties, especially as it affects the status of women in various societies. The task of applying principles in face of these difficulties was the major one of the Beirut meeting of the Commission and it was only by persistently making requests and recommendations to the UN that progress was effected. It is one thing to declare a right, it is another to accord that right and to implement its operation in the face of different laws and traditional customs. Thus women's international organisations discovered that their work is by no means done when principles are agreed, they have to integrate them in the life of each community.

The conference of the IAW held at Beirut at the same time as the Commission meeting was the first of the regional conferences to be organised by the Alliance. These were formed for the purpose of studying the needs of different areas, the working programme for which was divided into five regions: Africa, Asia and the Far East, Europe, Latin America and the Middle East. This first one was arranged in collaboration with the Federation of Lebanese Arab Women whose president I. Kaddourak welcomed the delegates, from societies in Syra, Iran, Iraq, Egypt and Palestine. Several board members and the Alliance president, Hanna Rydh also attended. Hanna Rydh gave a talk on the threshold of a new era, a theme much in line with the general spirit of the post-war period of building a new and better world.

One of the most important committees of the Alliance since the Geneva

Congress of 1920 had been that on Equal Moral Standard, Prostitution and Traffic in Women. The Alliance had reason to be pleased therefore when the General Assembly of UN adopted on 2nd December 1949 a Convention on the "Suppression of the Traffic in Persons and of the Exploitation of the Prostitution of Others". Although this was signed by 14 countries, with 27 ratifications and/or accessions its world wide application has been slow.

Amsterdam Congress 1949

The international coverage of the Alliance was greatly extended at the Amsterdam Congress in 1949, when women's societies of eight additional countries became affiliates, namely Ceylon, Ethiopia, Iran, Iraq, Jamaica, Pakistan, Trinidad and Tobago and Turkey. The last mentioned had previously been a member, but ceased to be so just after the Istanbul Congress of 1935, because it was considered by the Turkish Government that now women had the vote a women's society was no longer necessary and was disbanded, although it should have been obvious to the Turkish Government that to secure equality of men and women in all fields of social and economic life Turkish women had still much to put right. The return to the Alliance of the Turkish Women's Association was therefore especially welcome. The addition of Iran, Iraq and Ethiopia was due to Hanna Rydh's missionary activities, while that of Ceylon and Pakistan was largely a legacy of Carrie Chapman Catt's efforts.

It was not surprising that the resolutions at the Amsterdam Congress were made with a strong consciousness of the Universal Declaration of Human Rights of the UN. The first general resolution expressed profound satisfaction that in both the Charter of the UN and the Declaration "the nations of the world have recognised the principle for which the Alliance stands, namely equality between men and women", and it called upon the UN "to take urgent steps to secure the implementation of this principle". The belief was reaffirmed "that justice, and economic and political freedom for women is only finally to be achieved under a system of democratic government". What is and is not a democratic government has, of course, been differently interpreted. That of the Alliance which is one of the best interpretations, given in Chapter 15, was reiterated in the main at the Amsterdam Congress. The second resolution was concerned with peace, when approving reference was again made to the UN Charter and Declaration of Rights. In the third resolution on civil and political rights, the Declaration was again cited in each of its four sections, three of which were concerned with married women, their nationality, the abolition of legal incapacity, and property, all of which had been discussed at previous congresses. Equal moral standard and economic rights were the familiar subjects of the fourth and fifth resolutions, but the sixth was a new subject, related to efforts to avert future wars and to better ways of settling international differences, which had brought into being the movement for World Federal Government and the Council for European Union. Believing that there can be no real democracy if women do not take their share of responsibility, the resolution requested that the bodies mentioned should include among the representatives on their governing bodies women competent and active in international work from well-known women's organisations.

At this Congress the IAW formulated a programme of work during the next three years until the next Congress. The programme included the intention to continue all efforts to remove discriminations of all kinds which were largely enumerations of previous resolutions.

A second group of objects was concerned with work for world peace through the UN.

Preparing resolutions was done by the five special committees in collaboration with affiliates as follows:

Peace and United Nations: Chairman: Margery Corbett Ashby.
Civil and Political Rights: Chairman: Andrée Lehmann.
Economic Rights: Chairman: Marie Ginsbērg.
Equal Moral Standard: Chairman: T. Sandesky Scelba.
Equal Education Rights: Chairman: Andrée Lehmann.

Status of Women Commission

In this period 1949–1952 the Commission on the Status of Women continued to hold annual meetings, the fourth and fifth at Lake Success in May 1950 and May 1951 and the sixth at Geneva in April 1952. Hanna Rydh attended the meeting in 1950 and she was able to record (*IWN* July 1950) that "never has so much attention been given in Lake Success to the non-governmental organisations, the representatives of which were accepted as partners in discussions on the same level as the governmental representatives . . . the Alliance by its president and its permanent consultant to UN, Mrs Baker van den Berg".

The first subject discussed was the political rights of women. The Secretary General's report showed that in 53 countries women have equal legal rights with men in the political field. In 21 countries the legislation does not provide equality. In some of these countries, however, the women have such rights if they fulfil certain educational or property qualifications (Gautemala, Portugal, El Salvador, Syria). Amongst the rest the women in some other countries have the right to vote and be elected to municipal bodies (Bolivia, Mexico, Monaco and with restrictions Greece and Peru).

No election rights are given to the women of Columbia, Egypt, Haiti, Honduras, Iran, Iraq, Jordan, Lebanon, Lichtenstein, Nicaragua and Switzerland.

It was seen therefore that in 1950 there was still some way to go before complete political equality of men and women existed throughout the world. In Europe there was only Switzerland and Lichtenstein where it did not exist but alas they were to remain backward for many more years.

Among other subjects discussed was the nationality of married women and the Commission adopted a resolution requesting ECOSOC to ensure the drafting of a convention, embodying the principles: that neither marriage nor its dissolution shall affect the nationality of either spouse, and that nothing shall preclude a country (party to a convention) making provision for the voluntary naturalisation of aliens, married to their nationals.

Tineke Hefting attended the meeting of the Commission in 1951 on behalf of the Alliance and gave a fairly full report (*IWN* July 1951). She recorded that the main subject of discussion was the Draft Convention on Political Rights of Women, on which there was some difference of opinion. The text of the UN Secretariat was however adopted with several amendments. Contrary to the Bogota Convention the text contained, in addition to the rights to vote and to be elected, the eligibility to public office. The additional articles were:

(1) Women shall be entitled to vote in all elections on the same conditions as men; (2) be eligible for election to all publicly elected bodies, established by national law, on the same conditions as men; and (3) be entitled to hold public office and to exercise all public functions established by national law, on the same conditions as men.

Tineke Hefting referred to the questionnaire sent by the UN Secretariat to governments and NGOs on family law and property rights and she urged the societies affiliated to the IAW to do their utmost to reply, especially as stress was laid by several of its members on the willingness of NGOs to co-operate with the Commission.

At the meeting of the Status of Women Commission at Geneva in April 1952 the Alliance was represented by the president, Hanna Rhyd, Margery Corbett Ashby and Chave Collisson. A wide range of subjects was discussed bearing on questions of equality of the sexes. Margery Corbett Ashby who wrote the report for the *IWN* (May 1952) said that the proceedings were marred because of the two rival groups: the Russian group who would not vote for any proposal put forward by the USA or the UK and the USA and UK did the same in reverse. One result of this was that the majority of delegates often refrained from voting as they did not wish to be identified with either bloc. Margery adds, however, that this did not conceal the good work of the Commission.

A recommendation made to ECOSOC was that it should prepare an International Convention designed to eliminate all discrimination against women in the field of political rights and among other recommendations were these to governments:

(1) To guarantee women the right to work on an equal footing with men; (2) to guarantee girls and women access to all forms of training and apprenticeship; (3) to ensure provision of adequate facilities and opportunities for vocational training and guidance for all workers without regard to sex; (4) to promote such opportunities for women; (5) to bear in mind the needs of women in vocational guidance and vocational and technical education.

At this meeting the Alliance supported the action of St Joan's International Social and Political Alliance in bringing to the attention of the Commission the terrible sufferings of girls under the system of circumcision (excision) in various part of the world. From the information provided by the St Joan's Alliance it appears that female circumcision is a religious rite and has several forms, but there is really little justification for it on religious grounds. It is found chiefly in Africa, Arabia and Indonesia. The fullest documentation came from Sudan, but Islamic leaders stated that it is not part of Islamic Law but is a pre-Islamic practice which became embedded in the religion of the people. It was held that an expression of world opinion on the subject by United Nations would help to arouse world conscience on a barbarous practice.

In the discussion on the subject Margery records that: "In the comments made by the representative of the WHO one saw the vast abyss between the respect shown to men and that shown to women. Ritual murder which sacrifices an occasional man is treated as murder and cannot be sheltered under the plea of religion, but the mutilation of all women in certain areas of the world which causes life-long suffering is condoned under the plea of religion. The representative of WHO declared that this question had been raised 20 years ago, but that African men had defended the custom. The women of the Commission fortunately took a more human view."

Equal Pay

The question of "equal remuneration for men and women for work of equal value" was discussed at the Conference of the International Labour Organisation at Genoa in June 1950. Very few associations of employers accepted the principle although trade unions were more favourable. The matter was again discussed at a conference of the International Labour Organisation a year later at Geneva in June 1951. Women's societies set up an office in Geneva to keep in touch with the delegates to the conference and the Alliance held a board meeting there concurrently with the ILO conference.

The proposed recommendation was the same as discussed a year before at Genoa. It was realised by Women's International Organisations that a recommendation was not enough, but that a convention on the subject should be adopted.

After the matter was debated the question was put to the vote and the proposal for a Convention supplemented by a recommendation was carried by 59 to 39 with the United Kingdom voting against. The Convention on equal pay was finally adopted at the Plenary Session on 29th June 1951 by 105 votes to 33 with 40 abstentions, among them the United Kingdom. Some of the main points in the Convention are that each member of the UN shall "ensure the application to all workers of the principle of equal remuneration for men and women for work of equal value, and should be applied by (a) national laws or regulations; (b) legally established or recognised machinery for wage determination; and (c) collective agreements between employers and workers." There was also provision for objective appraisal of work and its value and of differential rates without regard to sex.

The adoption of such a convention was certainly a considerable achievement of International Women's Organisations. But they realised it was but a beginning and the next step was to secure its adoption and ratification in all the member states.

Naples Congress 1952

The affiliation of societies at the Naples Congress indicated that the membership continued to spread throughout the world with the addition of societies from Japan, Thailand, The Philippines and Haiti. Also the Alliance was very pleased to welcome a German society, the Deutscher Frauering back into the fold. At the same time societies from four countries had not continued membership since the last Congress, namely Hungary, India, United States and Uruguay, all, to some extent, for political reasons.

The first resolution at the Congress was a general declaration and consisted of a confirmation of the basic principle for which the Alliance exists, that of the "Equality of men and women in all personal, social and political rights and responsibilities both national and international", the resolution reiterated the belief in democracy, and in support for the UN Declaration of Human Rights, and pledged the Alliance, both by direct international and national action by means of its affiliated associations, to insist that the Declaration of Human Rights shall be implemented in action and not exist merely on paper.

Of the other nine resolutions the first five and most important emanated from the work of the five commissions or committees (the terms seem interchangeable in the record of the Alliance), a note of which was given early in this chapter in the account of the Amsterdam Congress. Margery Corbett Ashby's committee on peace, which changed its name from "Peace and United Nations" to "Peace and Human Relations", was responsible for the second resolution, which widened a little its scope to comprehend all human relations and concluded with an appeal to affiliated societies to press their governments to introduce legislation against all discrimination of race, colour or religious creed.

The third resolution on civic and political rights prepared by Andrée Lehmann's committee requested the Commission on Human Rights to submit to the next General Assembly an alteration of the French title of the Declaration, from Droits de l'Homme to Droits Humains. It also requested the inclusion of Article 16 in the Draft Covenants being prepared by the Commission on Human Rights.

Marie Ginsberg had been succeeded by Laurel Casinader of Ceylon as chairman of the Economic Rights Committee which was responsible for the fourth resolution. It noted with satisfaction that the Convention and Recommendation on Equal Remuneration for Men and Women for Work of Equal Value had been adopted by the ILO and it called upon its affiliated societies to form committees in their countries to adopt and implement the principle of equal remuneration. That was in 1952, and although by 1979 most countries in Europe had adopted the principle the implementation is far from being realised.

Andrée Lehmann was also chairman of the Educational Rights Committee which formulated a resolution (5th) containing several requests to the United Nations to recommend to its member states provision for the education of women and girls, especially as this had been much more neglected than for men and boys, and many suggestions were made of some of the facilities that should be provided. One request goes to the heart of discrimination: "to exclude all causes, preventing women from getting equal access to education on all levels, in all groups, whether economic or geographical".

Dr T. Sandesky Scelba had been succeeded by Chave Collisson as chairman of the Equal Moral Standard Committee, which was responsible for the sixth resolution concerned chiefly with prostitution. It expressed satisfaction that the General Assembly of the UN accepted the Convention (in December 1949) for the Suppression of the Traffic in Persons and the Exploitation of the Prostitution of Others, and urged that all member states of UN should abolish state regulation of prostitution and that third party exploitation should be a legal offence. Reference was again made to female circumcision and it was urged that in territories where it is practised that

Andrée Lehmann, president of La Ligue Français pour le Droit des Femmes became a member of the board of IAW in 1946 and a vice-president in 1949. She was a notable linguist and organised the interpretation facilities at congresses and meetings. In 1939 she was chairman of the Committee on the Legal Status of Women, from 1946 to 1967 of the Committee for Equal Civil and Political Rights, and in 1949–1952 of the Committee on Equal Educational Rights.

its eradication should be secured by education and the appropriate measures of prohibition.

The five special standing committees remained the same as after the Amsterdam Congress (1949). There were three new chairman, Laurel Casinader became chairman of Economic Rights Committee; Chave Collisson of Equal Moral Standards and Amy Bush of Equal Educational Rights Committee.

At the Naples Congress Hanna Rydh resigned the presidency of the Alliance after six years of devoted service to its work. She proved to be an inspiring leader and through her efforts women's societies in many countries in Asia became affiliated. Such work conscientiously done is very demanding and the calls of her chosen career of archaeologist[2] were insistent. Still the Alliance was fortunate in having such a leader for six years. I remember visiting Hanna Rydh in Stockholm, with my wife, years later in the summer of 1963. She was then in hospital but she left for an afternoon to receive us in her beautiful flat. She was dressed, I remember, in white and I have rarely experienced a more dignified and kindly person. She showed us her archaeological collection and spoke of her interesting years as president of the Alliance. After we left she returned to hospital and some months later we had news of her death.

Hanna Rydh was succeeded by Ester Graff from Copenhagen. She was 56 and managing director of the Copenhagen branch of Lintas Ltd (Lever Bros. International Advertising Service). In connection with her work she travelled in Europe and the United States and was a board member of *Dansk Kvindesam* fund, the oldest women's organisation in Denmark.

Several changes had taken place among the vice-presidents and board members during the six post-war years since the Interlaken Congress in 1946 and there were many new members who were destined to play very active parts in the work of the Alliance.

In addition to Margery Corbett Ashby and Hanna Rydh a few were prominent members before the war, among them Frau Adele Schreiber of Berlin who was a member of the board as far back as the Rome Congress (1923), and who became first vice-president at the Paris Congress in 1926, she continued a very active one through the thirties and after the second world war, and was part author of the jubilee history of the Alliance, *Journey Towards Freedom*, published in 1954. Among others prominent before the war were Nina Spiller of Great Britain and Marie Ginsberg of Switzerland, both of whom became board members at the Istanbul Congress (1935). The former became treasurer at Copenhagen (1939) and continued as such during the war and beyond up to the Amsterdam Congress (1949) when she was succeeded by Eva Kolstad of Norway. Nina Spiller continued to give great service in a variety of ways. Marie Ginsberg became a vice-president at Interlaken and a very useful and active one she proved to be. Andrée Lehmann of France became a member of the board at Copenhagen and a vice-president at Amsterdam—a very dynamic one.

Among the new post-war members who were later very active and valuable were Chave Collisson of Australia who became a member of the board at Amsterdam (1949) and hard working chairman of the Equal Moral Standard Committee, Amy Bush of Great Britain, was elected to the board at Naples (1952) and became a great asset in the educational field, becoming chairman of the Committee on Equal Educational Rights. Margaret Mathieson was another new member of the board from Great Britain who was to prove an asset to the Alliance, and who later was part author with Adele Schreiber of *Journey Towards Freedom*.

The IAW had been extending to include women's societies in the Near and Far East. At Rome in 1923 the Women's Indian Association was affiliated and continued until the Amsterdam Congress in 1949. In that year the Association of the All-Ceylon Women's Conference became an affiliate, and with it several delegates, of whom two became valuable and active members of the Alliance, namely Dr Ezlynn Deraniyagala and Laurel Casinader. The former became a board member at that Congress and vice-president at Naples, while the latter became chairman of the Economic Rights Committee.

Katherine Bompas, who had been Headquarters Secretary for 27 years resigned at the Naples Congress. She had proved a very efficient and resourceful secretary in difficult conditions especially during the hard times of the war and immediately afterwards when she undoubtedly contributed to the survival and revival of the Alliance. She later became a member of the board for a short time.

At the end of 1952 Elisabeth Hamilton-Smith relinquished the honorary editorship of the *International Women's News*, a task that she had efficiently performed since the journal again came under the control of the Alliance in January 1946. She maintained the high standard that it had achieved in the inter-war years, and her resignation was a real loss.

She was succeeded by Margery Corbett Ashby, who thus added yet another service to the many that she had already given to the IAW. She took control with the issue for January 1953, and was assisted by Nina Spiller who edited the French section.

The headquarters of the Alliance in the early post-war period was in England, at 45 Kingsway, Wembley, but when Hanna Rydh became president at Interlaken, the headquarters was transferred to her home in Sweden at Johanesgatan 20, Stockholm; and when Ester Graff became president at Naples, the headquarters was in turn transferred to her home in Denmark at Vester Søgade 48, Copenhagen, an indication that these were very much working presidents. In fact from the beginning and all through the long presidencies of Carrie Chapman Catt and Margery Corbett Ashby the hardest working members had been the presidents.

UN Convention on Political Rights for Women

On 20th December 1952 the Convention on the Political Rights of Women was adopted by the UN General Assembly with 46 voting for, none against and 11 abstentions. Six of the abstaining countries subsequently signed. The adoption of the Convention naturally gave much satisfaction to the Alliance for it had worked hard and conducted much international propaganda to achieve this. It had made many representations to the Commission when the Convention was being drafted. As adopted the Convention requires that women shall be entitled to vote in all elections, be eligible for election to all public elective bodies, established by national law, be entitled to hold public office and to exercise all public functions, established by national law, all on equal terms with men without any discriminations.

At its twelfth session in March 1958 the Status of Women Commission expressed regret that only 41 signatures and 29 ratifications had been obtained since March 1953 when it was opened for that purpose. The Commission also at that time adopted a resolution "regretting that discriminatory measures were still being taken in many countries against married women who apply for or occupy administrative posts", and this attitude was confirmed by ECOSOC at a meeting in 1960 when it recommended to governments of states members of UN that the necessary steps be taken to remove legal and other obstacles impeding the exercise of the right of married women to work.

These recommendations demonstrate that it is often a long way from the United Nations adoption of a principle to its implementation in the various member countries of the world. The international acceptance of the principle is only half the battle and women have to continue to persuade and fight so that the principle becomes a habit of thinking—often a very difficult matter.

REFERENCES

Article 16:
1 (1) Men and women of full age, without any limitation due to race, nationality or religion, have the right to marry and to found a family. They are entitled to equal rights as to marriage, during marriage and at its dissolution.
   (2) Marriage shall be entered into only with the free and full consent of the intending spouses.
   (3) The family is the natural and fundamental group unit of society and is entitled to protection by society and the State.
2 Hanna Rydh was very well known as an archaeologist and was author of many books including *The Land of the Sun God*; *Symbolism in Mortuary Ceramics*; *Seasonal Fertility Rites*; *The Death Cult in Scandinavia and China*; *Life in Pharaoh's Land* and several others.
3 To avoid ambiguities it should be explained that a United Nations Convention is an international legal instrument to which nations subscribe, thus committing themselves to be bound by its terms.
   A convention is usually drafted by one of the Commissions, and is then signed by national governments which is an expression of their agreement with its principles. For it to be adopted by a country it has to be ratified and accord, of course, with a country's own legal requirements.

Ester Graff of Denmark, president of
the IAW 1952–1958.

CHAPTER SEVENTEEN

1953–1958

Women in the Changing East. Colombo and Athens Congresses

The Alliance had been gradually extending its influence and membership to the Near and Far East, to the Asian and African countries in the inter-war period and this was vigorously continued after the second world war. Societies of Japan, India, Egypt and Palestine had become affiliates at the Rome Congress in 1923, and of Turkey at Berlin in 1929. Interlaken (1946) saw the addition of societies of Lebanon and Syria, but it was at the Amsterdam Congress of 1949 that the extension was most marked with affiliates from Ceylon and Pakistan, Iran and Iraq, and Ethiopia. The two first were to become particularly active and provided two presidents of the Alliance for twelve years from 1958 to 1970.

Ceylon had been a British Colony from 1802–15 until 1948 when it became a self-governing state and a member of the British Commonwealth. A new republican constitution was adopted in 1972 and the country changed its name to the old Brahma one of Sri Lanka. Here until almost the mid-twentieth century women had been very much in subjection, but a strong liberating movement had been generating in the inter-war years, and was much intensified after the second world war. Particularly active was the All-Ceylon Women's Association. Among the first of its enterprises in collaborating with the Alliance was to hold the second IAW Regional Conference in July 1954. The president of the Association, Ezlynn Der-aniyagala, was very energetic in organising this and made a two months' visit to London to make arrangements.

The theme of the conference was education of women and related subjects, and after inaugural meetings, attended by nearly 300, the conference divided into study groups. Societies from Pakistan, the Philippines, India, Indonesia, Nepal, Japan, and, of course, Ceylon, were represented.

The All Ceylon Women's Conference invited the Alliance to hold its next Congress in 1955 in Ceylon, and this invitation was accepted by the Board at the International Committee meeting in London in June 1954. Influencing the acceptance was the recognition that because of its convenient situation Ceylon was becoming a centre for international meetings.

Much preparation was necessary for a Congress so far afield. It was the first to be held outside Europe, and was also the Jubilee Conference,[1] so special efforts were made for its success.

Some changes were made in the arrangements. Hitherto, apart from preparatory meetings, Congresses had lasted about a week to 10 days. (Naples 8 days, Amsterdam 7 and Interlaken, 6) but that at Colombo was planned for 16 days, from 17th August to 1st September. This was partly due to the financial help given by Unesco which was conditional on the conference not being less than 14 days.

Delegates from 24 countries attended, also delegates from ten International Organisations, and representatives from the United Nations, UNESCO and the ILO.

The theme of the Congress was "Equal access of women and girls with men and boys to opportunities of education". The delegates were welcomed by Sir Oliver Goonetilleke, the Governor-General, by Mrs Ezlynn Deraniyagala, and by Dr N. M. Perera, Mayor of Colombo, who referred to the Alliance as a beacon light for the women of Asia, where the barriers of caste, creed, and sex were hard to break. Greetings were given by Mr James B. Orrick, the United Nations Director of Information for India. At the opening ceremony Sir Oliver Goonetilleke lit the pana, or candelabra and then the president of each affiliated society lit a wick, so that when completed there was a blaze of 30 lights. It served to symbolise Dr Perera's remark.

Resolutions on the subjects of the five commissions were the only ones adopted at the Congress and these formed the themes of the study course (now called seminar) which was an additional event for a Congress.[2] The resolutions were preceded by a General Declaration, in which it was noted that world tension was being lessened by the acceptance by groups of nations of principles of reasonable concession, mutual respect and understanding. The comment was justified and continued to be justified, although one might not get that impression often from the press and radio that depend unfortunately for much of their interest on trouble and sensation which they make the most of and sometimes exaggerate. Although there is much progress still to be made in international understanding it probably had reached a greater measure of success than at any previous time in history.

The Declaration continued by saying that the development of this world understanding is dependent on reforms which will ensure equality and spiritual freedom and a responsibility to each individual man and woman of every country, race, and kind, not only through legislation but through every-day practice, not only in the community but also in the family, the fundamental group unit of society. The IAW it continued, having striven through its organisation for 50 years for these principles, now proclaimed in the Universal Declaration of Human Rights, will increase its activity to ensure that these rights are applied, so that the obstacles which hinder women from exercising their educational, economic, civil and political rights as equal citizens are overcome. For no community can rise above the general status of its women, every community will gain by the inspiration women can bring and by the working together of men and women towards a richer life. The women's cause is today that of all mankind.

At Colombo, Ester Graff was re-elected president while the new board members were Begum Anwar Ahmed of Pakistan and Jur. kand Edith Anrep of Sweden.

Covenants on Human Rights

In the early fifties the UN Commission on Human Rights was preparing two draft Covenants one on Civil and Political Rights and the other on Economic, Social and Cultural Rights. These were studied by the Alliance, and, objecting to some of the provisions, as a consultant it made several recommendations to the commission concerned with wording to ensure more precision, the avoidance of ambiguities and temptation to delays in implementation. For example in the wording of the Draft Covenant of Civil and Political Rights, the Alliance was critical of "legislation . . . shall be directed towards equality of rights and responsibilities for the spouses as to marriage, during marriage and at its dissolution". It was pointed out that the word "directed" does not actually oblige the states to bring their legislation into harmony with the substance of Article 16 of the Declaration of Human Rights. The wording preferred was the spouses "are entitled to equal rights as to marriage, during marriage and at its dissolution". There were several more examples where it was felt that the wording was unsatisfactory, and on which recommendations were made. They signify the constant alertness of the IAW in serving the democratic cause of equality. There is also the important aspect that vague wording is open to many interpretations as that of the League of Nations showed, with such unsatisfactory results. The Commission on Human Rights completed its preparation of these Draft Covenants in 1954, and submitted them to the General Assembly of the UN, which referred them to the Humanitarian, Social and Cultural Committee, which adopted them in 1960. They were however, destined for further consideration and this will be mentioned later.

Also in the fifties a sub-commission of the Human Rights Commission concerned with the Prevention of Discrimination and Protection of Minorities was hard at work and held many sessions. This meant a tremendous amount of research by the experts who composed the commission as it involved a global study of kinds and conditions of discriminatory policies in education whether based on race, sex, religion or any form of bias or prejudice, contrary to the Declaration of Human Rights.

The NGOs with consultative status were asked in 1953 by UN whether they considered it advisable to convene a conference to meet and exchange views on the most effective means of combating discrimination and to consider the possibility of establishing common objectives and programmes. The IAW was in favour of this and sent to the UN a summary of its activities against discrimination, especially in that of sex discrimination, whether of a legal, legislative, conventional or moral character. The IAW was also asked for advice on a variety of relevant matters. It suggested in the matter of political rights that studies should not be confined to legislation but to factors which emanate from prejudice, and habits resulting from the traditional subjection of women. The offices of all religious communities should, it was stated, be open to both sexes and women should be able to participate in the function of cults equally with men.

The conference of the NGOs with the sub-commission was held in 1955 and at the ninth session of the sub-commission in the spring of 1957 a report was issued which prompted much discussion especially the sections dealing with sex discrimination and equality of access to education. It was considered that the report took a too optimistic view "in stating that Governments were making every effort to eliminate or diminish such discrimination". The report itself indicated that there was "a world-wide attitude of passive resistance" to educational opportunities for girls and women (See *IWN* August 1957).

At this session two reports prepared by the ILO on discrimination in the field to employment and occupation were considered. The statement that improvements in the employment status of women would have to wait until improvement of their status generally met with opposition, especially from the Status of Women Commission representative. Exception was also taken to the assertion that it was in times of war or other catastrophe when there was a manpower shortage that advance for women in employment could be made.

A further NGO Conference on the subject of discrimination was planned for 1958. This was held at Geneva in June 1958, at which five representatives of the Alliance were present, Nina Spiller, Mrs Bernard, Amy Bush, Andrée Lehmann, and Laurel Casinader. The main advocacies of the Alliance were:

1. Equal educational opportunities for men and women.
2. East-west collaboration for the mutual understanding of each other's cultures and problems. It was pointed out that this had been a special purpose of the IAW programme in recent years, which had included the first International Congress in the east.

3. The need for civic education by the holding of seminars and by other means, which contributes to the economic emancipation of women.

A seminar, or study course, as it was previously called, had already been held by the Alliance in connection with the Colombo Congress, and another in connection with the Athens Congress, but subsequently they were held in different years from those of Congresses except for that in India of 1973. Between the Colombo and Athens Congresses the UN General Assembly adopted the Convention on the Nationality of Married Women on 29th January 1957. 47 countries voted for the adoption, 2 against with 24 abstentions. This had been drafted largely by the Commission on the Status of Women with the assistance of International NGOs of which the IAW contributed much. The Convention provides that marriage, or its dissolution, or the change of nationality by the husband during marriage, shall not automatically affect the nationality of a wife. Contracting states agree that an alien wife may, at her request, acquire her husband's nationality through specially privileged naturalisation procedures.

Athens Congress and Study Course 1958

Accepting the invitation of the Greek League for Women's Rights the foundation of which was prompted by the Alliance in 1920, the eighteenth Congress of the Alliance was held at Athens from 25th August to 4th September 1958. It was preceded by a study course or seminar from 7th to 21st August which was held with the assistance of UNESCO and was organised and arranged by Amy Bush who was president of the Alliance Committee on Equal Education Rights, and directed by Helen Judd, Lecturer in Social Administration at the London School of Economics. The theme of the study course was the Civic Responsibility of Women of the East and the West. The subjects discussed were "Parental and Community Responsibility for the Child", "Women's Place and Progress in a Developing Economy", "The Education of Boys and Girls", "Women's Part in the Local Community", "The Meanings and Functions of Local Government", "Women as Makers of Policy", "Trade Unions, Friendly Societies and Co-operatives", "The Equality of the Sexes", "The Work of the United Nations and the Specialised Agencies for the Progress of Women" which included a study of the Declaration of Human Rights, and discussion on the meaning of Citizenship and the practical implications of accepting responsibilities in domestic, economic and political matters.

In addition to Amy Bush and Helen Judd, the study course was assisted by Eva Asbrink of Sweden, Laurel Casinader of Ceylon, while Egli Psaltis acted as interpreter and liaison officer. Ruth Lazarus of UNESCO took an active part in the course. Students and participants, many of them members of the Alliance affiliates, came from Brazil, British Guiana, Ceylon, Denmark, Egypt, Germany, Ghana, Greece, Iceland, Iran, Ireland, Japan, Kenya, Malaya, the Netherlands, Nigeria, Pakistan, Philippines, Sierra Leone, Spain, Switzerland, Vietnam and Yugoslavia. Such an extensive coverage from various parts of the world could hardly fail to be a valuable contribution to international understanding, because each of those attending would return to their countries and spread the knowledge and experience that they had gained, especially as among them there were journalists, teachers, those trained in social work and active members of women's societies.

The method in conducting the course was carefully planned. For example each day started with a short recapitulation by Helen Judd, so as to draw together the threads of the work of the previous day, while discussions were generally in three groups. Among the lecturers were Mr Orrick and Ruth Lazarus who spoke of the work of the United Nations, Andrée Lehmann on the work of the Alliance, Marios Raphael who outlined the growth of world population and the world famous planner Constantine Doxiadis who spoke of the urban environment and of enhancing the dignity of human life.

Four days elapsed and then the Congress began and most of the participants in the study course stayed on. Delegates from societies in 29 countries attended, with individual members and visitors from another six countries, and special representatives from the United Nations, ILO, USA, and fraternal delegates from 13 international organisations. Observers came from no less than 13 Greek women and girls' organisations.

The theme of the Congress was Yesterday, Today and Tomorrow. To amplify: it sought to get an answer to the question why with women having the vote in nearly all countries in the world there are so few in public life and so few in parliament. The Congress was directed to study the obstacles due to prejudice, and custom and to discuss means of overcoming them.

In her presidential address, Ester Graff gave a review of the many activities of the Alliance. She referred to the yearly board meetings since the last Congress taking place in Norway, Switzerland and the Netherlands; the choice of different countries serving the purpose of strengthening ties with many different members, and the conferences with presidents. She spoke of her visits during the period to Japan, Pakistan, Nepal and Egypt and of cementing the links of the societies in these countries with the Alliance. She also referred to the study courses and to regional conferences the first two of which, as we have seen, took place in Beirut in 1949, the second at Colombo in 1954, while a third had taken place in East Pakistan in 1956. Although she referred to that at Colombo as very

Ezlynn Deraniyagala, president of the
All-Ceylon Women's Conference, and
president of the IAW 1958–1964. She
was the first president from Asia.

promising, that in East Pakistan was devoted to the work of women in handicrafts and cottage industries and was less so. Unfortunately it was postponed from its originally projected dates because of serious floods causing a severe food situation. When it did take place only one neighbouring country sent delegates, but four others supplied specimens of their cottage industries for an exhibition which was one of the principal events of the conference organised by the host society. It may have been because of the difficulties encountered at the first three regional meetings that the board decided not to proceed with any further ones for the time being. They were however, revived thirteen years later.

The discussions on the theme of the Congress were led by Dr Andrée Lehmann who spoke on "Yesterday the Vote", describing how it was secured in various countries of the world, followed by Dr Maria Thanopoulous, the president of the Greek League for Women's Rights who spoke of Today and the regrettable maximum of only ten per cent of members of parliament being women; then Begum Anwar, chairman of the UN Status of Women Commission who spoke of Tomorrow and the aims to secure that fifty per cent of Members of Parliament should be women. The first woman MP in Europe, Mrs Tynne Leivo-Larsson of Finland also gave encouraging advice.

The resolutions again emanated from the work of the five committees, reiterating, emphasising often in different wording, the contentions of resolutions at former congresses. The titles of the committees and the chairmen or presidents as they were now called, remained the same with the exception of that on "Peace and Human Relations". It was succeeded by that on "International Understanding". Margery Corbett Ashby resigned the chairmanship of the former, and the chairman of the new committee was Edith Anrep of Sweden who had become a board member of the Alliance at the Colombo Congress.

Ester Graff resigned the presidency at the Athens Congress and was succeeded by Ezlynn Deraniyagala of Ceylon who had been a member of the board since 1949 and a vice-president since 1952. Reference was made to some of her activities earlier in this chapter.

The work of the president of the Alliance is exhausting and exacting, especially to one who feels an obligation to do her utmost for a world wide association with a great cause. The work involves travelling to many countries of the world to maintain association and contact with national women's organisations, and to secure new affiliations; it involves presiding at board meetings and meetings of national presidents, and of attending to a vast international correspondence. Ester Graff who had performed her task very conscientiously during her six years of office, felt that she had neither the strength nor the means to continue, and she thus reluctantly handed over to her successor. During her term of office she worked consistently for the main object of the Alliance: the equality of the sexes in all fields of life. She realised that the IAW was the only women's international organisation with that as its main purpose.

At both the Colombo and Athens Congresses the programme of work for the ensuing three years took the form largely of briefs for the five commissions which followed the adopted resolutions. For the Committee on Equal Civil and Political Rights the principal aim was "to achieve a more proportionate number of women members of parliaments and local councils", and partly to further this, widespread efforts were advocated to impress on women their responsibilities as citizens. Among the suggestions made were meetings, lectures, study courses, education in general to create a habit of thinking and the exercise of influence on the press, radio and television. The directives to this committee at Athens also repeated the recommendation at the Colombo Congress to seek to secure the inclusion of Article 16 (that concerned with marriage and the family—see Chapter 16) of the Declaration of Human Rights in the Covenant of Application, as previously discussed.

For the Committee on Equal Education Rights the plea was again made for equal education for boys and girls. Included in the brief for the Committee on Equal Moral Standards was the resolution to press for a draft convention of the UN on (1) Minimum legal age of marriage; (2) Free consent to marriage; and (3) Compulsory registration of marriages.

The work proposed to the Committee for International Understanding followed the main lines of creating conditions for peace and international understanding and the removal of discrimination of race, sex, and creed, and in addition to influence the UN to create a convention on human rights, and to press governments to ratify the Genocide Convention.[3]

The setting of each Congress, and the social activities attending them have not received a great deal of attention in this history, as there has been a concentration on the work directed to securing the main aims of the Alliance. The social activities and the tours generally arranged at the Congresses served, however, to lighten the arduous work of participants, and I can testify from extensive evidence and a little from my own experience that they were hard-working Congresses, which were generally made very pleasant and agreeable by social functions and the attractions of the local scene. Notes of these were generally given in the Congress numbers of *International Women's News*. The description of social events and tours given for the Athens Congress in *IWN* (September–October 1958) made very entertaining reading. It was anonymous but was possibly from the pen of the editor. In referring to the zeal for learning being handed down from Plato and Aristotle, the remark is made that "fortunately Plato's teaching about the role of women in the community is followed and not that of Aristotle". Among the memorable experiences to the writer of the article was that of seeing the Iphigeneia in Aulis of Euripides in the ancient theatre of Herodes Atticus at the foot of the Acropolis. With the full moon rising slowly above, and the glorious silhouette of the Parthenon behind us, we listened to the tragic story of the girl who was sacrificed by her father to appease the gods and allow the Greek fleet to sail against Troy. Rejecting the offer of Achilles to save her, she cried: "Better to lose a thousand women than that one man should die!" The women's movement has travelled far along the *Journey Towards Freedom* since her day.

The writer gave a picturesque description of a visit to Cape Sonium. "Here", she said, "on a lonely headland stands the temple of Poseidon. We watched the sun setting behind its milky columns, and then the rising moon turned the wine-dark sea to liquid silver." (Homer sometimes referred to the wine-dark sea.)

REFERENCES

1 The inceptive or preparatory meeting at Washington in 1902 could hardly be called a Congress. The first real Congress was at Berlin in 1904.
2 A report of this study course at Colombo was given by Margaret Mathieson in the Colombo Congress Report 1955.
3 The Convention on the Prevention and Punishment of the Crime of Genocide was adopted by the General Assembly of UN on 9th December 1948 and came into force on 12th January 1961. By 1970 seventy-three countries had ratified it.

CHAPTER EIGHTEEN

1959–1964

Working with the United Nations. The Status of Women Commission. Dublin and Trieste Congresses

During the fifties and sixties the Alliance was working increasingly with the United Nations. This was greatly facilitated by its having been accorded consultative status in 1948. The Alliance worked mainly with the advisory commissions of ECOSOC, on Human Rights, Social Matters and Status of Women, and the specialised agencies, mainly the International Labour Organisation and the Educational, Scientific and Cultural Organisation. Some of the work of these commissions and agencies was of major consequence to the central aim of the Alliance and involved close collaboration, which was often very fruitful. The Alliance was able to provide a two-way channel between its affiliated societies from nearly fifty countries of the world and the United Nations. Communication from affiliates was through their own liaison officers to the chairmen of the special committees, while affiliates were able, by communicating with the Alliance HQ to propose subjects that they would like discussed by UN commissions and agencies.

Women had participated as representatives and advisers in the United Nations from the beginning, but at first their representation was very small, only 20 at the first General Assembly. Twelve years later this had more than trebled to about 70 whereas men's representation had less than doubled, but still they outnumbered women by five to one. In the work that more directly affected women's interests, representation by women, however, was strong, such as in the Status of Women Commission.

After the early years, the work of the Status of Women Commission was necessarily in some degree repetitive, concentrating on improvements of wording, amendments, increased comprehensiveness to make resolutions more effective for incorporation of principles into covenants. One important matter that was discussed at the 12th session (1958) was the principal theme of the Alliance Congress at Athens in 1958: the access of women to public offices and functions. It was agreed at this session of the Commission to ask NGOs to provide information to enable a new resolution on this subject to be made at the 14th session at Buenos Aires in the spring of 1960. The Alliance Committee for Equal Civil and Political Rights wrote therefore to the affiliates asking in May 1959 for this information to be sent by 1st July. A reminder was given in March 1960 but with no result. It was a serious default and contrasted rather sadly with the enthusiastic responses that had always been received in the earlier years of the Alliance. The Alliance Commission reported to the Dublin Congress its "great sorrow that no affiliated society sent in an answer". "This silence", it continued, "is completely opposite to the aims of the Alliance." It was pointed out that "associations met in Congress, adopted resolutions, and by their own votes agreed to work in their respective countries with the object of implementing these resolutions at some future date. From this silence one must deduce that if it was because they had not worked—it threw doubt on the entire efficacy of our Alliance, if because they had neglected to inform us of the results of their activities—this deprived us of a way of evaluating the efficacy of our efforts".

This fortunately seems to have been the only occasion, when the affiliated societies of the Alliance failed to play the part of supplying information. Perhaps the difficulty of providing up-to-date information in an orderly form where statistical work had not been extensive was mainly responsible.

In the three years from the Athens Congress in 1958 to that at Dublin in 1961 the new president, Ezlynn Deraniyagala travelled extensively and a record of this was given in her report to the latter Congress. She visited 18 affiliated societies of the Alliance in 13 countries: Australia, Egypt, France, Germany, Great Britain, Iran, Ireland, Israel, Nepal, Pakistan, Turkey, Lebanon and the Philippines, while she also visited four countries without affiliated societies, India, Indonesia, Singapore and Afghanistan with the hope of securing the affiliations of further national women's societies. In the case of India she made several efforts to obtain the reaffiliation of the All India Women's Conference, but a series of mishaps seemed to prevent this.

In addition to Ezlynn's travels, Margery Corbett Ashby visited affiliated and other women's societies in the Near East and Hanna Rydh travelled to the Far East, Helen Judd represented the IAW at the UNESCO Nigerian Seminar and visited the women's societies there while Amy Bush attended the World Conference on Adult Education in Montreal with the interests of women and the Alliance very much at heart.

Ezlynn Deraniyagala's visit to Israel was especially rewarding in the picture she was able to obtain of the social position of women there. She was assisted and provided with facilities for study by Dr Brachyahu, president of the Women's Equal Rights in Israel, and Jenny Blumenfeld, president of the Council of Women's Organisations, while two board members, Tehilla Matmon and Zilla Shoham gave much assistance. Ezlynn had a useful and profitable talk with Mrs Golda Meir, a member of the government, who was then (1959) acting for the Prime Minister.

Ezlynn formed two pictures of the women of Israel at this time: one bright containing all the colours of progress, the other sombre and quiescent. Ten of 120 members of the *Knesset* or Parliament were women, while in other spheres of public life they appeared to be increasingly active, in municipal government, in diplomacy, in the civil service and in law where there were several judges and attorneys. Large numbers were employed in education, in the academic professions and in the health and social services. After recounting this and much more (*IWN* November 1959) she concluded "enough has been said to show that the social and economic position of Israeli women is good". "However," she continued, "in those branches of private law which are of intimate concern to women such as marriage, divorce and inheritance, there are grave instances of discrimination against them more than medieval in severity. This despite the Declaration of Independence which assured the women of Israel that their absolute equality with men in rights and duties would be maintained by the state in all respects."

The conjugal relationship and all it implies is governed by the Rabbinical Courts who have sole jurisdiction over Jews in this respect. There is no civil marriage or registration. Marriage between members of different religions is not allowed and the non-Jewish partner is obliged to accept the Jewish religion. If this law is defied the children of such unions are "bastards" who in turn may marry only "bastards". In all marriages the husband must provide for his wife, but all moveable posessions and her earnings after marriage are legally his unless a prenuptial contract is drawn up. Divorce in the Rabbinical Court is by mutual consent and as in other countries where this ground exists it is seldom that mutuality is genuine. If a married woman becomes insane, her husband may divorce her at once, but if he becomes insane she can never re-marry. The same discrimination exists in the case of desertion. A childless widow must obtain a *Halitza* or permit from her deceased husband's brother before she may re-marry, and sometimes she suffers indifferent or malicious treatment in consequence.

As for inheritance, as recently as 1958 a bill was presented to the *Knesset* in which it was proposed to enable the husband to bequeath all the property which has accumulated during the lifetime of the couple to whoever he sees fit, which seems utterly to abrogate the principle of one law, one judgment, for men and women which is the basis of the State of Israel. Two of our affiliates, Wizo in Israel and the Women's League for Equal Rights, have protested vigorously against this unrestricted power for the husband, urging that he be limited to a right to bequeath only up to half the property within his possession. A daughter cannot inherit as much as a son and a widow must share the guardianship of her children with a male relative.

Needless to say, Israeli women have not been idle about this weight of discrimination against them, and foremost amongst its combatants are the three affiliates of the IAW and their leaders.

To assist women in the many problems which arise from this sadly archaic state of affairs, the Women's Rights Association instituted a free legal aid service as long ago as 1920. With little money or specialised training its members studied the religious law, struggled to assist women in their suits before the Rabbinical Courts, and gradually established centres in all the cities where there were such courts. The efforts of the Equal Rights Association were insufficient to meet this great need, and so four years ago it joined forces with Wizo in Israel in order to strengthen and spread its excellent work.

This is an indication that in a country that has been very progressive in many fields of economic and social life there is still considerable discrimination against women due largely to traditional habits of thinking emanating partly from religious doctrine. It is in such fields that progress towards equality is especially difficult, and demonstrates that the journey of such organisations as the IAW is still in parts an uphill one.

In her visit to Pakistan Ezlynn Deraniyagala was met by an Alliance vice-president, Begum Anwar Ahmed, who was also chairman of the UN Status of Women Commission, and a member of the All-Pakistan Women's Association which she represented, with one other, on the Family Law Commission. This had produced a parliamentary bill concerned with registration of marriage and divorce and the establishment of matrimonial courts which represented considerable advance for women.

In Kabul, the capital of Afghanistan, Ezlynn Deraniyagala found a community where apparently for several decades women were emerging to a fuller and freer life. The Women's Welfare Society, the first women's organisation to be established in Afghanistan, was founded immediately after world war two in 1946. The Queen was patron and the chairman was Kama Khanum, daughter of Marshall Shah Mahmood Khan Ghazi. The purpose of the society was to improve the status of women in Afghanistan, to provide them with guidance and to stimulate education. Women occupied at the time (early sixties) many positions in commercial and industrial life formerly occupied only by men, and many traditional habits like the wearing of the *chaudri* had largely disappeared. Still, many restrictions continued to exist, as for example, the prohibition of school—which means education—for the married woman.

The changes coming fairly quickly for Afghan women are necessarily accompanied by difficulties of adjustment. Ezlynn Deraniyagala remarks that they are full of interest and significance for the Afghan woman. "Modestly and with great dignity she is striving to adjust herself to the new social conditions which confront her as she discards the *chaudri*. She realises that with social freedom come many strange new responsibilities, and is sometimes a little puzzled as to what these responsibilities entail . . . the success which attends her striving is a shining augury for her future."

Dublin Congress, August 1961

Delegates of societies from 24 countries attended the Dublin Congress— two-thirds of the countries with affiliated societies. In addition there were observers from seven countries without affiliated societies and several international fraternal delegates. In her report the president gave an account of her travels and of the women's societies in the countries she visited and announced the affiliation of six new societies: two well-known ones in Great Britain, the Fawcett Society[1] and the National Union of Townswomen's Guilds;[2] The Women's Suffrage Movement of the Bahamas, the *Amicale des Elués Municipales of France*, the Sierra Leone Women's Movement and the Council of Women's Societies in Nigeria.

Much that was resolved at this Congress was inevitably a repetition of resolutions at previous ones although sometimes couched in different wording as suited the trend of events. The first committee devoted its first section to the means of achieving a more proportionate number of women members of parliament which it had previously advocated. The second section of the resolution was concerned with the incorporation of Article 16 of the Universal Declaration of Human Rights in Article 22 of the Draft Convention on Civil and Political Rights. Article 16 states that men and women "are entitled to equal rights as to marriage, during marriage and at its dissolution" whereas the draft for Article 22 of the Covenant by the third Commission of the General Assembly of UN states that the legislation of states should "tend towards" this equality. The United Nations was reminded that the eighth session of the Status of Women Commission passed a resolution asking that Article 22 of the Draft Covenant should be exactly the same as Article 16 of the Declaration, and the Alliance asked all its affiliated societies to request the leaders of national delegations to the next General Assembly of UN to ask for this. That this action met with some success is testified by the Covenant on Civil and Political Rights adopted in 1976. Article 22 had become 23, and the wording on the matter in question became "State Parties to the present Covenant shall take appropriate steps to ensure equality of rights and responsibilities of spouses as to marriage, during marriage and at its dissolution".

A new item in the resolutions was concerned with age of retirement and pensions. It noted that ECOSOC suggested that the ILO should study the subject and it was recommended to affiliated societies that they should

Board meeting of IAW in Berlin 1959. From left to right in the front row are: Leila Basnayake, then treasurer of IAW; Ezlyn Deraniyagala, president and Dr Hedi Flitz, vice-president of IAW 1961 and Member of Parliament and City Councillor of Wilhelmshaven for 20 years. Second row: Dr Hanna Rydh, Elizabeth Halsey for some years secretary of IAW, Margery Corbett Ashby and Mrs Baheega Rasheed. Back row: Edith Anrep, Marie Thanoopulos, Margaret Ingledew and Chave Collisson.

"take steps to educate and convince women workers of their ultimate advantage in acquiring an equal age of retirement and equal pension rights with men". The general acceptance of this principle in 1979 still seemed a long way off.

In the autumn of 1961, shortly after the Congress, Margery Corbett Ashby resigned the editorship of *International Women's News*. She gave her reasons in a note in the journal for September–October—that her eyes were giving trouble and she felt that the paper should be edited by a younger woman. Margery was then in her eightieth year. In this note she remarked that "the success of the women's movement over my three-quarters of a century has been staggering in its speed and world-wide extension. I can hardly believe that the Alliance I saw starting with a few European countries and the USA could now embrace so many countries in Asia and Africa, to link together women with the same high ideals of service and responsibility." It could be added that no person had contributed more to the success of the international campaign for women than Margery herself. The world wide extension of the Alliance is illustrated by the countries of the principal officers after the Dublin Congress: the president from Ceylon, the first vice-president, Maître Andrée Lehmann from France; the second vice-president, Mme Safiyeh Firouz from Iran; the third vice-president, Begum Anwar G. Ahmed from Pakistan; the Hon. Secretary Miss Egli Psaltis from Greece. The countries represented by the Executive Board members were Sweden, UK, Philippines, Turkey, Germany, Switzerland, Sierra Leone, Lebanon, Norway, Iceland, Australia, Nigeria, Egypt, Liberia, Italy, Ireland and The Bahamas.

The president Ezlynn Deraniyagala expressed her sadness at Margery's relinquishment of the editorship of *IWN*. She was, however, able to welcome her successor, Helen Whittick, president of the National Women Citizens' Association, who led the British delegation at the Dublin Congress. Margery very graciously alluded to her successor in saying that "she felt she was marrying off a beloved son to a very nice girl".

The work and value of the Status of Women Commission

At its sixteenth and seventeenth sessions held at the New York headquarters of the UN in March 1962 and 1963 the Status of Women Commission continued its discussions on methods to improve the position of women in modern societies with a view to making recommendations to ECOSOC. Matters considered were equal pay for equal work, vocational guidance and training for women and girls, access of women to training and employment, the age of retirement for women and equal pensions with men, and the problems of working mothers.

The sessions were attended by representatives of twenty-one countries. The chief difficulties in agreeing about recommendations were the habits and traditional prejudices that, although existing in all countries, had various manifestations. In the discussions on vocational guidance for women and girls for example, among the difficulties were the (1) traditional dependent status of women in many countries; (2) the prejudice of parents in giving preference to the education of boys; (3) the tendency of girls to take short-term unskilled or semi-skilled jobs; (4) the categorization of work which is traditionally men's and traditionally women's; and (5) the attitude of considering women's work as subsidiary or marginal. All this mostly outmoded thinking provided obstacles that had to be overcome. The answers to the questions posed by the common habit of thinking led to recommendations. One was to indicate to governments their responsibility to their country by including women's work in their economic planning which involves determining the future needs of the labour market. It was also proposed that parent-teacher associations should bring pressure on educational authorities to introduce vocational guidance in the senior forms of girls schools, and that the ILO should conduct research into the particular problems of women workers. It was agreed that all women, including mothers of young children, should have the right to work, and be free to take up paid employment, and that day nurseries and crèches should be increased and improved.

It will be remembered that at the Dublin Congress of the IAW the age of retirement and pensions for women were discussed and affiliates were recommended to campaign for equality with men in the matter. The question was considered at the seventeenth session of the Status of Women Commission which recommended that "with due regard to national, social and economic policies and conditions, the provisions concerning the pensionable age and right to pensions under social security and insurance schemes affording economic protection to retirement pensioners should be sufficiently flexible to meet varied and changing circumstances, individual needs and reasonable individual preferences as regards effective retirement."

This is quoted in an article by Laurel Casinader in *IWN* (May 1963). It was stressed "that to eliminate possible disadvantages to women an equitable employment pension scheme should include shorter periods of employment and part-time employment and also allow for a flexible retirement age for men and women". The need for voluntary rather than compulsory retirement was urged and that the adequacy of retirement benefits should be kept in line with changes in prices and wages. It was noted, that although there was a wide divergence of views among governments and women's organisations, there was a trend towards equal provisions in retirement for men and women.

It may be questioned whether the recommendation of the Commission in this matter was not a little too vague and indefinite. After all, in commerce and industry there is a definite retirement age, although varying in different countries. Generally in UK, to cite one example, it is 65 for men and 60 for women. The question is should it be the same for both with equal pensions, with a woman, whether married or unmarried, treated as an individual in the same way as a man.

One useful reaffirmation made at this session was that men and women should have equal access to vocational training.

Recommendations are made to ECOSOC which considers them and determines whether they should be passed to the General Assembly and, if so, what changes or modifications should be made, if any. This procedure no doubt partly prompted Joan Vickers, MP, the British Government's representative on the Status of Women Commission, to question the need for the Status of Women Commission in an article entitled "Is it really necessary" in *IWN*, September 1963.

"As the Commission", she writes, "has to work through the Economic and Social Council (it does not even elect its own members), and also has one representative on the Human Rights Commission, might it not be better to enlarge the membership of these committees instead of this special commission for women which meets for three weeks each year in a rather isolated position?" She remarks that resolutions are passed and handed on to ECOSOC and many are never heard of again. She stresses the theme that "the only way in which women can improve their status is through education, not necessarily through the vote", and stresses the aid and guidance given by voluntary organisations without which the work done by the Commission would be much slower. The views of voluntary associations, she added, might be still more influential if they were published in advance of meetings of the Commission so that delegates have an opportunity of studying them. She concluded the article with repeating the question whether it would not be better to abandon the Commission and have larger representation of women on ECOSOC, ILO and UNESCO.

In the light of the history of the Status of Women Commission and the strenuous preliminary work to get it formed both in the days of the League of Nations and during the inceptive period of the United Nations, to follow the advocacy of Joan Vickers and abandon it for bigger women's representations on other bodies can hardly be regarded as anything but a retrograde step. It will be remembered that in 1936 the liaison committee at Geneva that represented women's organisations throughout the world urged the Council of the League of Nations to appoint a committee of experts on the Status of Women and this was appointed early in 1938. The expert committee did much research work in collaboration with women's organisations as described in Chapter 12. The work was continued by United Nations and a Status of Women Sub-commission to the Commission on Human Rights of ECOSOC was appointed and held its first meeting in April 1946. It submitted a valuable report to the Commission on Human Rights briefly outlined in Chapter 15. Late in 1946 the Commission on the Status of Women reporting direct to ECOSOC was established.

In the *IWN* January 1964 Marguerite Bowie replied to Joan Vickers. She mentioned that at the deliberations of the formation of the United Nations at San Francisco in 1945 a separate commission on the status of women was proposed by Bertha Lutz of Brazil (a prominent member of the Alliance who was elected to its board at the Interlaken Congress) and supported by the Latin American Countries; but opposed by Virginia Gildersleeve of USA who contended that the work should be done by the Human Rights Commission. The USA delegate received the support of the two women in the British delegation: Ellen Wilkinson and Florence Horsburgh, "whether", she says, "speaking from conviction, optimism or merely their Foreign Office brief".

Marguerite Bowie continues: "I was appointed as 'Adviser' to the British Delegation at the second session, at that time agreeing largely with the cagey Foreign Office brief. But I have learned my lesson, as have many brought into contact with very different national and political conditions.

"None of the achievements of the Commission on the Status of Women", she continues, "would have been possible if left to the Human Rights Commission. On that commission, for years, we did little but draft Conventions, still not accepted by the General Assembly, and left long agendas on other matters unconsidered. Only the persistence of the women in continually sending back their requests and drafts to ECOSOC finally got through a Convention on Political Rights of Women (still not signed by the United Kingdom) and a Convention of Nationality of Married Women. Incidentally, their first effort, to be fair to the men too, and have a Convention on the Nationality of Married Persons, was severely snubbed! Both these conventions have had a wide effect on women's rights and the Commision's last effort, which had an equally rough passage, the Convention on Age of Marriage and Consent to Marriage, is already having great legal and social consequences.

"There are questions no committee of men would have 'touched with a barge pole' such as that of circumcision of girls, which the women have bravely and boldly tackled. Theory and practice are so often miles apart, and there is a lot still for the women to do before women in all countries can stand free and equal with men.

"The small number of women serving on commissions and committees other than the Status of Women is deplorable, and the record of the United Kingdom, a so-called 'democratic' country, is particularly bad."

She concludes the article by saying that "While the men regard visits to the UN as a privilege rather than a crusade you are not likely to get more women delegates. As more women come into the professions and into government employment one finds more women appointed as 'Advisers' to delegations. But we want them as policy-makers. I think that is a problem as much for women as for men to solve."

This line of thinking was strongly supported by Ruth Tomlinson, (IWN May 1964) who was for three years the representative of the UK government on the Status of Women Commission and who subsequently worked for several years in close co-operation with it. She speaks of the leadership, stimulus and understanding of the Commission as indispensable to the work for the advancement of women in Africa, Asia and South America, and in promoting their rights in the political, economic, civil and educational fields in accordance with the principles of the UN Charter.

Meeting in June 1962 of the board of
the IAW at the headquarters of the
National Union of Townswomen's
Guild, Cromwell Place, London.

KEY

1. Mrs. E. Deraniyagala, *President*
2. Mrs. M. Corbett Ashby, *U.K.*
3. Dr. Hanna Rydh, *Sweden*
4. Mrs. Nina Spiller, *U.K.*
5. Miss Ester Graff, *Denmark*
6. Maître Andrée Lehmann, *France*
7. Mrs. Amy Bush, *U.K.*
8. Mrs. Edith Anrep, *Sweden*
9. Mrs. Laurel Casinader, *U.K.*
10. Miss Chave Collisson, *U.K.*
11. Mrs. Pearl Grobet Secrétan, *Switzerland*
12. Mrs. Margaret Ingledew, *U.K.*
13. Mrs. Eva Kolstad, *Norway*
14. Mrs. Sigridur Magnusson, *Iceland*
15. Mme Baheega Raschid, *Egypt*
16. Mrs. Hilda Tweedy, *Ireland*
17. Mrs. M. C. Walker, *Bahamas*
18. Mrs. Elizabeth Halsey, *Administrative Secretary*
19. Begum Rashid, *Pakistan*
20. Mrs. Katigbak, *Philippines*
21. Mme Volli, *Italy*
22. Mrs. Elizabeth Griffiths, *Australia*
23. Mrs. Helen Whittick, *Hon. Editor, I.W.N.*

Ruth Tomlinson remembered "the third session of the Status of Women Commission held in Beirut in 1949 and how women from the Lebanon, Syria, Iraq and Egypt flocked to sessions in order to have direct contacts with representatives of the Commission and of NGOs. These women felt something from these first-hand contacts which encouraged them to struggle (and they did) for the political rights of their own women, and for their rightful status in the family and community. Here was the spirit of co-operation at its highest—a real mingling of the Status of Women Commission. NGOs and local women's organisations of all kinds. I was fortunate to witness similar 'contacting' at the 14th Session of the Commission held at Buenos Aires in 1960. The representatives of the Commission definitely held the front of the stage, and representatives of NGOs and local women's organisations rallied round, seeking answers to their problems. . . . From my knowledge of the working of the Human Rights Commission, I cannot see this body tackling these problems with anything like the same crusading zeal as the Status of Women Commission. On the plane I have outlined, progress could be fairly rapid but I still think it will be some time before the Commission works itself out of business." This question of the future of the Status of Women Commission was discussed at the IAW Congress at Trieste in 1964 (see p. 257).

Women in Africa

Among the activities of the Alliance in the triennial period 1961–64 was the international committee meeting at Monoravia (Liberia) in July 1963 followed by a seminar of African women. This continued the work of a seminar held at Ibadan, Nigeria in 1961. Many prominent members of the Alliance attended the Monoravia seminar including the president and most members of the board.[3] In addition to Liberia there were representatives of Nigeria, Sierre Leone, the Cameroons and Senegal, and a representative of UNESCO.

The seminar was directed by Norma Nelson Cole of Nigeria, and the first session was devoted to reports of the activities in the two years since the seminar at Ibadan. The second and third sessions were devoted to "Participation in Citizenship" and "International Relationships" followed by "Fitting Programmes to Objectives" which was directed to a consideration of how to achieve the aims for which they were working, in which education and training for employment figured prominently.

This is an example of the activities of the Alliance extending to the undeveloped countries. It was followed two months later by a seminar on the role of women in urban development held at Lagos (Nigeria) organised by the UN Economic Commission for Africa, (attended by members of the Alliance including a former president, Ester Graff) occasioned by the rapid growth of African towns consequent on the increased industrial and commercial concentrations providing employment, often of a new kind, to both men and women. This meant a considerable migration of population from rural to urban areas, such as had taken place in the developed countries for over a hundred years. This migration in Africa took place first mainly among men, especially those who acquired skills for the better paid jobs; the migration gradually included more and more women, who with well paid jobs acquired an independence and a consciousness of rights unknown in her former life.[4] It was to discuss this evolution of the role of women in Africa, and to help with knowledge, understanding and experience that these African seminars took place.

Trieste Congress

The twentieth Congress of the Alliance was held at Trieste from 19th August to 1st September 1964. It was attended by delegates of societies from 28 countries (of the 36 affiliated) with fraternal delegates from USA and Canada and a representative from UNESCO. Two new affiliates were the Kenya African Women's Association and the Women's Rights Movement of the Philippines.

Held at Trieste University the opening ceremony was in the handsome Magna Aula. Presiding with the president was Anna Volli the president of the Alleanza Femminile Italiana, the hostess society.

In her report the president, Ezlynn Deraniyagala, gave some account of her travels and her visits to affiliated societies during the three years since the Dublin Congress. She visited Japan, the Philippines (where she obtained a new affiliate), Thailand, Liberia, Nigeria, and in Europe: London, Helsinki, Stockholm and lastly, Trieste, to prepare for the Congress: fifteen affiliates in nine countries. Altogether she had visited as president thirty-three affiliates in twenty-three countries. She asked the question is it all worthwhile and invariably the answer she said is "yes" because, "it redounds to the strengthening and consolidation of the Alliance". She pointed out that the rank and file of affiliate membership remain ignorant of and indifferent to IAW but a visitor, especially the head of the international organisation inspired with a missionary zeal, can bring home to large audiences the work that is being done and the fact that through the IAW there is a channel to the United Nations and to some 114 governments available to every woman, and the visitor can obtain an insight into the problems of each visited group and the adjustments in understanding prompted by the knowledge gained.

Inevitably the resolutions, prepared mainly by the five standing commissions, were again largely reaffirmations of resolutions at previous Congresses. There were, however, a few items or new approaches to subjects

Begum Anwar Ahmed of Pakistan, president ot the IAW 1964–1970. She brought to the IAW the realisation that if women's status in the "third world" was to be raised, then attention must be paid to family planning.

occasioned by the work of the various sections of the United Nations. In a general declaration affiliates and individual members were urged to intensify their efforts to secure the realisation of the ideals of equality given in the UN Declaration of Human Rights, so that women everywhere can enjoy these rights and add their full strength to the community. In the section on Equal Civil and Political Rights the argument for equality in home life was put in new terms. A mother in a family who has a paid job, should not have a double day's work, which renders her unable to find time for political and social work, and it was therefore asked that home economics and child care be taught to both sexes at all levels of education.

The resolution of the Equal Economic Rights Commission welcomed the report of the International Labour Conference on women workers in a changing world and requested it to organise regional meetings and urged affiliates to hold national seminars on the subject.

The Equal Rights on Education Committee called attention to Article 26 of the Declaration of Human Rights[5] and called upon governments to ratify the Convention against discrimination in education adopted by the 1960 Unesco General Conference.[6]

Among the Equal Moral Standard Commission's resolutions affiliates were asked to study and support for signature and ratification by their governments four UN Conventions:

1. On Abolition of Slavery, the Slave Trade, and Institutions and Practices similar to Slavery.
2. On Free Consent to Marriage, Minimum Age of Marriage, Registration of Marriages.
3. On Recognition and Enforcement Abroad of Maintenance Obligations.
4. On Suppression of Traffic in Persons and of the Exploitation of the Prostitution of Others.

In view of the discussion on the abandonment or continuance of the Commission on the Status of Women (see pp. 250–253) the expression of appreciation of its work at the IAW Congress at Trieste in 1964 is apposite. This work it is claimed has led to significant improvements in the political, economic, social and cultural position of women all over the world, and the Congress stressed the importance of strengthening the structure and programme of the Commission. It welcomed the decision of ECOSOC that the Commission shall meet annually, and it recommended that countries which have no elected seat on the Commission during any given year should appoint women observers to attend, and affiliates should urge their governments to make appointments.

At this Congress Ezlynn Deraniyagala resigned the presidency and was succeeded by Begum Anwar G. Ahmed of Pakistan, who was a vice-president and had served as chairman of the UN Status of Women Commission.

Ezlynn Deraniyagala during her six years of office proved to be a very sensible, inspiring president who was an untiring propagandist for the Alliance and its causes as her world-wide travels testify.

Partly stimulated by her own activities she had a world picture of the position of women in modern communities which contributed to the expansion of the Alliance. She was a worthy successor to Margery Corbett Ashby, whom she joined as an honorary president. Two new vice-presidents, in addition to Princess Safiyeh Firouz of Iran, were Edith Anrep of Sweden and Dr Hedi Flitz of West Germany, while Olive Bloomer of Great Britain became honorary treasurer in succession to Leila Basnayake of Ceylon.

REFERENCES

1 The Fawcett Society was originally the "London Society for Women's Suffrage" founded in 1866 (see Chapters 2–4 for the early suffrage activities in which it played a part). In 1926 the name was changed to "London and National Society for Women's Service", and in 1953 to the "Fawcett Society". During the century the Society gradually formed a library relating to women's suffrage, which since 1926 was organised and expanded by Verie Douie who continued as librarian for 41 years. It became one of the world's finest libraries of books on the women's movement. Since 1976 it has been at the City of London Polytechnic.

2 The Townswomen's Guilds were founded in Great Britain in 1929. The beginnings resulted from discussions between Eva Hubback and Margery Corbett Ashby. As women received the franchise in 1928 on equal terms with men it was felt that there should be some national organisation devoted mainly to the education of women for citizenship. After women over the age of 30 had received the vote, at the 1918 election the National Union of Women's Suffrage Societies changed its name to National Union of Societies for Equal Citizenship and this provided the genesis of the first Townswomen's Guild. The first four guilds were established at Haywards Heath (near Margery Corbett Ashby's home), Burnt Oak, Moulescoomb and Romsey, and by the end of 1929 twenty guilds had been founded and affiliated to the NUSEC. Margery Corbett Ashby was its first president. Like the National Union to which the guilds were affiliated they engaged at first in political propaganda in the cause of women, but in 1932 it was decided to drop all political propaganda and devote activities to the education of women as citizens, and to recreational interests such as the arts and crafts, music, drama, to social interests in fact to comprehend the full life for a woman.

It was decided at the same time to make the national organisation a separate body and re-name it the National Union of Guilds for Citizenship, changed a year later to National Union of Townswomen's Guilds. By 1976 there were about 2,700 guilds in Great Britain. An excellent account of the Guilds is given in a jubilee book by Mary Stott entitled *Organisation Woman – The Story of the National Union of Townswomen's Guilds* London 1978 (Heinemann).

3 See Reports by Amy Bush, Edith Anrep and Laurel Casinader in *IWN* October 1963.

4 See: *African Women in Towns – an Aspect of Africa's social revolution* by Kenneth Little (Cambridge University Press) London 1975.

5 Article 26 of the United Nations Declaration of Human Rights states:
    Everyone has the right to education. Education shall be free, at least in the elementary and fundamental stages. Elementary education shall be compulsory. Technical and professional education shall be made generally available and higher education shall be equally accessible to all on the basis of merit.

6 In 1959 UNESCO circulated the Draft Convention to member states and non-governmental organisations for comment. The Fourteenth Session (1960) of the UN Commission on Status of Women considered this Draft and requested ECOSOC to ask the General Conference of UNESCO to make a few amendments. UNESCO General Conference, Eleventh Session, held November-December, 1960, adopted, with some modification, the Draft Convention concerning Discrimination in Education. It was then referred to governments for ratification.

CHAPTER NINETEEN

1965–1968

The UN Declaration on the Elimination of Discrimination against
Women. African Seminar 1966. London Congress 1967

In 1963 the General Assembly of the United Nations was concerned that
there was still considerable discrimination against women, and passed a
resolution inviting the Commission on the Status of Women to draft a
declaration directed to eliminating such discrimination. ECOSOC asked the
Commission to prepare this with a view to consideration by the General
Assembly at its 20th session.

There was no meeting of the Commission in 1964 but at its meeting
at Teheran in March 1965 a drafting committee was appointed to prepare
this declaration. It had several meetings and submitted a draft to the Commission. A majority of delegates considered that more thought should be
given to the substance and wording, and it was felt that the declaration
should not merely repeat principles that had been given in conventions
but should aim to advance on the present position, and set standards for
future achievement. A further draft was prepared for the next meeting
of the commission at Geneva in 1966 (the 19th) and was further discussed and revised, but it was not until the Commission Meeting in New
York in February-March 1967 that the draft revisions were completed in a
form acceptable to the Commission. It was then finally agreed and
submitted to ECOSOC for presentation to the General Assembly. A few
further amendments were made by the Third Committee and it was then
adopted by the General Assembly on 7th November 1967.

The Declaration follows the principles given at the UN Charter and
the Declaration of Human Rights as they affect matters of the equality of
the rights of men and women. The principles embodied in the Declaration
represent a considerable advance in ideas which some might consider to
be almost revolutionary in character in face of centuries of customary
and habitual thinking, yet they are very much in line with what the IAW
had been advocating during the previous half century. The essential note of
the Declaration is set by the first article in which it is stated that denying
or limiting woman's equality of rights with man constitutes an offence
against human dignity. This can be amplified in many ways, constituting a

criticism of that traditional thinking which implies an inferiority in women for which there is no reliable evidence or justification, and thus seeks to denigrate half the human race which is inconsistent with its dignity. The use of the term dignity can be appreciated and is valuable because it comprehends much that is finest of human character—moral worth and honour combined with intelligence and understanding.

The third article of the Declaration is concerned with the very important matter of education "towards the eradication of prejudice and practices based on the inferiority of women". Here is one of the most difficult things to propagate because it means, in many cases, a total change in habitual thinking leading to the operation of practices different from centuries of custom. This obsolete thinking is familiar in most of the professions, of which the church is a conspicuous example, and in domestic life. Provision for the implementation of accepted principles is given in the second article of the Declaration in which it is stated that they "shall be embodied in the constitution or otherwise guaranteed by law", and that they "shall be ratified or acceded to and fully implemented as soon as practicable". This is a matter for individual governments, but also for non-governmental organisations (NGOs) and voluntary bodies concerned with their realisation. The IAW was careful, for example, to request that all its affiliates should bring pressure on their governments to take measures of implementation.

Although this Declaration was the principal matter discussed at the Status of Women Commission of 1965, 1966 and 1967, other important matters concerned with equality continued to be considered. At Teheran in March 1965 much time was devoted to various aspects of equal political and economic rights and the position of women in marriage and family life. It was noted that while more women were elected to local government little progress had been made to elect women to parliament, and various proposals were made to increase the prospects of a greater proportion being so elected. It was agreed that training in voluntary leadership was important, and that NGOs should take the initiative by holding seminars on civic education with the help of governments. The pamphlet by the UN Secretary General on the Civic and Political Education of Women originally published in 1951 was reissued in 1965 and was well received by the Commission which discussed measures to get it widely known. The IAW representative mentioned that as the Alliance was disturbed by the small number of women in parliament its affiliates were being asked to make a study of how women use the vote.

As previously implied NGOs of consultative status take part in the discussions of the Status of Women Commission. An interesting sidelight was given of this collaboration by Frieda S. Miller, the IAW consultant to the Commission reporting on the meeting of the Commission in New

Statue of Emmeline Pankhurst in Parliament Gardens, London, erected in 1966. Each year on Mrs Pankhurst's birthday on 14th July a commemorative meeting is held at the statue by the Suffragette Fellowship. In this photograph taken at the first meeting in 1966, Mary Leigh an ex-suffragette is carrying the flag she often carried in protest marches. On her left is Gwyneth Dunwoody, MP, daughter of Baroness Phillips.

York of February-March 1967 (IAW May 1967). "As always", she says, "NGO attendance was substantial and persistent. There was a more active hostility to the NGOs on the part of the representatives of the USSR than at some previous sessions. This same atmosphere had existed in the meetings of the Sub-commission for the Elimination of Discrimination earlier in the year. I want to call it to your attention because, if it turns out to be a general acceleration of opposition to NGO functioning in the international framework, it might be well for the NGOs concerned to review their tactics and practices and adjust their patterns as seems most effective."

This was said less by way of criticism than "to suggest building support for the original concept embodied in the United Nations' Charter of the part that citizens need to play in the development of national and international policies".

It might be added that there are always those who believe that policy making should be left to elected representatives, and that the expression of opinion by voluntary bodies and independent individuals should not influence or deter the work of the elected representatives who have full responsibility. This view is hardly consistent with a free democracy. Only a small minority of persons are sufficiently informed to vote intelligently on the many matters that are involved in governmental and international policy; most people vote for a political party whose principles are for the most part vaguely understood, and are those which voters consider are most likely to serve their own individual interests. On numerous international and national issues they are ignorant. Specialist organisations, both international and national make studies of special subjects and are often better informed on these than government departments. Most of the advance and improvements in civilised communities have arisen in the first place and in the early stages from individuals and voluntary bodies propagating ideas and ultimately converting governments. Very rarely do they spring in the first place from members of a government. The government minister who advocates and implements a policy has been converted to his line of thinking by decades of voluntary propaganda. That is why the NGOs are of inestimable value to the United Nations, and that is why the attitude of the USSR representatives cited by Frieda Miller suggests a dictatorship of elected representatives rather than a true democracy.

IAW activities in Africa

At the Congress in Trieste in 1964 the wish was expressed that the Alliance should extend and intensify its activities in the developing countries, especially in Africa. It was also felt that the Hannah Rydh memorials project which had been initiated shortly after her death should be devoted to helping African women to advance their status in society. In implementation of these intentions the president Begum Anwar Ahmed made a tour of West Africa visiting Senegal, Guinea, Sierre Leone, Ghana, Dahomey and Nigeria and meeting the leaders of African women's organisations and helping in every way possible. Anwar Ahmed was well equipped for this task, for as a former chairman of the Status of Women Commission and she herself belonging to a developing country, she was able to understand readily the problems of African women and to appreciate the efforts they were making to raise their status in communities by means of greater participation in the economic, political and social life of their countries.

Anwar Ahmed gave a full report of her mission to the Alliance board meeting at Zürich in June 1965. Following Anwar Ahmed's tour the Hannah Rydh Memorial Seminar was held in Freetown, Sierra Leone[1] in April 1966. It was made possible largely by grants from the Swedish affiliate, Fredrika Bremer Forbundet, in memory of Hannah Rydh, and from the Ford Foundation. The theme was "The Role of Women in the Economic Development of West Africa", divided into four sections:

1. The Position of Women in Economic Life.
2. Development of Resources—Human and Physical.
3. Women in Employment.
4. Women's Voluntary Organisations.

Many prominent members of the Alliance took part including Edith Anrep, a vice-president, two of the chairmen of commissions, Amy Bush and Laurel Casinader, and Elizabeth Halsey the secretary. Other members came from the UK, the USA, France, Sweden, Switzerland and Ceylon, thus a fair representation from various parts of the world. Forty delegates represented twelve West African countries: Dahomey, Gambia, Guinea, Ivory Coast, Liberia, Mali, Nigeria, Senegal, Togo, Upper Volta and Sierra Leone. The Prime Minister of Sierra Leone, although unable to attend the opening, came in at the end and addressed the gathering while the Mayor of Freetown—Mrs Constance Cummings-John spoke at the opening and attended throughout.

In the first section of economic life Jeanne Cisse Martin gave a paper in which she traced the gradual awakening of African women from drudgery, slavery and apathy to modern times where they are beginning to find themselves in the dual role of home maker and worker outside the home. She urged women to take a more active interest in education, training and leadership, because, she said, "women are rapidly moving their sphere of interest and influence from the family to the nation, from the nation to the region, from the region to the continent and from here to the international field". Therefore she must be well qualified to meet all her responsibilities.

Speeches and discussions were related to women's position in the family and the home, in professions, industry, trade and agriculture. African women tended to be individualists but in this way they dispersed their energies and therefore in order to meet the needs of an expanding economy, it was necessary to form co-operatives. For market women[2] in particular it was essential to do this. The problem of delinquency was referred to as probably resulting from the absence of the mother from the home and the consequent neglect, but, as one delegate put it, the child was the responsibility of two persons and needs the care and attention of both parents.

The second section was concerned with the more general questions of the utilisation of resources. Several papers were given on women in employment. It was stated that in West African countries the striving for a higher standard of living resulted in the acceptance of the idea of a wife working to supplement the family income. Although women here did not have the same bars and hindrances and male opposition to their entry to employment as do women in the western world, they had to be equally qualified as men. Therefore it was necessary that girls should have equality of opportunity with boys in education and often it was ignorance of available curricula which made girls miss the available opportunities. Women's organisations could help here by giving this information. If equally qualified, women had the right to equal pay but they should also have an equal sense of responsibility.

The dual role of women necessitated the provision of welfare facilities to help the family and sometimes the provision of part-time work was necessary for those with family responsibilities. Among welfare facilities maternity benefits rated high and these had to be accepted as the right of the mother although care had to be exercised in demanding rights and privileges which could perhaps endanger her employment opportunities.

Planned parenthood had a different connotation in West Africa because here the problem was one of underpopulation: their main concern was that urgent measures had to be taken to reduce the high infant and maternal mortality and therefore planned parenthood had to be geared to this project.

The fourth subject—women's voluntary organisations—was introduced by Laurel Casinader and several papers were read by delegates on the ways women's organisations could help in the promotion of women's participation in their different countries. The subjects of the papers were the methods already employed in western countries and their application to West Africa. Valuable points were made in the papers and ensuing discussions ranging from balancing the family budget to the financing of industrial projects. Austerity regimes for the family and the country were mooted and it was felt that governmental action could set an example and

London Congress of IAW, August 1967, inaugural luncheon at Wandsworth Town Hall. Left to right: Baroness White, Dame Margery Corbett Ashby, Princess Alexandra who opened the Congress and welcomed the 200 delegates, the president Begum Anwar Ahmed and Alderman W. W. Carnie, the Mayor of Wandsworth.

that the wanton spending of money on ceremonial occasions often made people incur debts beyond their means. The dower system and its merits and demerits were debated. Again it was the pressure power of women on central authorities that was urged as important in developing countries where so much had to be undertaken by governments or aided by them, and here too women could act as a body to induce governments to implement Conventions and recommendations passed by the UN and its Commissions.

Fifteen conclusions were formulated at the termination seminar. These covered, among other subjects, the dual role of women; literacy; co-operatives, especially for market women; the presentation of African culture, including dress; and the recognition of vocational and technical training side by side with academic education. In the first conclusion it is stated that although woman is now pressed to engage in gainful employment or voluntary work outside the home, her primary desire is to care for her home and family. This would appear to shift emphasis a little. In most European countries up to 1939 the married woman's essential function was the home. Since the second world war her freedom to take employment outside the home has been emphasised, consistent with her domestic duties. At the same time it has been stressed that the husband should share equally in those domestic duties. In connection with this however the claim is made in another conclusion (11) that in view of the dual role of women the recognition of part-time work is desirable.

Under the heading of Education it was stated that organisations should assist by:

(a) Encouraging parents to send their girls to school at the earliest possible legal age. Proper schooling is essential to help them to compete in the labour market, as, even after marriage they may need to work.

(b) Ensuring that school curriculums for girls and boys should be the same, while co-education is desirable. Some training in domestic science should also be given. Fathers and mothers should be equally responsible for the training of their children.

In the matter of health it was stated that education is the key to better health. "This", it is added, "should include the elimination of taboos and prejudices, as well as encouragement in the use of modern scientific methods" and women's organisations should influence public opinion for these purposes. It might be questioned whether it is wise to lump prejudices and taboos together, for some anthropologists would say that not all taboos are bad, and that it would occasionally be of advantage if some were introduced into modern society.

Further points were made in such matters as the modernisation of farming, partly to ease the burden on women; on the place of part-time work especially in view of women's family and domestic obligations; equal pay for men and women for equal work and responsibility. The desire to increase population in Africa was considered in relation to family planning which is important for working women. The valuable point was made that the first step in maintaining and increasing population is to lower the high rate of maternal and infant mortality.

Prospects of parliamentary franchise for women in Switzerland 1965

At the board meeting at Zürich in June 1965, the opportunity was taken of holding a public propaganda meeting in the Aula of the University of Zürich, Switzerland, other than Liechtenstein, was then (1965) the only European country where women still had not the parliamentary franchise. Dr G. Heinzelmann, vice-president of the Association Suisse pour

London Congress of IAW 1967, the newly elected board and honorary members in the garden of Southlands College, Wimbledon, where the Congress was held. In the centre is the president, Begum Anwar Ahmed, and among those on her right are Andrée Lehmann, Amy Bush, Laurel Casinader, Irmgard Rimidini and Helen Whittick; among those on her left are Dame Margery Corbett Ashby, Edith Anrep, Margaret Ingledew, Hedi Flitz, Anna Voll and Chave Collisson.

le Suffrage Feminin presided and contributions were made by many members of the board.

Elizabeth Halsey, the administrative secretary of the Alliance, made a valuable contribution when dealing with prospects of women's vote under the Swiss system of so many major decisions being reached by referenda. She claimed "that the vote had been given to American women by a referendum of American men; that the system is in use for many purposes in a large number of American communities today and much civic and national business is conducted by a system similar to that of Switzerland." She thus refuted the commonest argument against the enfranchisement of Swiss women, 'it could not be made to work under our system'.

This meeting was an excellent use of the board and even if it did no more than encourage the women who are fighting for the right to share in the making of the laws by which they are governed, was well worth while. Not a few hopes had been raised when the audience heard of the stimulating effect 'in the right places' of IAW Congresses and Board meetings at Berlin, Istanbul and Teheran.

At a dinner given by the Mayor of Zurich to the ASSF and the board on the following evening, at which the Regieningsrat Ernst Brugger, the Minister of Justice and Social Affairs of the Canton of Zurich was present. in his speech the Minister gave an assurance of the intention to introduce a bill giving women parliamentary franchise. He acknowledged, what has indeed never been denied, the great contribution that Swiss women are making to the life of their country and said that "no longer can we do without the talent of women in this hitherto closed department of life". He urged his audience, however, to get to work on those women folk of the men who would be asked to vote on the issue, not all of whom are convinced of the need. "Why do we want to make life more difficult", said one working woman to me, "the men can manage without us: let them do it". The Mayor of Zürich confirmed the promise of the minister and it is evident that opposition from the top is almost non-existent; one feels "it is just a matter of time—but what time" and to those who wait it seems long indeed.

London Congress: 1967

Delegates representing women's organisations from thirty countries (of a total of thirty nine) attended the twenty-first Congress in London from 1st to 10th of August 1967. In addition several fraternal delegates and representatives from the United Nations, UNESCO and ILO attended. The Congress was under the patronage of Princess Alexandra and a supporting committee which included Barbara Castle, Lena Jeger, Baroness Phillips, Lady Summerskill, Margaret Thatcher, Dame Joan Vickers, Dame Irene Ward, Eirene White and Shirley Williams.

The inauguration ceremony took place at Wandsworth Town Hall with the Mayor of Wandsworth, Alderman W. W. Carnie presiding. (Incidentally this position was held three years previously by Amy Bush, a vice-president of the Alliance.) Princess Alexandra made a short speech declaring the Congress open, in which she said that women can only give of their best if they have equality of opportunity with men for education, training and entry into the professions. In this way the best talent can be trained for the service of mankind. She was followed by Margery Corbett Ashby who had recently received the honour of Dame of the British Empire. Dame Margery reminded the gathering that it was gratifying to the four hostess societies that the 21st Congress was being held in England for the first time since 1909. Begum Anwar Ahmed the president in her opening speech congratulated Dame Margery on her well deserved honour.

In her report the president referred to her travels in the three years made in the interests of the Alliance. In addition to her visits to women's organisations in West Africa to which reference has already been made, she attended the UN seminar at Manila on measures required for the advancement of women with a view to a long-term programme, and was elected chairman of the 26 NGOs that had sent observers which prepared several recommendations. From Manila she made a tour of the Far East and visited and spoke to women's organisations in Tokyo, Hong Kong, Jakarta, Singapore, Kuala Lumpur and Bangkok.

The Congress in its general declaration expressed satisfaction at the imminence of the UN Declaration on the Elimination of Discrimination against Women, drafted by the Status of Women Commission and presented by ECOSOC to the General Assembly. This gave great impetus to the Congress, and every delegate was conscious of it when the resolutions were discussed and agreed. These resolutions were grouped under the work of the five Commissions. Those concerned with equal civil and political rights, economic rights and rights to education, and with equal moral standard included references to discrimination against women and welcomed the declaration prepared by the Status of Women Commission. Much other matter in the resolutions was inevitably a repetition of those of previous Congresses, but sometimes put in different and more effectual wording. The items of the first resolution of the International Understanding Commission were rather vague, and were really a little too general in relation to the main purposes of the Alliance. The second resolution of this Commission, however, concentrated on the designation of 1968 by the UN as the International Year for Human Rights. The resolution noted with appreciation that ECOSOC deemed it essential that women's rights should be included in the programme for the Human Rights Year and in the agenda for the International Conference on Human Rights, and had asked that the standards of the proposed Declaration on the Elimination of Discrimination against Women should provide goals for the year. The resolution, therefore, requested that affiliated societies should give vigorous support to the proposed actions of the United Nations and designate 1968 for renewed national activities on behalf of women's rights.

In an emergency resolution affiliates were urged to ask their governments to instruct their delegates to the UN General Assembly in September

London Congress 1967, Dame Margery Corbett Ashby, Edith Anrep of Sweden and Dr Hedi Flitz of West Germany in conversation with the editor of *IWN*, Helen Whittick.

1967 to ensure that NGOs of consultative status in the field of human rights be invited to the International Conference on Human Rights to be held in Teheran in 1968 to commemorate the twentieth anniversary of the Universal Declaration of Human Rights.

Preceding this Congress the 21st session of the Status of Women Commission was held in New York in February–March 1968. The meeting was under some pressure partly because it was held at the same time as those of three other commissions on Human Rights, Social Development and International Trade, and partly because reports of the Human Rights and Status of Women Commissions were needed for the Teheran Conference due in a few weeks time.

A working party of the Status of Women Commission was set up to make proposals on the Declaration on the Elimination of Discrimination against Women. It prepared a resolution that the UN should urge governments, NGOs and individuals to do all in their power to implement the Declaration and that the opportunity of the International Year for Human Rights should be taken to give publicity to the Declaration, and that the Secretary-general should make funds available for the purpose.

Another working party of the Commission was formed to study the position of women in private law and it proposed in its report that Article 16 of the Declaration of Human Rights should form the basis of the work of the Commission in the field of private law. (Article 16 is given in the first reference to Chapter 16).

The report, which was accepted by the Commission, emphasised that Article 16 focused attention on the family as a unit of society and that greater attention should be paid to its legal protection. It recommended the Commission to study, within the framework of Article 16: (1) Legal capacity; (2) Property rights; (3) Domicile and residence; (4) Dissolution of marriage and judicial separation (including maintenance obligations) and parental rights.

At this meeting the UK delegation asked for a long term programme for the advancement of women which was agreed. This really meant the implementation by persistent propaganda of the Declaration on Elimination of Discrimination against Women, and it welcomed the inclusion of this on the agenda of the Teheran Conference. Many other matters were discussed at this busy meeting, among them the value of seminars and how they should be organised. Some reference to this is made in the next chapter.

The Teheran Conference 1968

The Conference on Human Rights was duly held in Teheran in April–May 1968, and was attended by 350 delegates (including 50 women) from 84 countries and 120 observers representing 47 non-governmental organisations. The Sharinshah of Iran struck the right note in opening the Conference when he said that "political rights without social rights, justice under law without social justice, and political democracy without economic democracy no longer have any meaning". In short, equality of opportunity and democratic principles must range through the whole of human activity.

U. Thant, the Secretary General of UN followed with an enumeration of the instruments for the protection of human rights adopted by the General Assembly during the past twenty years, and referred to the international conventions on the elimination of all forms of racial discrimination and the two international convenants of human rights. The coming into force of these covenants he felt, would be a great moment in the history of mankind.[3]

The rights of women had its place in the Conference and was discussed at some length. Begum Anwar Ahmed attended as the representative of the Alliance and in her report she said that debate on women's rights "was animated but not controversial. Equality of the sexes is obviously no longer disputed. Male delegates were as vehement as the women in their exhortation for the need for overall improvement in the status of women. All agreed that legislation alone was not enough. It had to be accompanied by measures for the social, economic and cultural development of women to ensure them a position of equality with men."

Regarding those countries which withheld equal rights for women for fear that emancipated womanhood may upset the balance in society it was requested that the United Nations carry out studies concerning the deeply rooted values which interfere with the promotion of the equality of women in some cultures. During the debate it became quite clear that outmoded attitudes were the biggest obstacle in obtaining for women their full human rights. Reference was made to the UN Declaration on the Elimination of Discrimination against Women, and member states were asked to give wide publicity to this Declaration. A comprehensive resolution adopted by the Conference requested member states to:

(a) Set up national commissions on the Status of Women.
(b) Ratify the eight basic UN Conventions for promoting the Status of Women.
(c) Promote national plans to provide for optimal utilisation of woman power.
(d) Promote vocational guidance programmes and professional training at all levels for participation of women in the economic life of their countries.
(e) Promote a ten year unified long term plan for the advancement of women. (See IWN: June 1968.)

The importance of family planning in relation to human rights was emphasised. It was pointed out by represenatives of UN specialised agencies that an excessive increase in world population was a danger to human dignity. A 2 per cent annual increase was the maximum that could be afforded if a higher standard of living was to be secured. The declaration on population of 10th December 1966, signed by 30 heads of states would, it was hoped, receive more signatories in 1968. Family planning in relation to the status of women was also discussed.

During Human Rights Year there was activity throughout the world among the affiliates of the Alliance to implement some of the recommenda-

Nina Spiller for many years a prominent and hard-working member of the
IAW. She was treasurer from 1939 to
1949, edited the French section of the
IWN for many years. She travelled
widely in the interests of the women's
movement and became an honorary
vice-president of IAW. She died in
December 1967 at the age of 90. Dame
Margery said of her "a dauntless
spirit in a small frame".

tions of the Conference. Some of them, including Norway and Guyana
recommended to their governments that a National Status of Women Commission should be appointed.

The Headquarters of the IAW since the second world war had been
at the residence of the president, or in the same city. When Begum Anwar

Ahmed became president in 1964 the Alliance Headquarters was moved from Ceylon to Washington where her husband was Pakistan Ambassador to the United States. About the time that they were due to return to Pakistan, in the spring of 1966, Elizabeth Halsey, the administrative secretary of the Alliance resigned. She had rendered good service to the Alliance since 1958, but had now become executive director of the Committee of Correspondence in New York, and was, understandably reluctant to leave that city. Begum Anwar Ahmed felt the disadvantages of locating the headquarters at Pakistan because of remoteness and difficulties of communication and thought it would be better to have a permanent location. Another difficulty was that the Alliance was without an administrative secretary. Consultation with a few board members and the spirited action of Amy Bush solved these difficulties. A London address was chosen at 13, Prince of Wales Terrace and in the words of the president "Amy Bush showed a fine spirit of selfless co-operation, and accepted full responsibility for the administration of the headquarters. She has been doing this job in an honorary capacity for the last 16 months, and has carried a very heavy burden on behalf of the IAW. Words fail me. I do not know how to express my sense of gratitude for the great and voluntary help she has extended to the Alliance. I must also thank those board members in London who have assisted Mrs Bush in this task, especially Mrs Spiller for finding the premises for the office".

REFERENCES

1 This account of the Seminar at Sierra Leone is based mainly on the report by Laurel Casinader which appeared in *International Women's News* for June 1966. In this report the fifteen conclusions are given.

2 For meaning and significance of the term "market women" in Africa see Kenneth Little *African women in towns*, 1973 (Cambridge University Press), pp. 49–51. Little explains that in many African regions "the market has become virtually a woman's world." For many "market women" it is much more than trading, it is an important part of their social life.

3 As each covenant required a minimum of 35 ratifications to bring them into force it was not until several years later that these were obtained. The International Covenant on Economic, Social and Cultural Rights came into effect on 3rd January 1976, and The International Covenant on Civil and Political Rights on 23rd March 1976.

CHAPTER TWENTY

1969–1972

Status of Women Commission. Seminars. Königstein Congress. Women's Liberation Movement

By the late sixties nearly all possible advocacies for sex equality in political, social, economic, educational and vocational fields had been made by the Status of Women Commission and by the IAW so that at the twenty-second session of the Commission held in New York in late January and early February 1969 there was the feeling that delegates and other participants were going over the same old ground. Such principal items on the agenda as political and economic rights, opportunities for women, status of women in private law and access of women to education were becoming well worn topics of discussion. Yet familiar as they were at the Status of Women Commission meetings the principles were only fully accepted by a minority of countries; while adoption and translation into law, and the practice were not then fully appropriated by any country. Efforts had to be directed to making the peoples of the member states of the UN and their governments fully aware of decisions in the forms of conventions, declarations and covenants. In this work circumstances that were unfamiliar such as difficulties of acceptance because of various social customs and religious observances in different countries, were brought to the notice of the Commission by delegates and others. As Margaret Bender the IAW representative at the session said, "there is new material and there are new facts being brought out under the familiar items" (*IWN* May 1969).

Difficulties were experienced in getting the Declaration on the Elimination of Discrimination against Women known, understood and accepted. These difficulties were deplored at the twenty-second session of the Commission, yet they indicate the challenge to be met. The difficulties mentioned ranged from the indifference and apathy of women themselves to the indifference of the news media to the importance of the Declaration. Although efforts had been made by the Secretary General of UN by some member states and by NGOs to get the Declaration widely known and accepted, there was still much to be done.

Discussion on the Declaration continued at the 23rd session of the SOWC at Geneva in March 1970.

The reactions of various countries were given by delegates. It was stated that in Canada the Government intends to revise old laws as they affect this subject and to legislate for equal opportunities. The UK delegate stated that a national commission had been established with members consisting of representatives of voluntary organisations, trade unions and professional women's organisations. The second step was a bill on equal pay which would become law at the end of 1975, as it did.

Inadequate publicity and difficulties of promoting a general awareness of the Declaration were cited by the French delegate and methods of propaganda were discussed. Two of the IAW observers spoke. Laurel Casinader said that although the Alliance uses the information from UN sources, it makes its own investigations. She spoke of the importance of seminars and indicated the value of regional seminars in which the Alliance had usefully participated. Laurel Casinader also referred to the value of male participation in the women's movement and she remarked that it is encouraging to see at that session men taking a lively interest in and contributing to the discussion. She added that "They are here, we hope, voluntarily, and not as the victims of a big stick. Only a short time ago the odd male present was a curiosity". She regarded this as a happy augury for the future when men and women will sit together and discuss all problems. She also referred to the IAW's enquiry into the use women make of the vote.

It might be remarked here that in the vigorous activities of the IWSA for political equality in the few years before the first world war, men were prominent participants (see Chapters 3 and 4), but once this equality had been obtained in some countries this participation lessened although it has been the endeavour of the Alliance to encourage it with, it must be admitted, rather meagre results.

Irmgard Rimondini in her comments referred to the belief of the IAW that Status of Women is strongly hampered by the lack of family planning facilities. She mentioned that at all the regional seminars family planning formed an important part of the discussion. Parents, she contended, have the exclusive right to determine freely and responsibly the number and spacing of their children, while family planning enables women to devote more time to community responsibilities, and thus develop their own personalities. She said that the IAW urged its affiliates to encourage women to take advantage of family planning facilities and spread knowledge in all possible ways. If health centres do not exist then there should be a demand that they be established.

Five resolutions were agreed on a long-term programme for the advancement of women, and for their participation in the economic and social development of their countries. The assistance of the United Nations in these activities was sought. The first resolution was to get information and opinions from working women on their family responsibilities, and on the task and difficulties of carrying out both the activities of outside work and home duties. The results of the surveys would determine whether there is a need for an educational campaign and resulting guidance.

The second resolution asked that the United Nations and related organisations should take appropriate measures to ensure equal opportunities for the employment of women in senior and professional positions and that they should set an example to all member states by so doing.

The third resolution was really an extension of the second to include opportunities to fill vacancies in the highest ranks of the international civil service, specifying ILO, FAO, UNESCO, WHO and UNICEF.

The fourth resolution was directed to securing the participation of women in projects of a technological character and to their having access to training for this purpose; while the fifth dealt with the organisation of seminars. Access of women to education and training in all fields was also discussed at some length and recommendations made.

International Labour Organisation fiftieth anniversary 1969

An International Labour Conference was held in Geneva in June 1969 and during the Conference on the 18th there were celebrations of the fiftieth anniversary of the foundation of the ILO. Prompted by this a special seminar was held by the IAW in collaboration with its Swiss affiliate, the Association Suisse pour le Suffrage Feminin at Fribourg (Switzerland) in July on the theme of "Men and Women in Modern Society". Directing the seminar was Dr Lotti Ruckstuhl with Dr Hedi Flitz presiding. The seminar was divided into three main sections. (A) Education of boys and girls; (B) Husband and wife in the home; and (C) Men and women in the labour market.

In the first section education was considered both at school and the home. In the second, questions were discussed of family responsibility, the changing roles of men and women in this context and the relation of the family to working parents. The third section included reviews of the existing occupational structure, education and training in relation to equal employment opportunities and equal pay.

The keynote speech at the seminar was given by Marianne Gatzke who gave an overall picture of the changing roles of men and women in modern society both in Europe and in the developing countries. After reviewing the many advances in the various activities of modern society she emphasised that these are no longer only masculine concerns, but equally men's and women's. She remarked that often the interests of writers and scientists are directed almost exclusively to women's problems, and even when studies are made on the necessary integration of men's and women's roles they deal mainly with the position of women and very little with the position of men. Social matters demand the joint action of men and women. She referred to a conference at the University of Chicago's Centre for Continuing Education in 1965 in which several pertinent questions were raised on the role of boys and girls. Here are some:

1. Why do girls consider jobs and boys consider careers?
2. Why do boys and girls often act in terms of each other's expectations?
3. Why emphasise in the curricula and materials being used in schools the traditional occupational roles of boys and girls?
4. Why do girls continue to choose conventional vocations?
5. What are the prejudices which impede and limit women's spheres of activity?

Marianne Gatzke referred to the desirability of modifying the traditional role of husband and father which had occupied Swedish sociologists, and she mentioned the coined expression "male emancipation" which meant freeing men from traditional roles. She also spoke of the freedom of the individual in a democratic society to choose among life's different patterns, but "women's choice, compared with men's is still rather restricted". According to a Swedish report on the subject, "married women have less leisure time than any other group in society, and they do not have the same opportunities for promotion as men owing to employers' reluctance to train and promote them. Matrimony in its character as an institution for the support of women is an indirect obstacle to their emancipation in modern industrial society. It is necessary to advocate the economic independence of every person outside as well as inside marriage. The social security of the parent who stays at home to care for children should be the same as that for the working parent." Possibilities for greater contact between father and children was stressed. The so called primary female role deprives women of equality in vocational training and employment and equal representation in political and trade union organisations. The question of the roles of the sexes is therefore one of our chief problems. "Male prestige" tends to preserve the philosophy of segregation.

The Swedish labour market policy is determined to do away with a sex division of labour and of jobs. It is found that the existing division tends to consider married women as a reserve labour force which can be dispensed with when necessary.

Second Hanna Rydh Memorial Seminar

At the 21st session of the Status of Women Commission in New York appreciation was expressed of the value of seminars in disseminating in-

formation about the emancipation of women and the resulting education
of the general public on the subject. After considering the increase of
seminars it was agreed to request the Secretary General to examine the
possibility of making larger contributions to financing them and so contribute to the spread of knowledge. Certainly the IAW had found seminars
valuable and had appreciated the assistance given by the UN in financing
and organising them.

Edith Anrep of Sweden, President of
IAW 1970–1973.

Encouraged by the success of the first Hanna Rydh Memorial Seminar
at Freetown, Sierra Leone in April 1966, for West Africa (see Chapter 19),
a second for East Africa was held at Addis Ababa in October 1969. Hanna
Rydh when president had visited Addis Ababa and persuaded the Ethiopian Women's Welfare Association to become affiliated to the Alliance. The
president of the EWWA was Princess Tenagne Worq, daughter of Emperor
Haile Selassie, and when Edith Anrep, the first vice-president of the
Alliance, visited Addis Ababa early in the year to make preparations for
the seminar the Princess agreed to be its president, which gave considerable status to the occasion. This preparatory visit by Edith Anrep was a

very happy 10 days for her partly because she exchanged the winter scene of Sweden, with its short days, for the warmth, clear blue skies and sunshine of Ethiopia.

At the happy instigation of the president of the Alliance, Begum Anwar Ahmed, a meeting of the International Committee (the board and presidents of affiliates) was arranged to precede the seminar, so that in addition to twenty-seven delegates from Ethiopia, Kenya, Somalia, the Sudan, Tanzania and Uganda, several members of the Committee attended, thus increasing the diversity of participants from various parts of the world.

The theme of the Seminar, Women's Participation in Society, was divided into three main sections:

1. "The role of Women's voluntary organisations."
2. "Participation in community development."
3. "Employment."

Most that was was discussed and decided for future action was a repetition of previous seminars, and was very familiar to the representatives of the UN and the Alliance, but for most of the delegates and their friends from the six countries of East Africa it was a revelation of the progress in thought on the relation of the sexes. Great stress was laid on self help, because, however much assistance is given to women of developing countries, the advances must be made by the women themselves by their own actions. The value of seminars, such as the two in East and West Africa, is to fortify the women of these countries with the knowledge of what is being done throughout the world and thus encourage them to make their own efforts in the most effectual manner. The seminar gave information on working with governments, on educational needs, family planning and many other matters to enhance the position of women in society. One useful conclusion or directive was that a brochure should be produced by the Ethiopian Women's Association in collaboration with delegates from associations of other East African countries on "self-help programmes in community development". Another directive was that delegates on their return to their own countries should set up sub-committees in their own associations to study and apply the recommendations made at the seminar.

In 1969 the IAW was given liaison status to the United Nations Food and Agriculture Organisation, which gave the Alliance facilities for attending meetings of the FAO with some measure of participation. This is not only valuable for the Alliance but it provides a source of information for the FAO because many of the IAW affiliates are in the developing countries where agriculture and agricultural occupations are prominent and in which women are conspicuous. Although in many of these countries women form a large part of the rural labour force their status and remuneration is generally much less than that of men. Also there was widespread ignorance of the activities of the FAO among the agricultural developing countries and the Alliance was subsequently able to perform a useful function by helping to spread such information among its affiliates in these countries.

Königstein Congress 1970—Education in the Technological Age

At the international committee meeting that preceded the seminar in Addis Ababa (September–October 1969), the Committee accepted the invitation of the Deutscher Franuenring and the Deutscher Staatsburgerinnen-Verband to hold the 22nd Congress of the Alliance at Königstein in the Taunus Mountains near Frankfurt from 9th to 16th September 1970. It was duly held according to plan.

Representatives of fifty-one affiliated societies from forty countries attended including two new ones from Ghana and Morocco, with several fraternal delegates and observers making an assembly of over 300, including four men of whom I was one. I took part in several of the discussions. The actual participation in a Congress was a valuable experience. The theme of the Congress was "Education in the Technological Age", prompted by its being the United Nations International Education Year.

It is difficult to be definite on what emerged from the Congress because so much that is valuable to social progress comes gradually in an indefinite way. The most precise record of progress was that of the work of the five commissions in the last three years based on the resolutions of the London Congress of 1967, and the further resolutions for another three years' work. Less precise, but challenging and illuminating were the papers relating to the theme of the Congress—and the interchange of views in the many discussions, with the emphasis on international understanding and co-operation. Not the least valuable were the informal meetings of so many peoples from so many countries who talked to each other about their lives, customs and habits, often related in some measure to the common cause of equality of citizenship.

It is the international character, the fraternity of so many peoples, and the good fellowship at such a congress that makes it especially stimulating and inspiring. It is doubtful whether many conferences of the period had such a wide international character.

Herr Ehrenfried Willke, Mayor of Königstein, welcomed the delegates and others to his very pleasant town in the Taunus Mountains, and Dr Hedi Flitz, vice-president of the Alliance, and principal German hostess, welcomed the gathering to Germany. Announcements and outlines of programmes by Amy Bush, vice-president and honorary executive secretary, who had done a tremendous amount of work in arranging the Congress, gave a sense of organised control.

After the president, Begum Anwar G. Ahmed, had declared the Congress

IAW Congress at Königstein, West Germany, September 1970. Left to right: Helen Whittick, editor of the *International Women's News* (the Alliance Journal); Amy Bush, vice-president and organiser of the Congress; Begum Anwar Ahmed, president; and Olive Bloomer, treasurer.

open, the Mayor of Bad Homburg, where the inauguration took place, welcomed the delegates. A message of welcome was given by the Patron of the Congress, Hilda Heinemann, wife of the president of the German Federal Republic, who was unable to be present because she was paying a state visit to Norway with her husband, but, towards the end of the Congress she entertained the board and representatives of affiliates at a luncheon in Königstein.

In her opening address Begum Anwar Ahmed recalled some of the early days of the Alliance. Referring to the first Congress in 1904 held in Berlin, she mentioned the progressive spirit of Dame Margery Corbett Ashby who attended that first Congress in Berlin in 1904, who was president for 23 years (1923–1946) and who is with the Alliance today.

The president was followed by very gracious speeches of welcome by Dr Gisela Naunin, president of the Deutscher Frauenring; Margarete Schukert, president of the Deutscher Staatsburgerinner-Verband and Liselotte Funcke, vice-president of the Deutscher Bundestag.

Then came a very forward-looking opening address by Hildegard Hamm-Brucher, Secretary of State in the German Federal Ministry for Education and Science. After a personal word of greeting she said that "in a world in which male concepts of life still predominate, our efforts to achieve equal status and equal responsibility are still in the initial stage. In all spheres of public and professional life we are still somewhat remote from the goal of fair partnership. We are all striving in our own spheres—usually dependent on ourselves—to establish a more just, a more peaceful, a more human relationship."

The Minister dealt with the mental development of young children, and with their early awareness "that all is not right with the world" and with the restlessness of the younger generation. She disagreed with the prevalent male attitude that this is a temporary phenomenon. She then went on to consider the deficiencies of our educational systems and the wide-spread illiteracy. Although there is the increasing spread of education, especially in the developing countries "illiteracy continues to increase at an alarming rate" showing an increase from 1950 to 1960 of from 40·9 to 41·2 million as a result of population growth. 60 per cent of the adult population of all UNESCO states together are illiterate. This indicates the tremendous task confronting educational policy in the future.

Turning to the more qualitative aspects of education the Minister dealt with the effects of the age of science and technology in which we live, and she spoke of the interests of the individual and of the community which are not always the same: she made a plea for more and more international co-operation in education. She concluded her address by summarising three principles of education in the technological age.

First, all forms of education must aim to arouse understanding and a constructive imagination for the possibilities of technological developments, whilst at the same time focussing on critical reflexes against meaningless and inhuman consequences that may ensue from such developments.

Second, education in the technological age must instil an ability to live together with other generations, religious, races and nations, to communicate and co-operate with them.

And third, education in the technological age must guarantee the basic rights of equal opportunities and equal treatment whilst enabling the young to reach maturity, to determine their own lives, and to participate in decision making.

The main theme was continued throughout the Congress by further addresses on various aspects of education. Marianne Gatzke spoke on "education as a continuing process"; Lakshmi Menon on "education as a social force" and Eva Kolstad on "education as a means to international understanding".

In her address Marianne Gatzke concentrated largely on the changes in our educational systems and the needs of the developing countries She posed the questions put by the Uganda Education Commission in 1963— "When over half the nation is illiterate and the people rightly clamour for education, when teachers are in short supply and inadequately trained, when government and industry demand trained recruits, when unemployment is widespread and increasing, when the nation is poor—what policy should the government pursue?" Moreover when the means to provide education are limited, what kind of education is required, and at what level? Trained manpower is recognised as an essential condition for economic and social development—and also in maintaining effective political institutions and sound government. Robert K. A. Gardiner, Secretary General of the Economic Commission for Africa was cited as saying: "After independence it was considered that . . . large scale expenditure on all and any form of education would lead to progress. Most governments now spend more than 20 per cent of their national budgets on education and yet the systems they have established are turning out growing numbers of primary school-leavers, ill prepared for employment. . . . The institutions of higher learning still follow classical courses and ignore critical areas of specialisation for accelerating social and economic development. And, then there is the prospect of adding graduate unemployment to the unemployment of school-leavers." She was critical of her own Western Germany that "our educational concept is still oriented towards the values of the past. We give the highest reputation in the liberal arts and we still undervalue the technical and technological sciences and the status of those who teach them. What is necessary", she argued, "is a radical reassessment of our educational values and requirements. Curricula should be changed completely to fit the needs of the age of technology—a new 'functional' educational emphasis is needed."

Lakshmi Menon gave an outline of some educational developments in India. She remarked that education "has replaced birth and descent as the criterion of high social status". "Wealth", she continued, "can now be acquired by training in skills, so that a person can rise in the social scale and attain fame and fortune. In countries like India there is now no ban against inter-caste and inter-religious marriages as there once was. Educated people of the different castes and religions are abandoning their old traditions and accepting these changes happily—whereas the illiterate are still traditional in outlook and rigid in their thinking on these matters. Changes in the law and public opinion have been brought about by the educated. Legislation to improve the status of women is sponsored generally by individuals with a high level of education who set the pace of reform. It is their intervention and impetus, their awareness of rights and responsibilities, their insight and inspiration, that have led the country to modernisation."

"Education fulfils also the important role of national, political and social integration, holding together diverse groups, linguistic and ethnic. It reduces the gap between the traditional cultures and the modern ones, and between rural and urban societies. In India educated landlord classes have transmitted an urban and national point of view to their rural kinsmen and brought an awareness of rural needs to cities. Social integration cannot be achieved by legislation. It is a long process hastened by sharing common concerns and living together in neighbourliness."

She made some pertinent remarks about the desirability of changes in the home. "For the education of women", she said, "changes must be made in the home if it is to be a continuing process and prevent violent revolution."

"Today's discontent and unhappiness", she continued, "are largely due to lack of education among women, especially in the developing countries. How can the generation gap be bridged if mothers remain illiterate and children are drawn into the vortex of the space age? But if there is natural understanding between the parents at home and the children growing into adulthood, through opportunities to share experiences and exchange ideas, much of the dichotomy that we find between belief and behaviour can and should be avoided. The socialising of the individual begins at home and education to be effective as a social force should take the home and woman into account."

In speaking of education as a means to international understanding, Eva Kolstad referred to International Education Year 1970 and the work of UNESCO, and the themes specially selected for the programme which were Teaching about (1) the aims and work of UN and its related organisations; (2) human rights; and (3) other countries. She had some very pungent things to say about education, democracy and dictatorship. She asked "does education foster the development of democracy, in particular parliamentary democracy? Experience has shown that this is not necessarily the case, and we are faced by the fact, for instance, that since their independence many of the governments in Africa have been overthrown by military leaders. In the last generation in countries where educational standards were high, a dictator could turn individuals into a mass man, willing to surrender his sacred rights and become the servant to a state completely contemptuous of democracy. Thus the absence of education and military take-overs go together—and even with education, odious dictatorship can exist. So that we must conclude that education in itself is no guarantee for democracy or for international understanding. It all depends on the character of the education, the way it is given and the way it is taken—in fact, the point was well brought out last year (1969) by the deputy Director General of UNESCO, speaking about education for parliamentary democracy and the schools, when he said:

" 'The school system must be a prototype of democracy. . . . The school system based as it is on compulsion and conformity, instils anti-democratic attitudes. Its goal-oriented, antediluvian and autocratic teaching and learning methods must give place to role-oriented techniques of instruction and thought which can become the basis for dialogue and tolerance of disagreement. . . . We will have taken a long step forward toward the achievement of democracy when our institutions of education are themselves democratically organised and operative.

"Also old forms of education, in which nationalism was stressed, must be supplanted by education as an instrument for international understanding.' "

Eva Kolstad stressed the desirability of a school system and adult education system that is open and equal for boys and girls, for men and women. It is essential, she said, that we—the Alliance—"see that our governments ratify the important UNESCO Convention against Discrimination in Education and implement its ideas". She referred also to the resolution of the Commission on the Status of Women recommending co-education at all levels, as a help in preparing boys and girls for a more equitable distribution of tasks and responsibilities in the family and in society. The Status of Women Commission had recommended that further studies on co-education were desirable to determine its effects on education and training performance, career opportunities, moral behaviour and the psychology of boys and girls. This subject of co-education was referred to in the General Declaration of the Congress and again in the resolution of the education committee referred to later.

The president's address was mainly a report of activities of the previous three years, but her chosen theme, "The Changing Pattern of the IAW" prompted some speculations about the future. Begum Anwar Ahmed referred to the work of seminars beginning with that held in Karachi, at the invitation of the All Pakistan Women's Association, in July 1968, jointly organised by the IAW and the Associated Country Women of the World. This fine collaboration by two international women's organisations was much appreciated by UNESCO which sponsored the Seminar.

Delegates from the five participating countries—Ceylon, India, Iran, Nepal and Pakistan—brought to the seminar a variety of views and experience in the field of adult literacy. The two common factors which emerged were the enormity of the problems and the paucity of human and material resources necessary for its solution. . . . The most valuable achievement of the seminar was the draft curriculum which dealt with the vital subject of how and what to teach the illiterate adult.

Anwar Ahmed also referred to seminars at Fribourg, and Addis Ababa of which some account has been given.[1] Continuing she said: "In the past triennium the Alliance has effectively operated in three continents helping the women of each area to come together to define problems and discuss solutions.

"As we gather together, it becomes abundantly clear that seminars, workshops, and allied forms of field work are the best implements the Alliance can use to further its aim of promoting the universal acceptance of inherent human dignity and the equal human rights of women.

"The resolutions we adopt at our congresses, whether directed towards the United Nations or its specialised agencies, or even towards our own affiliates, should never be considered an end in themselves. It should remain the constant endeavour of the board and headquarters of the Alliance to translate these resolutions into meaningful action wherever and whenever possible. I would strongly recommend that the Congress keep this principle in view when formulating the working programme for the next triennium."

Anwar Ahmed gave the re-designation of the International Standing Committees or Commissions which had been agreed by the International Committee, as (1) Civil and Political Rights; (2) Education; (3) Economic; (4) Social; (5) United Nations; and (6) International Understanding. Two of these, the first and last, were the same as formerly at the London Congress, the second and third previously included "Equal" and "Rights". The fifth Commission was additional. The most radical change was the fourth from "Equal Moral Standards" to "Social". These changes were from preciseness to more generalised and vague titles and in the opinion of many persons more was lost than gained.

Later in her address Anwar Ahmed said that in her opinion the major work of the Alliance lies in three channels:

1. Information on important matters pertaining to women—at a global level—disseminated through the *International Women's News*.
2. Stimulation and guidance of national affiliates through the various commissions of IAW.
3. Exchange of views, experiences and ideas through the seminar and workshop technique.

The *International Women's News* therefore occupies a significant place in our work programme . . . the quality of *IWN* continues to be most satisfactory, but you should be made aware that its publication without a regular paid editor puts a great strain on headquarters. We are fortunate that Helen Whittick is once again our Honorary Editor, and we hope she may be persuaded to stay on with us for another triennium.

Helen Whittick spoke at the Congress of the difficulties of editing the journal and asked for more contributions from the affiliated societies about women's activities in their countries. She quoted from *International Women's Suffrage News* of February 1929 which said, "There are societies affiliated to the Alliance in forty-two different countries; for news of the work of these societies we are too often reduced to a study of the public press. . . . Is this as it ought to be? Is it suitable that a paper which is to reflect the opinions and to give information about the activities of the most highly educated and intelligent women in forty-two countries should eke out its existence from month to month with such chance-found scraps of information as its Editor can manage to collect?" The position, Helen Whittick asserted, was very much the same in September 1970 as it was in February 1929, and she reiterated the appeal to affiliates to send her information about the activities of their societies so that she would be in a position to select from valuable first-hand information, rather than having to scout round for items to fill the journal with second-hand material.

Instructive and enjoyable were three evening meetings, one a forum on Asia, another an African Baratze (also a forum) and another, a group discussion organised by the youth committee. Much information was gleaned on family life and marriage customs from delegates of the Asian and African countries, some of which seemed strange to European ears. One of the speakers for an Asian country remarked that when a woman married she married a family, not unknown in Europe, but not usual in recent years.

Session of the Youth Committee

Among the exciting sessions was that organised by the youth committee. A gratifying circumstance of this 22nd Congress was the large proportion of young women who attended, and they certainly gave a very good account of themselves at the youth forum. Among the many notable contributions from the platform was that from Annelise B. Truninger, of Switzerland, who protested against the sex discrimination that still existed in numerous social fields, which she would like to see eliminated, including the special things for women, as if like children, they were not a fully adult section of the community. She objected to the women's page in newspapers, the women's journals and to women's features on the radio. In this point of view she was supported by one of the four men, who attended the Congress as observers, who said that carrying her argument logically to the IAW he looked forward to the day when it was no longer entitled the "International Alliance of Women", but the "International Alliance for Equality of Citizenship", which, he admitted, brought in questions of race.

The General Declaration of the Congress related to its theme. It stated that much more effort is needed to bring about a real equality of men and women in the home, in industry and in the professions in this technological age, and that due to lack of education many women are hindered in developing and using their full potential. The effort must be directed to a change in customs and attitudes of mind which lag behind legislation that is often not enforced. Affiliates were urged to see that all means of education and training for technical jobs are open to women.

Most of the resolutions inevitably repeated those of previous Congresses, although with different wording and varying emphasis. Conscious that it was International Education Year, the Education Commission asked affiliated societies to request their governments to give support to activities to secure equal access of men and women to education. This was still far from universal and action should therefore be taken by affiliated societies to request governments to ratify and implement the Convention on Discrimination in Education of 1960, and to make all forms of education equally accessible to boys and girls and men and women, although no specific mention was made of co-education in the resolution. The inclusion of this can hardly be implied because of the psychological questions mentioned earlier by Eva Kolstad's citation of UNESCO's request.

There were many activities additional to the Congress for which it provided the opportunity. Before it opened a tour was organised by the Deutscher Frauenring for twenty delegates from developing countries to study welfare projects in several towns. After the Congress nearly half of the participants enjoyed a three-day visit to Berlin which included lunch at the Rathaus, the harrowing spectacle of the Berlin Wall, the happier experience of *Simon Boccanegra* at the splendid new opera house, a visit to social centres of various kinds in the new urban area of Neukolln known as Gropius City and a delightful concluding evening by candlelight in the Palace of Charlottenburg.

A study morning was spent in the Bundeshaus with a talk on "Berlin—its function for Germany and Europe" and the difficulties of this island city. After the Berlin visit a few board members—Hedi Flitz, Amy Bush, Irmgard Rimondini, Olive Bloomer and Helen Whittick—spent a few days in Strasbourg and attended a session of the Council of Europe. They were also received by the Secretary General with whom they had a long discussion on the role of NGOs.

Family Planning

A new subject for a resolution at the Königstein Congress was that of family planning. Although it had been discussed at various meetings of affiliated societies, and the subject had been broached at previous congresses, there was some difficulty in reaching agreement as it affected religious susceptibilities. But at this Congress of 1970 it at last became the theme of a principal resolution of the Social Commission. It gave convincing justification for family planning by affirming that a woman has an equal right with her husband to decide the size of her family. It recognised that the status of women is affected by family planning, and that the economic and social status of women has a direct effect on the economic and social development of the country. It stated that family planning enables women to devote more time to community responsibilities, thus developing their own personalities and helping to create a healthy, happy family which should lead to a healthy community. It urged affiliates to encourage women to take advantage of existing family planning facilities and, where they are not available, demand that health centres, including family planning services, be established, and to spread knowledge of such services by means of books, pamphlets, mass media and other educational means.

This became a principal subject for discussion at sessions of the Status of Women Commission and at UN seminars. Eighteen months later at the 24th session of the Commission in February and March 1972, it was discussed and a resolution was drafted. The Commission had before it a progress report on the subject which was introduced by the Special Rapporteur, Helvi Sipilä, who said that more detailed studies at national levels were needed. She hoped to present the completed study to the Commission at its twenty-fifth session in 1974 which had been designated by the UN as World Population Year. (See next chapter).

Following the 1972 Status of Women Commission meeting a seminar was held by the UN in July of that year at Istanbul at the invitation of the Turkish Government on the effects of family planning on the status of women. The seminar was attended by delegates from 30 countries half of whom were from IAW affiliated societies, and Laurel Casinader, vice-president and Irmgard Rimondini, board member of IAW, also attended. The seminar was memorable partly for a valuable address by Helvi Sipilä on the scope and nature of family planning. Irmgard Rimondini spoke of the work of the IAW in this field and on the necessity of follow-up work after seminars. Sixteen resolutions were formulated of which the most pertinent to the theme were "family planning services should be free of charge and integrated in overall health and welfare services", and "regional and national seminars on the status of women and family planning should be held".

Women's Use of the Vote

With women having the vote in nearly all countries of the world, the question why there are so few in public life and so few in parliament, was a recurring one at the congresses. It was a principal theme at the Athens Congress of 1938 when Maria Thanopoulous and Anwar Ahmed both regretted that not more than about ten per cent of members of parliament were women in most countries of the world and that the aim should be to make it 50 per cent. Many suggestions were incorporated in the resolution of the Committee on Equal Civil and Political Rights for propaganda to accomplish this; and it was felt useful to find out how women used the vote in various countries. As mentioned by the Alliance observer at the 23rd session of the Status of Women Commission in 1970 a questionnaire was being conducted by the Alliance on the subject. Some of the results were published in the *IWN* for February 1971. Twenty-one countries replied to the questionnaire, and in addition seven made statistical surveys.[2]

The replies gave a useful picture of how women vote and they are very much in line with what trained observers have noted, although the questionnaire could not always be conducted by the approved systematic methods to get the most accurate results. The following summary is based on Margaret Ingledew's article "Women's use of the Vote" in *IWN*.[3]

After the IAW Congress at Königstein in September 1970 a few members of the board visited the Council of Europe in Strasbourg, and were received by the Secretary-general with whom they are here seen in conversation. Left to right: Laurel Casinader, Hedi Flitz, Amy Bush, Irmgard Rimidini and Helen Whittick. Olive Bloomer was also there but is just out of the photograph on the right.

Tradition and custom are given as the chief reasons for the lack of success in getting women into parliament, while women's indifference and lack of interest are also factors. In some countries the scarcity of suitable qualified women is another reason. More women are willing to stand for local than for national government. Nearly everywhere the party system is all-important, and parties will not nominate women while so many men want to stand, while women are generally less likely to attract votes than men.

Practically all countries consider that it is becoming less common for women to feel they ought to vote the same way as their husbands, though in Indonesia in the country areas they still do, and the Netherlands is pessimistic enough to think 70 per cent of their women do.

In Trinidad and Tobago and in the United Arab Republic both men and women are ready to vote for women, and Ceylon notes that both men and women voted in their thousands for Mrs Bandaranaike. Italy and Switzerland declare that men never vote for women; Denmark that a small percentage of men genuinely want some women in parliament; Finland that really good women do get men's votes; and the United Kingdom feels that better educated men are more likely than less educated men to support women. In Germany as women lack confidence in themselves, there is little confidence in women candidates. In Trinidad and Tobago although there are often more women than men on the committees that "pre-select" candidates, few women are nominated, possibly because not enough are willing to stand. In Germany, Norway, Iceland and Sweden, where there are lists of candidates for each party, it has become the custom for some women's names to appear. In the last Icelandic elections women were at the head of several lists. In France the parties of the "left" give women more prominence that the parties of the "right".

The electoral laws do not anywhere officially discriminate against women, but there is still widespread prejudice against them. In Australia there have been only 41 women MPs in all the 66 years of women suffrage. The political parties everywhere encourage women to become members, but the women usually undertake fund raising and the donkey-work at elections. Until there is public confidence in the ability of women they are unlikely to attract votes. In several countries women's organisations ask candidates for their opinions on matters affecting women and study party programmes and election addresses, and in some—France, Germany, Pakistan and UAR—go so far as to advise women not to vote for candidates who do not support progressive legislation for women.

The only difference recorded between voting rights of men and women was in the UAR where it is compulsory for men both to register and to vote, but optional for women, who may even withdraw from registration if they wish.

This is but a brief indication of the trend of the replies. They probably do not give any further information than that already held by keen and experienced observers. Mostly they confirm that it is tradition and custom (which foster prejudice) that are the main obstacles to progress. The ability to think things anew on a logical basis is given to few, but it is for those few to influence the many. As the philosopher A. N. Whitehead says, "The art of free society consists first in the maintenance of the symbolic code; and secondly in fearlessness of revision, to secure that the code serves those purposes which satisy an enlightened reason".[4] The societies, he says, which cannot combine these must ultimately decay. Prejudice, it could be added, can have no place in an "enlightened reason".

Sex equality in the home

One of the most difficult conditions to achieve in the campaign for equality of the sexes, and one that was receiving increasing attention in the early seventies, is equality in the home and an equal sharing of domestic tasks, which logically follows equality in the spheres of political, economic and social life generally. When these are secured in all the professions, and in employment, in education and the law, and in all activities outside the home the natural corollary to this is that there should be an equal partnership in the home. Yet it is probably in this domain that man finds it most difficult to adjust himself. When both the man and his wife have full-time jobs, then the domestic chores of house cleaning, food preparation and dish-washing should obviously in fairness be shared equally between the partners. Yet frequently the wife does the major part of such work. It is a matter of degree, and some husbands do as much as their wives in the home, but evidence indicates that they are still a minority. Often a woman has two jobs, a full-time job in an office, shop or factory, and another in the home, while the husband has still his one job.

Women have traditionally looked after the home, and if they obtain a full-time job or a part-time one it is often tacitly expected that they should continue with their traditional tasks in the home. Such a notion dies hard and it will probably take many decades to change to an equal division of domestic work. Yet the mid-twentieth century saw the beginning of the change.

There are interesting signs. In the BBC film item on reporting Scotland the title of instruction in "Mothercraft" for Aberdeen Schools was changed —in 1969—to "Parentcraft" in order to include boys. An experiment in Norway by the Norges Familierad (Family Council) was the subject of an article by Cedric Thornberry in The Guardian (21st January 1971). In this experiment the husband and wife took turns in going out to work and staying at home to look after the house and family which can be done on a half-day, half-week or alternate weekly basis. For the experiment to be economically viable the salary or wage of both husband and wife should be roughly the same. It can be appreciated that such an experiment could be conducted also with husband and wife both in full employment.

Four industrial concerns agreed to participate in this experiment and women trade unionists were especially interested, for the experiment gave "ordinary working women the chance to participate. Discussions had previously been 'about women with higher education and potential incomes' who if they wanted had managed to go to work somehow. Now they think discussions may centre on the position of women who have had no chance to do this because it is too expensive to replace their own domestic services."

Cedric Thornberry quoted Ola Rokkones, the Director of Norges Familierad, as saying that they hope "to lay the foundations for a family policy which is more compatible with current social needs. It's obvious that the family form we have today and its apportionment of roles and responsibility is incompatible with modern industrial society."

"All previous attempts to achieve equality in the family, have", he says, "failed", and "work division in the home itself must therefore be investigated", and he makes the valuable points that "the current apportionment of work keeps women away from the 'stimulating productive process' and thus from having real influence over the creative and reforming agencies in society. Men", he suggests, "are also deprived and have become mere productivity factors with little contact with their children and non materialistic values."

This Norwegian experiment has been watched with interest. The spirit which actuated it was much in line with Annelise B. Truninger's contribution to the youth forum of the 22nd IAW Congress (see page 232).

This change to a more equal division of labour in the home can probably be most speedily accomplished by equality in education as suggested by Annelise Truninger. Propaganda would thus be directed to ministries of education and various education authorities and teachers.

In an address by Betty Lockwood, chairman of the Equal Opportunities Commission on Equal Opportunity—Changing Social Attitudes, she recorded that she had occasionally received requests for part-time employment from husbands so that they could share work in the home equally with their wives. This is valuable evidence of progress in this field of equality.

Dame Margery Corbett Ashby's ninetieth birthday celebration

The ninetieth birthday of Dame Margery Corbett Ashby on 19th April 1972 was a fitting occasion to recall her great work in improving the condition of women in modern society. Much of this has been in association with the International Alliance of Women and she has probably contributed more to its activities than any other woman.

Many of her activities have been recounted in the first half of this book covering the period from 1904 to 1935 in chapters two to eleven, but it is appropriate to underline some of them and to cite a few not already mentioned.

It will be remembered that the first Congress at which she officiated as president was held at the Sorbonne in Paris in 1926. She rose nobly to the occasion and gave one of the finest speeches on international co-operation and the women's movement that has ever been made. She presided without fail at every Congress until 1946, at the jubilee Congress at Berlin in 1929, at Istanbul in 1935, Copenhagen in 1939 and at Inter-laken in 1946. One of the proudest events of her life was connected with the Istanbul Congress. Six months before she visited representatives of the Turkish Government and pointed out that a Congress of the Alliance was being held in Istanbul, an Alliance which had as its principal object universal suffrage for women, yet Turkish women were without it. When the Congress was held Turkish women had the vote.

At the first Congress after the war at Interlaken in 1946, the question was raised whether the Alliance should continue now that its main objects had been secured. Dame Margery was insistent that it should carry on because although "the theory of equality of status and opportunity is now accepted . . . we have to battle not for the principle but for the application". Thirty-three years later that is still true.

At the birthday dinner at the English Speaking Union on 8th May at which Baroness Seear presided, Dame Margery's health was proposed by Dame Kathleen Courtney who was then ninety-four. Dame Kathleen re-called some of the outstanding events of Margery's career and referred to Margery's work as a British delegate at the Disarmament Conference and how she was exasperated and saddened by the lack of any positive policy by the British Government. Several other speeches were given by promin-ent women. Hilda Denny, president of the National Women Citizens Association mentioned that in 1968 Dame Margery was selected by the Turkish Women's Societies as the "Woman of the Year". In a graceful final tribute by Edith Anrep, the president of the Alliance, speaking on behalf of the affiliates of over 40 countries, a valuable point made was that Dame Margery "kept progressive theories alive". The gift of imagina-tively restating them is rare but it is one Dame Margery possesses.

Dame Margery's reply to all these tributes was characteristically to incite women to further efforts to apply the accepted principles. There was perhaps slight regret in the comment "that today there was a natural reluctance among men and women to take on extra responsibilities, and there was a note of disillusion in the comment that she had expected women would work for peace, but they seemed just as susceptible as men to defence propaganda".

The Women's Liberation Movement

Because it was much in the public mind from about 1965 to 1975 it is desirable, at this stage, to glance briefly at the Women's Liberation Movement which has received much publicity during the period first in America and then in Western Europe, chiefly in Great Britain, The Netherlands, France and Sweden.

The UN Status of Women Commission had periodically suggested that member states should set up National Commissions on the Status of Women and among the first was President Kennedy's in 1961 with Eleanor Roosevelt as the first chairman. Its first report in 1963 revealed how women continued to be discriminated against and denied many rights and opportunities. Later, Status of Women Commissions were set up in each of the fifty states, their establishment being greatly facilitated by politically active women.

The reports and work of these commissions covering most areas of the USA served to confirm the first report of discrimination against women and denial of opportunities. As a result in the early sixties a great wave of indignation among women seems to have spread across the country, especially as the revelations so often verified individual experiences. It was fortified too by the ineffectiveness of the Civil Rights Act of 1964. Women formed protest groups and the incipient movement found a powerful voice in Betty Freidan's *The Feminine Mystique*, published by Gollancz in 1963. It became a best seller and made its author famous.

The "feminine mystique" is the traditional notion of the housewife—mother established by custom as the model for all women—the glorious goal of their lives. This cult in the American mind was supported by distorted presentation of Freudian theories and sociological ideas which sprang from them, both of which have been exploited by American big business, and by primitive animalism.

Betty Freidan emphasises the dangers to society of these attitudes and in her last chapter entitled "A new life plan for women" outlines the possibilities of the full life for women in modern society where "she can fulfil a commitment to profession and politics, and to marriage and motherhood with equal seriousness".[6]

Three years later in 1966 the "National Organisation for Women" was formed in the USA with the aim of promoting sex equality. Betty Freidan was the first president. Chapters were formed throughout the country and it had a big membership of about 60,000 by 1975. It became a power-

Ruby Rich, MBE, of New South Wales,
Australia, member of the board of
IAW 1964–1971 and an honorary
member since 1971. She has worked in
the interests of women in Australia
for nearly half a century.

ful and influential organisation and was ultimately listened to. It was greatly assisted in its rapid spread by the network of communications set up previously by the Status of Women Commissions in the States. The Women's Liberation Movement can hardly be said to have an official organisation but NOW more than any other fulfilled the role. Another body is the Women's Equity Action League formed in 1968 which has slightly different aims concentrating mainly on education, legislation and litigation.[7]

"Women's Lib" spread to Great Britain in the late sixties as the result of American influence partly through the media of American women in London engaged in propaganda against the Vietnam war. It has never had the success in Great Britain that it had in America. It has had little influence on existing women's organisations in Great Britain who have largely ignored it, and believers in the equality of the sexes have sometimes been careful to say that they have no association with "Women's Lib". The supporters of the movement, on the other hand, have sometimes expressed impatience with existing women's organisations as getting nowhere as did the suffragettes with the suffragists in the early years of the century.

Virginia Novarra, a member of the Alliance Board from 1974 to 1976 was awarded a Winston Churchill Travelling Fellowship to study the means used to publicise equal opportunity legislation in USA and Canada, and as a result she produced a valuable outline of women's activities and advance towards equality in those two countries.[8] She compares the extent of discrimination in USA and Britain and gives evidence that it has been greater in recent years in the former. In conclusion she comments that "the outlook at present (1976) is for continuing pressure towards improvements in the status of women in Britain but nothing like a crash programme. The majority of women will accept these changes as they come, but will probably not press for speedier progress". In her view there are "few signs of that burning indignation over injustice to women and neglect of their talents which have made NOW, WEAL and other pressure groups a power in the land over the other side of the Atlantic. It may be that such a mood will come to pass here, but it is difficult to see what will create it".[9]

Reference to this question will be made later, but it is pertinent to observe here that as sex discrimination in the sixties and seventies appears to have been more conspicuous in USA than in Britain there are not quite the powerful reasons for indignation and protest which perhaps explains the comparative mildness of its impact. A revival of sex discrimination and flagrant or cryptic evasions of the provisions of the Sex Discrimination Act might provoke the mood of which Virginia Novarra speaks.

REFERENCES

1   Reports were published by IAW Headquarters.
2   See article by Margaret Ingledew, *IWN*, Vol. 66, No. 2, Feb. 1971. The twenty-one countries replying were Australia, Ceylon, Denmark, Finland, France, Germany, Iceland, Indonesia, Israel, Italy, Japan, Netherlands, Norway, Pakistan, Sierra Leone, Sweden, Switzerland, Thailand, Trinidad and Tobago, the United Arab Republic and the United Kingdom.
3   "Women's use of the Vote." *IWN*—Feb 1971.
4   A. N. Whitehead. *Symbolism, its meaning and effect.* Cambridge, 1928, p. 104.
5   Given at the annual general meeting of the National Council of Social Service in November 1976.
6   Betty Freidan, *The Feminine Mystique*, 1963, p. 375.
7   There are many books that give some account of the Women's Liberation Movement. Among the best are Kate Millett *Sexual Politics*, London 1971 (Rupert-Hart-Davis); William H. Chafe: *The American Woman*, New York 1972 (Oxford University Press); Juliet Mitchell: *Woman's Estate*, London 1971 (Penguin Books), Judith Hole and Ellen Levine: *Rebirth of Feminism*, 1971 New York (Quadrangle), Joan Huber (Editor) *Changing Women in a Changing Society*; a series of essays by different authors. Especially pertinent is Jo Freeman's *The Origins of Women's Liberation Movement*.
8   Virginia A. Novarra *Right on, Sister! – Impressions of the movement for equal opportunity in North America*. London, 1976.
9   Ibid., p. 106.

CHAPTER TWENTY-ONE

1972–1974

Status of Women Commission. New Delhi Congress. Seminars

The 24th session of the Status of Women Commission took place at Geneva from 14th February to 3rd March 1972. Eugenia Stevenson of Liberia was elected chairman, and one of the four vice-chairman was again Eva Kolstad of Norway (a prominent member of the board of IAW). The session was attended by the permanent representatives of the Alliance: Marie Ginsberg and Irmgard Rimondini, while Amy Bush, the senior vice-president also attended for the first week, followed by the second vice-president, Laurel Casinader, for the middle period, while Edith Anrep, the president, attended in the last week. This strong representation by the Alliance was doubtless because it had submitted statements or memoranda on the subjects of many of the resolutions adopted by the Commission, covered by the first eight as follows:

1. Influence of mass communication media on the formation of a new attitude towards the role of women in present-day society.
2. Implementation of the Declaration on the Elimination of Discrimination against Women.
3. Programme of work and establishment of priorities.
4. Equal pay for work of equal value.
5. International instruments or instruments relating to the status of women.
6. Status of women and family planning.
7. Status of women in private law.
8. Status of the unmarried mother.

The Secretary-general was requested to invite NGOs to comment on the first resolution and was also requested by UNESCO to consider the possibility of inter-disciplinary studies.

Women and mass communication media

The IAW memorandum on the subject of the first resolution was based on a questionnaire and statement sent to affiliates in several countries.[1] In response all said that the subject needed time and research but useful comments were received from affiliates in Australia, Egypt, Finland, India, The Netherlands, Norway, Sweden and the United Kingdom.

The statement recalled that in accordance with the objects of the IAW it endeavours to place emphasis on mass communication media aimed towards:

(1) Arousing in women awareness of their actual status in present-day society; (2) Informing women on how to grasp new opportunities; (3) Influencing mass communication media to eradicate the derogatory image of women and create a new image based on the dignity of the human being.

All affiliates thought that the most important forms of mass media were radio and television. "The spoken word" it was alleged "is the most important factor in mass media in developing countries where the leap from the drum to the tranisistor is fantastic". The Indian affiliates stated "that transistors are the rage among the old and young men and women in every village. Therefore, in India the radio is the most important means by which new attitudes towards women could be presented". The Egyptian affiliate agreed, and added that "Deep-rooted traditions could best be eradicated by enlisting sympathy and co-operation and not by provocation. Women's organisations in the Netherlands have invited men and women to speak on subjects relating to the role of women in the economic field; e.g. on part-time work, crèches, job counselling, in order that the general public be made aware of the new concept of women."

In India, TV was available in 1972 only in the largest towns and so can be used as a medium of communication only for a proportion of the urban population but it is spreading. For the promotion and dissemination of new ideas this channel of communication is important. In Egypt, the first line of attack is thought to be the educated classes, through whom new patterns concerning women can then be broadcast to less educated groups. The Norwegian affiliate stated that although TV is not used for advertising, programmes still perpetuate the traditional sex role of women. In Sweden, although many programmes still maintain existing prejudices, there is a tendency to broadcast on programmes which reflect the new position of women in the family, on the labour market and in society. That so few women are in high decision-making posts of mass media is deplored while more women as commentators would be welcomed. A Finnish analysis of sex roles on TV emphasised the current conceptions of discrimination against women: of those who appeared on TV 70 per cent were men compared with 30 per cent women and this pattern ran throughout all activities of men and women as given on TV.

A major part of mass media operations is based on currently accepted attitudes—the exploitation of the traditional feminine characteristics of dependence on the male, confinement of women to the kitchen sink, household chores, care of husband and children, the traditional role of men as fighters, thinkers, providers, protectors, exploiters of willing women. The influence of this form of mass media is subtle and effective. This most insidious form of mass media perpetuates the derogatory image of women as sex symbols and as an inferior class of human beings. Women are used as sex objects to promote sales or portrayed as glamour girls to induce women to buy commodities which normally they would not dream of purchasing. Advertisements of objects enhancing social status are generally directed to men, and household gadgets and products to women. Stress was laid by the Dutch affiliate on the necessity of correct information regarding women in order to promote equality, and through pressure women have been appointed as advisers on TV and radio programmes.

The Australian affiliate referred to objectionable advertisements since 1969. It urged its State affiliates to investigate these. It issued a manifesto which was widely publicised in press, radio and TV. Letters of protest were sent to many advertisers as well as to film censorship boards, and a "white list" was prepared of commended advertisers. Some reaction and improvement was noted as well as rousing interest by mass media.

News reports, documentary material, interviews, tend to reinforce concepts of the traditional role of women, writes the Finnish affiliate, and as those seem to be constantly repeated they appear to be the only possible or natural ones. Moreover, the existence of women's magazines as apart from men's is founded on the existing concept of the differences of the two sexes, so that sex equality is not likely to be emphasised.

Affiliates stated that there is a scarcity of books on women's roles and at the request of the IAW Congress of 1970 they are now making enquiries as to the availability of a good bibliography on the status of women, and if this is found to be inadequate to press for its improvement. Nigeria is endeavouring to meet this need for the dissemination of information regarding women by requesting the authorities to publicise and distribute reports of seminars. The German affiliate stocked some libraries with pamphlets on social and political activities of women, and also provided a list of basic literature on the status of women with the request that some of these books be obtained. The dissemination of UN information on the status of women and the achievements of the Status of Women Commission and the Human Rights Commission in eliminating discrimination against women was undertaken by the headquarters of IAW. Resolutions, recommendations and conventions were distributed to affiliates who were requested to distribute the information to their members. The Finnish affiliates stated that social changes affecting the status of women arouse attention only if they are of news value and are most likely to reach the ears of a wider section of the population than if they are related to reform or to new legislation or to equal rights.

In Norwegian schools there are plans to work for the equality of the sexes and to change text books. Literature offered to children, including comics, should be re-oriented so as to present women in their new role. Also advocated is the use of mass media for children to change the prevalent images of men and women. All the Scandinavian countries work along these lines.

It would not be wise to over-estimate the influence of radio and TV or to state that they are the most important media of communication and information in present-day life; yet through these media new attitudes and social patterns can be introduced to the public and reach the widest possible audience while they are particularly effective in reinforcing ideas and opinion already held. While there are frequent examples that mass media like radio and TV are open to put forward new ideas, the IAW survey showed at the same time that there is a tendency to maintain outdated patterns concerning the role of women in society. The survey also stressed the importance of investigations and studies on mass media and of their concept not only of women's but also of men's roles in present-day society. These studies would have to be made on a national basis. IAW welcomed and appreciated every effort which could be made by the Commission on the Status of Women to promote such studies. More adequate representation of women in decision-making posts in mass media would lead to the promotion of a new image of women and add to the foundation of new attitudes.[1] In this connection it is interesting to look at the position of women in the administrative sections of what is perhaps the principal agency of mass media in the UK, the BBC. In 1971 Political and Economic Planning in collaboration with the Tavistock Institute published *Women in Top Jobs—Four Studies in Achievement, Women in the BBC* by Isobel Allen is the third of the four studies.[2] It gives a historical review of the employment of women in the BBC up to 1971, of the kind of careers open to them, the methods of entry and the schemes of training. One chapter is significantly entitled "Reasons for women finding it difficult to move into more senior posts" and among these is the difficulty of breaking into a man's world. The BBC appears to be very much a man's world, evidence of which is provided by men in senior positions. One says "Some women will get on just because they're so good. But it's the ones just below the alpha plus level that are discriminated against", and he goes on to say that women are "a distracting influence" in what is "a closely knit little circle of men meeting". When women are introduced into this little circle "it gets very disturbed and it doesn't like it. It doesn't know how to cope". Poor men, it might be remarked, and these help to run the BBC.

Another man in a senior position expressed similar antipathy to women, and a third spoke of the difficulties of working with women; and a woman in a senior position speaks of the difficulties created for women. It seems that a large number of men in the BBC, judging from the evidence here provided, are not comfortable working with women, and that many things stand in the way of harmonious collaboration. Perhaps it is partly explained by one woman's comment: "At one time I should have said that women were discriminated against. Now I should say they don't play the game the right way." And Isobel Allen adds to this "that the socialising, the drinking in the right pubs and clubs, and above all the easy social contact which men have with one another, all militated against the advancement of women". Isobel Allen rendered a public service in revealing this aspect in the life of the BBC. It could be added that this common attitude of men in the BBC is not exceptional, but rather typical of many men in top jobs, educated in single sex public schools and universities.

The other listed resolutions at the 24th session of the Status of Women Commission had been preceded by considerable discussion in which the memoranda of the IAW were noted. The implementation of the Declaration on the Elimination of Discrimination against Women and 'Equal pay for work of equal value' were discussed at several meetings. With regard to the latter, Amy Bush made a brief statement on the work and aims of the Alliance in this field, pointing out that unless governments and other responsible bodies make apprenticeship and technical training available equally for both sexes with women and girls encouraged to participate, discrimination will always exist. Furthermore, tied up with equal pay for work of equal value are the questions of an equal flexible age of retirement and equal pension rights for women and men.

In addition to the resolutions mentioned a tenth was recommended to the General Assembly for an International Women's Year in 1975 and the reasons for it. The next chapter is devoted to this.

Family Planning

As mentioned in the previous chapter the status of women and family planning was the subject of one resolution introduced with guidelines by Helvi Sipilä who prepared an exhaustive report on the subject for the 25th session of the Commission at New York in January 1974.

This report, entitled "The Inter-relationship of the Status of Women and Family Planning", covered most aspects of the subject including the concept, its importance for women as individuals and its impact on their roles in society, the status of women as a factor influencing fertility, and the implications for the status of women of current population trends. Of prime importance is the effect on the individual woman.

It is pointed out that "the widespread dissemination of family planning information and services is sometimes rejected on the grounds that it is not compatible with national needs" and that "less attention has been paid to the human rights aspects of family planning, that is, to the necessity of providing family planning information, education and services for the direct purpose of guaranteeing to all persons the right to determine freely and responsibly the number and spacing of their children, regardless of the population factor in the countries concerned. And even less attention has been paid to the necessity of providing family planning services as a means, among others, of enabling women to free themselves as individuals and to exercise fully their rights to social, economic and political equality with men."

A valuable point is made when it is stated that the knowledge itself of how to regulate births, regardless of its direct effect on fertility, gives women the power to plan their lives in ways undreamed of by those who have never questioned the inevitability of their childbrearing, or who have resorted in desperation to cumbersome, ineffective and often dangerous methods to stop unwanted births. As the Netherlands response points out, "family planning will greatly enhance people's awareness of the possibility of shaping their own destinies".

The value of family planning in providing better opportunities for education among girls and young women and for women's participation in public life is dealt with at length. "Delaying the onset of childbearing, either through delaying marriage itself, or by postponing the first birth within marriage, is the most relevant aspect of fertility regulation. Postponing the first birth should have the greatest impact on a woman's opportunities for vocational training or for secondary, college or university education in those countries or among socio-economic groups in which (a) she had a high probability of pursuing an education beyond the normal first years of childbearing to begin with, while (b) the birth of a child would effectively limit her chances of staying in school."

In the note on participation in public life we are reminded that "the United Nations has declared the right of women to participate in public life and political decision-making on equal terms with men. In particular, women are to be assured of the right to vote in all elections, to be eligible for all publicly elected bodies, to hold public office and to exercise all public functions."

"In so far as family planning contributes to freeing women from heavy domestic responsibilities, it can facilitate their active participation in community, national and international affairs. And in so far as the act of planning the spacing and number of births accustoms women to the possibility of acquiring greater control over their own lives, it may encourage them to play a more active role in public decision-making as well."

Congress at New Delhi 1973

At the Alliance board meeting in London in June 1971 the invitation of the All India Women's Conference to hold the 23rd Congress of the IAW in India in 1973 was accepted. It was confirmed at the international committee meeting at Helsinki in August 1972 and duly held in New Delhi from 7th to 14th November 1973. The theme of the Congress was "partnership for progress" which was interpreted on the basis of equality and implied equal partnership in the home, in law, in economic and social fields. Representatives of affiliated societies from twenty-four countries (of a total of forty-two countries with affiliated societies) and representatives from United Nations, USA, and USSR attended.

The Congress took place in the vast ballroom of the Imperial Hotel with the colourful decor of the gold and white banner of the Alliance flanked by the flags of twenty-four countries. The inaugural speech was given by the president, Edith Anrep, who warmly welcomed Mrs Indira Gandhi, the Prime Minister of India. Edith Anrep said that the IAW having attained the first goal, the suffrage, has spread its work to embrace women's conditions in all walks of life according to its slogan "Equal Rights—Equal Responsibilities". The IAW still holds its position as a spearhead organisation for women's rights. New social patterns are emerging all over the world, and great changes in the situation of women have been accompained during this century, but with few exceptions women are missing on decision-making bodies, including international conferences when vital global questions are discussed. In every country there is an elite of women who have reached high positions—we have but to look at India—but the journey towards freedom has not yet ended for many women. The theme of this Congress "partnership for progress" will bring about new creative thoughts and practical suggestions to promote a true partnership between women and men.

After Lakshmi Raghuramiah, the president of the hostess society, the All India Women's Conference, had welcomed the delegates, Mrs Gandhi addressed the Congress. She referred at the outset to the oil crisis and remarked that "as societies and economies grow more complex the simplest obstructions seem to throw them off balance". After mentioning that in spite of technological progress there are still large sections of populations starved, neglected and denied what the privileged enjoy, she spoke of the spirit of revolt among them, that of women. "Almost everywhere", she said, "women have won impressive political battles for franchise or for inheritance of property or equal wages. Yet they find that in many subtle ways the equality that is legally extended to them is withheld in practice.

Hedi Flite—has been a member of the board of IAW since 1961 and a vice-president since 1967. In West Germany she was a Member of Parliament and a City Councillor of Wilhelmshaven for twenty years.

Amy Bush—was chairman of the International Committee for Equal Educational Rights from 1952 to 1967, and chairman of the Projects Committee in 1967 and onwards. She became a member of the board of IAW in 1952 and a vice-president in 1967.

Laurel Casinader—was chairman of the Committee for Equal Economic Rights from 1952 to 1970. She became a member of the board of IAW in 1958 and a vice-president in 1970.

Olive Bloomer. Treasurer of IAW since 1964. She has been a very active member and taken part in many seminars. She was director of the Cairo seminar, sponsored by UNESCO, in 1978.

It is also true that it is far more difficult for a woman to make the same mark as a man in academic, economic and political spheres. Hidden persuaders of the various media and scientists who fit observations to theory, flatter women in order to enslave them. So we in India can understand the motivations of the Women's Liberation Movement which is active in many societies which are technologically advanced but not necessarily psychologically advanced to the same extent.

"Traditional societies were able to enforce conformity and obedience to authority by restricting the opportunities for education. The spread of education stimulates doubt and questioning. Unless society works for objectives which enthuse different sections, there will be increasing tensions between the individual and the state. Indian society is in transition. Many trends are simultaneously at work. The age old apathy and attitudes of resignation have been shed. Poverty is no longer accepted as divine dispensation. Education is expanding at a tremendous rate and reaching to groups which have so far been deprived."

After references to population, family planning and democratic rights she said: "Much earlier in our history, because of the ancient tradition of regarding Shakti or energy as a goddess, female in form, Indian society had made it possible for exceptional women to be accepted by society. A woman ruler or a woman in any other important position was never an oddity. So our history is sprinkled with the names of great women, rulers and generals, mathematicians and philosophers. Yet the mass of women had a raw deal and I am afraid this still continues. The important place that our social reformers of the nineteenth century gave to the removal of disabilities against women in education and law and the bond forged later in the Gandhi–Nehru phase of the freedom movement, has once again opened the doors. My party the Indian National Congress, has had several women presidents, two of them of British origin. We have had women chief ministers, as Sari Radha Raman told you, and today women are working in administration, in business and the professions in increasing numbers.

"But legal equality, or the opportunity for a few women to make their mark, does not mean that the majority of women have ceased to suffer from handicaps. They continue to be economically dependent and victims of custom and tradition. The *Vedas*, our ancient scriptures, had called husband and wife equal, like the two wheels of a chariot. And *Manu*, the ancient codifier of our society, said: 'Where women are honoured the gods rejoice; where they are not honoured, there all sacred rites are fruitless'. But the same *Manu* denied women the right of sacred learning. This contradiction between the ideal and the actual has persisted in our society to the present day. It can be ended only by women asserting their rights more vigorously and by being equally forthright in accepting responsibility and the burdens."

"I do not normally consider myself a feminist", Indira Gandhi said, "that is why I appreciated what the president said about partnership between women and men. But if 'feminist' means that there should be no discrimination against a woman using her ability and talent, if it means equality of rights on the basis of merit, then I am a feminist. But it seems to me that some women feminists want to escape from being women. There are certainly differences, biological and biofunctional and I personally entirely agree with the French senator who is reported to have once declaimed 'Vive la difference!' But there are also basic human qualities which are common to men and women and which are no less important. Hence one should not imitate but try to deepen and strengthen one's own personality. I view the fight of women for greater social and political rights as part of the larger struggle of groups which have been historically oppressed for their due share of freedom to develop in their own way and to shape the future for their children and the generation to come."

Among the keynote speeches[3] on the theme of the Congress was a long one: "Women and Men, Partners in the Community", by Krishna Iyer, an Indian judge, but it was not too long because it was one of the most eloquent addresses ever given to an IAW Congress, and is therefore worth quoting substantially. He began by speaking of the appropriateness of India as the venue for the Congress as the largest democracy in the world with a constitution which guarantees the equality of the sexes and has an outstanding symbol of Indian womanhood at the pinnacle of the power pyramid, although he warned his audience that law and life may vary, one political swallow does not make a common people's summer and Indian women have their sorrows.

Judge Iyer referred to himself as a 'committed' man "in the justice of the woman's claim for self-determination and share in undertakings beyond the bedroom and the household; but I also hold the tragic view that the backwardness and obscurantism of the home-bound women are being preserved as a vested interest and exploited as a convenient instrument by male opponents of human progress. My point is that your battle for a juster man-woman fellowship has to be fought against two enemies, the traditional female and the conservative male. The subtle weapons used against you are many, including religion, culture, law, biology and family, duty, not to speak of glamourising and its opposite, vulgarising. Please don't be lullabied by romantic writings or soothing celluloid about your looks or be brow-beaten by manifestations of masculine arrogance. Be conscious of your strength, be sure of your conviction, be clear that you ask for equity, not charity, partnership, not poetry, recognition of separate personality, not mere merger in man. Our century, I am confident, belongs to the suppressed and our world will witness the wiping out of the

Reception after the IAW Congress,
New Delhi 1973. Left to right: Mrs
Valborg Hagstrom, Sweden; Irène de
Lipkowski; Edith Anrep; and Indira
Gandhi, Prime Minister of India. It was
at this congress that Irène de Lipkow-
ski succeeded Edith Anrep as president.

unjust past and the emergence of the human person so long denied to
womankind. And when woman has found her soul and broken free from
the bonds of old, when a new natural but spiritual mutuality within and
without the home has been woven both would fulfil themselves. I believe
that heredity has not denied the female equal faculties or biology inflicted
disabilities now that science has solved problems of haphazard pregnancy
or necessary breast-feeding. The myths which hold women down are man-
made, not god-given and the villain of the piece is our cultural bias. . . .

"Every struggle for equal justice is against exploitation, tyranny,
indignity. When a woman worker is paid for equal labour less than a
man's wages it is naked exploitation. When a women is denied due share
in public offices it is plain discrimination. When a female is banished into
the kitchen, demanded to bear children and ordained not to meddle in

public affairs it is social oppression. When she is indoctrinated into a sense of divinely decreed inferiority it is cultural suppression and religious perversion. When women, or, as in some cases, married women are denied, under colour of law and usage, employment, even certain types of public service, or separate property, equal inheritance, matrimonial and divorce rights, political franchise or religious priesthood—the list is only illustrative, not exhaustive—it adds up to legal tyranny. And most offensive of all, when a culture and literature poetize the fine flesh of the female, idealise her obedience as a paragon of domestic drudgery and fail wilfully to see her soul or recognise her equal potential for science and society, we have to designate them as masculine manacles draped in legend, arts and religion. God who created us equal is made guilty by man. Women must prove His innocence by their performance!"

Judge Iyer referred to women's participation in national struggles against oppression and exploitation, and he cited the example of the USSR where the acknowledgement of women's right has "made woman equal partner with man as citizen, as producer, as consumer and even as communist leader". Other observers would perhaps comment that as in other countries this is true in principle if not wholly in implementation.

Continuing, Judge Iyer said: "India in its long struggle against imperialism has stressed the importance of social justice to the downtrodden, including women, and has done much to raise the dignity of that sex by conferring, in a comparative sense, higher legal status, cultural opportunities, personal rights and effective, though yet insignificant, role in public life. Gandhi, the father of the nation, and Nehru, the architect of free India, together contributed to the broad-based struggle for freedom with a social dimension, in which countless heroines, known and unknown, took part and thus laid the basis for the new road in free India for independence of women."

Judge Iyer went on to speak of the concept of "Women and Men— Partners in the Community" as equal association for achieving socially-directed goals. He referred to the campaign as a war by the weak against the strong, and he suggested the steps to create universal opinions in favour of practical equality apart from theoretical acceptance. "The conscience of humanity expressed in the Charter of the United Nations," he said, "has reaffirmed faith in the equal rights of men and women. The universal declaration of rights has proclaimed the equality of the sexes. The Indian Constitution, apart from highlighting social justice in its preamble, has prohibited discrimination by the State on grounds of sex and has insisted that no disability with regard to access to public places shall be imposed based on sex. Equal opportunity in matters of public employment has been assured regardless of sex. Nay, more, power has been given to the state to make special provision in favour of women and children to overcome disabilities. Indeed, equal rights of citizenship, of the right to elect and to be elected are conferred on women as much as on men. Equal pay for equal work, regardless of sex, humane conditions of work and maternity relief, provision against moral and material abandonment are directive principles of state policy in India although in actuality the distance to accomplishment is long. In the eye of our constitution and the laws, there is a total obliteration of sex distinction. So much so, in political life and public affairs, in social activities and educational attainments, in the civil services and other state action, the law is fair and equal to both the sexes. It is right to point out that there are many constitutions in the world which guarantee the fundamental equality of the sexes and confer universal adult franchise upon women. For example, Article 122 of the Constitution of the USSR proclaims that women have equal rights with men in all spheres of economic state, cultural, social and political life. These rights are further ensured to women by granting them equal right with men to work, payment for work, rest and leisure, social insurance and education, prematernity and maternity leave with full pay and the like. Article 137 declares women's rights to elect and to be elected on equal terms with men. The Constitution of the German Democratic Republic in Article 7 confers on men and women equal rights. It is unfortunate but true that in certain western countries, political equality has not been completely established. The judiciary has been a powerful, progressive instrument for equality in the United States.

"In India the religious and personal laws still persist in discriminating between men and women although after freedom a great deal of amelioration has come about. However, certain communities—and there is a chain reaction in this area, of one community claiming after the other, saying 'touch me not', and for conservatives in each community arrogating to themselves the right to speak for the whole community—still insist on the perpetuation of the discrimination against women in family laws including inheritance and matrimony. It is unfortunate but true that as late as 1973 the parliament of India which had very nearly passed a provision in favour of destitute divorcees, sensitively apprehending objections from male leaders of one community, withdrew from that step provisionally. I mention this to emphasise that perfect legal equality does not exist even in the books. Of course, even in effervescent African countries, and amongst the advanced white nations, large legal disparity in status and politics remains. So, the first part of the campaign has to be for constitutional and legal equality for women with men as an article of civilised life."

Continuing, Iyer claimed that "in the field of science and research, given equal opportunity, women can contribute as much as men. In the learned professions, the Soviet experiment has established that women are excellent lawyers, judges, doctors, farmers, manual workers and even police and army people. In the roles of intellectuals, thinkers, artists, executives, inventors and administrators, women can shine. None of these is funda- mentally incompatible with biological femininity. It is a slanderous story, when women astronauts and cosmonauts are realities, that the woman is fit only to be a housewife and to bring children forth periodically."

After speaking of the value of family planning he went on to speak of equal partnership in the home and concluded with some wise remarks on the Congress theme of "partnership for progress". "A mere demand for liberation and equality of status", he said, "is negative and may lead to excesses and perversions, while an egalitarian alliance for community development is positive and wise. If man and wife are each independent of the other economically and otherwise, the home may yet not be happy. But if both are free and equal and combine to build up a fine family the blend would be wholesome and soul-satisfying. Similarly, if women are able to stand on their own feet and defy and deny men, the race breaks up. But if manpower and womanpower are fruitfully united, the finished product will be an asset to possess. So you must set your sights rightly and look beyond simple liberation. You must have a sense of correct per- spective so that the new frontiers of human advance may be a joint achieve- ment. You must shape your means not in hostility to man but hand-in-hand with him to end exploitation of the weaker by the stronger. A new order, with aware women and understanding men, a value system where mother and father, sister and brother, are real contributories, a way of life which overrules the barbarous past and humanises mutual relations—such is the challenge which you are called upon to take up—at once a fighting faith and a constructive job."

In her address on Partnership in the Economic and Social Field, Annelise Truninger of Switzerland had, justifiably, a few bitter things to say about men and women in employment. "Men", she said, assign to women the jobs they dislike doing themselves. Socially and economically, women are men's auxiliary forces, not their partners. Today many women perform a double task; they go out to work as well as running a home. So women are doubly exploited, not only do they get underpaid and mechanical jobs but they are expected to keep house for a husband and children. In addi- tion, they are socially restricted and regarded as the inferior part of man- kind."

Speaking of social planning in the future she said that "women could contribute a great deal to the humanisation of our world. It is up to women to maintain the quality of life: men are too preoccupied with increasing the quantity of things by conquering nature."

She then defined the kind of partnership—"Women can be partners of men", she said, "not by imitating them to competing for their jobs, but as indispensable complements. Obtaining equal rights is not itself a synonym of partnership."

Covering the political field Leela Damodara Menon confirmed Indira Gandhi's mention of women's high position in earlier Indian societies. "In ancient India", she said, "woman was called man's partner in all things and enjoyed equal status with her spouse, but these golden days disappeared when for various reasons man became the master and woman the slave." Yet she was able to catalogue some of the achievements of women in the modern world. "It is a matter of pride for all", she said, "that there are three women Prime Ministers today [1973], guiding the destinies of their nations as well as or better than men. They are not there because they are women, but in spite of their sex. The German parliament has a woman president. The Atomic Energy Commission in USA has a woman chairman. There have been two women presidents of the UN General Assembly. There are a few women ambassadors, cabinet ministers, governors, parliament members and legislators, and some of them have blazed a trail of glory by their exceptional performance. However, for many women there is a gap between the law and practice. After each election, women's representation seems to get smaller and smaller."

Edith Anrep, the president, gave a report at the Congress of IAW activities in the triennial period 1970–1973 and in particular of her own work and travels and that of other officers during the period. She concluded her report by saying that she had done her best to follow the policy of the IAW as strictly as possible. "Thanks to our firm action programme", she said, "we can serve as an organisation with expert knowledge within our field work. In spite of our age—we could almost celebrate our 70th anniversary[4]—we have an up-to-date programme, and, as is usual at Congresses, we come together to give it new life following the trend of time." Then she asked questions that others were asking: "Is it sufficient to be up-to-date with our programme? Have we got the imagination and vision to be ahead of time like our pioneers?"

In this there is an implied criticism which is healthy. Up to about 1950 the IAW was always very much ahead of its time, but during the seventies there appears to be a tendency for it to fall into line with current vague thinking. This is indicated perhaps by the change in the title of the commissions that occurred at the Königstein Congress (1970) when, as mentioned in the last chapter, the terms "equal" and "rights" were dropped, and the "Equal Moral Standard Commission" became the "Social Commission". These changes indicate a degree of timidity and a move towards generalities and less precision and provide fuel for the criticisms of the women's liberation movement. The IAW should not be concerned with falling into line with current thinking, but, as in former days, being ahead of it. There are still not equal moral standards, nor is equality widespread in any other field. Symbolical is the less than 10 per cent of women members of parliament throughout the world.

Still, it is perhaps inevitable that with the principles the IAW so vigorously promulgated in the first half century of its life, largely accepted by many governments of the world with a fair degree of implementation by some, that the far-sighted pioneering of early days no longer has quite the same incentive. Yet only the partial implementation of accepted principles spells a need for further imaginative propaganda that Edith Anrep clearly had in mind.

Sadly Edith Anrep had decided to resign the presidency after only three years. In the history of the Alliance the president had generally been not only the leader but among the hardest working officers, and with the activities becoming so wide flung involving for the president much travelling to attend seminars and visit affiliated societies the strain to a conscientious worker like Edith Anrep was considerable. She occupied the office with dignity and efficiency and her resignation was a matter of widespread regret.

She was succeeded by Irène de Lipkowski of France who had had a varied and notable career. During the second world war her husband was a member of the Resistance Movement. He was arrested by the Gestapo, deported and died at Buchenwald. At the time of the liberation Irène de Lipkowski became Deputy Mayor of Orly, and in 1951 a Member of Parliament, and later Mayor of Marennes. She has many honours. She is an Officer of the Legion of Honour, and Commander of the National Order of Merit. Her son was a former French Secretary of State for Foreign Affairs.

In accepting the presidency, Irène de Lipkokski realised the heavy task of the office. She remarked that the differences of evolution in the different countries stressed the delay of equal status of men and women, but the new ideology of equal rights was beginning to influence more and more the feminine population. She reminded the delegates that it was owing to the Alliance that they all have a valuable contact with the United Nations and its agencies. She spoke of the valuable medium of the *International Women's News* and she asked for more news from affiliated societies of women's activities in their countries so that they stimulate each other.

The resolutions at the Congress were formulated by the six commissions. It was difficult to say or claim anything new in the resolutions, and they were inevitably mainly reiterations of things said before, sometimes more forcibly, sometimes less so. They served in many instances to reinforce recommendations of the Status of Women Commission. The value of family planning giving more freedom to women and enhancing their status in society, was first included in a resolution at the Königstein Congress, was referred to again at the Delhi Congress, while it had recently received much attention at the 24th and 25th Sessions of the Status of Women Commission (1972–74).

Three important seminars

In 1972, 73 and 74, the IAW organised three important seminars on "The Demographic Implications of Women's Participation in Society", the first at Georgetown, Guyana, 5–15th November 1972; the second at New Delhi, 9–29th November 1973; and the third in Accra, Ghana, 17–27th July 1974.   Each of these seminars was sponsored by the United Nations Fund for Population Activities. The first two were directed by Edith Anrep, the president of IAW, the third by Irène de Lipkowski who had succeeded Edith Anrep as president. Amy Bush, first vice-president, was the organiser for all three seminars, and Olive Bloomer the hon. treasurer of the IAW was the rapporteur throughout, Several other officers of the IAW gave assistance. These three seminars constituted one of the most notable enterprises of IAW.

That at Guyana was the first time the IAW had organised a regional seminar in South America. 40 participated; 22 from the Guyana Women's Leage of Social Service and 18 from the Caribbean territories of Antigua, Bahamas, Grenada, Haiti, Jamaica, Trinidad and Tobago. The main guest speaker was the indefatigable Helvi Sipilä, the United Nations Assistant Secretary-general for Social and Humanitarian Affairs. On each of the ten days there were 90 to 150 observers, including the UN resident representative, government officials and representatives of voluntary organisations.[5]

The subject of the successive sessions were civil, political, economic and social rights, civic education, literacy, self-help, women in employment, the creative use of leisure, family health and welfare and the role of women's organisations.

Helvi Sipilä in her address mentioned that two groups of NGOs were meeting in South America at the same time discussing the utilisation of human resources and the implications of the participation of women in development. In these meetings of women's organisations the participants were women. They followed an inter-governmental regional conference dealing with population problems in the ECAFE at which 24 governments were represented by 137 persons, apparently nearly all men, and Helvi Sipilä remarked that it was "extraordinary that there were practically no women in a meeting of government representatives who have the authority to formulate population policies and plan for the next decade." The report of the meeting was to include a section called "Social Development Programme" under which there was expected to be an assessment of the social development plans and achievements to permit more effective action in the light of prospective population trends and their implications. Among topics to be considered were changes in value systems affecting the family and the role of women in society. The topics would cover finance, social developments, and the implications of population which were to be considered in connection with nutrition and food supply, health services, education and training, housing, youth, the status of women and social security. "Are not women interested in these questions of paramount importance for their families and their countries? Why were women not there?" asked Helvi Sipilä.

"The reason is", she said, "that in spite of all the progress made by UN, its agencies, governments and non-governmental organisations, the participation of women in decision making procedures at all levels is nearly non-existent. It is of little help that there may be a few female heads of states, there is a minimum of participation by women in matters concerning the future of mankind. When you see women gathered at meetings

Irène de Lipkowski, president of the
IAW 1973 and re-elected 1976.

of their own, one must ask, has not the time come to stop talking about participation and begin participating in reality. Has not the time come for us to put an end to distinction as to sex instead of promoting it by our own activities?"

She said later that much as we appreciate the positive examples of the achievements of women as the heads of government and in prominent positions in some of the professions, "we must not forget the mass of women whose lot has hardly improved at all in spite of national and international efforts. For millions the Declaration on the Elimination of Discrimination against Women is just a piece of paper, even if they know it exists. Here the activities of non-governmental organisations both men's and women's are of great importance. Women must act as pressure groups, but why should men remain indifferent if they believe the clause adopted by the General Assembly "that the full and complete development of a country, the well-being of the world, and the cause for peace require the maximum participation of women as well as men in all fields."

Towards the end of her address Helvi Sipilä dealt a little with family planning and the status of women. She referred to the study of the subject by the UN which had begun in 1968 to be completed in 1974 which she said is expected to answer three main questions:

(a) To what extent does family planning, i.e. the way in which couples decide on the number and spacing of their children, affect the status of women in their possibility to participate in the social and economic development of their country?

(b) To what extent does the status of women, i.e. education, employment and political participation and equality within the family, affect the possibility freely and responsibly to decide on the spacing and number of her children?

(c) To what extent does the population trend in each country affect the status of women?

The answers to these questions are contained in the lengthy report on the subject prepared for the 25th session from which some quotations have been given.[6] Helvi Sipilä concluded her address by speaking of the action of the UN and its specialised agencies, but to achieve the goals the contributions of all citizens are required and the assistance of NGOs who, she said, in their influential membership and determined political approach will assist governments to make a better world for every human being.

The second seminar in the series followed the IAW Congress at Delhi in November 1973; 24 participated, 10 from India and 14 from Asian territories: Bangladesh, Indonesia, Malaysia, Nepal, Philippines and Sri Lanka, while about 30 to 40 observers attended each day. Mr Jyoti Singh, assistant secretary for world population year gave an address.

In this seminar there was stronger emphasis on family planning. In the first plenary session an address was given on "The right to plan a family" by K. Tambunan-Maulini of Indonesia. In the third session a general discussion on family planning as a necessity in raising the status of women, was followed by an informative address by Suratmi Iman Sudjakri of Indonesia on the important subject of how to direct religious customs, laws and attitudes towards the promotion of family planning. She quoted from the Koran, the Bible and the Hindu religion showing that rather than religion putting barriers to the promotion of family planning many concepts in them can be interpreted as favouring the practice. She spoke of the customary attitudes in rural areas of her country towards the bearing of children, how each child is regarded as a God-send. New social norms she claimed need to be extended to bring about the acceptance of family planning for laws are often the outcome of religious beliefs, customs and traditions. She asked for the re-thinking of these, and for new laws.

Her contentions were reinforced by those of Tara Ali Baig of India, who spoke on new family and social legislation, and who stated that social custom is still against the limitation of families or even the rights given by modern legislation such as the very advanced Termination of Pregnancy Act passed in 1971. In this, the wife has the right to abortion even without the consent of her husband, but doctors, to avoid unpleasantness, often refuse to do an abortion in these circumstances.

Following, Mahra Masani, also of India, speaking of "the role of communication in changing attitudes" stated that India has been a pioneer in adopting family planning as a part of national policy since 1952, yet more than 70 per cent of the people are not yet convinced of its need, which indicates that much persuasion is necessary to make the entire population conscious of its urgency, an urgency it might be added which is amply demonstrated by its population of 550 millions, a population which is still increasing and which has to be fed.

In the discussion that followed these three addresses, it was agreed that while religion is an essential part of everyday life, it is often misrepresented in matters of family planning and wrongly interpreted and it was recommended that the statements of enlightened religious leaders should be collected and publicised to remove doubts and misgivings.

In stating in a keynote speech on the evaluation of family planning programmes in developing countries, Dr S. N. Agarwala of India said that the over-all objective of a family planning programme is to reduce the birth rate, but surely this is only a partial objective, and Dr S. N. Agarwala should think further. One of the main objectives is freedom, to free women from the thraldom of continuous unpredictable child bearing and instead plan her life so that she can play a more useful part in all forms of social and economic activities.

The President of India, Varah Venkata
Giri greets Dame Margery Corbett
Ashby at the IAW Congress at Delhi
in November 1973. Standing to the
left of President Giri is Edith Anrep
who was then president of IAW.

In the same session Maniben Kara of India considered "Trade Unions
and Development and Family Plannang" and she complained that in the
campaign for family planning little attention is paid to women and their
rights, and she summarised what trade unions can do in the field of family
planning. Most of the nine points she made were concerned with ways
of making available a full understanding of the subject in all its aspects.

In the last seventh session Jyoti Singh, spoke on World Population Year
and referred to the contribution NGOs can make towards family planning.
He said that the work of the voluntary sector really needs to be strengthened
and that the involvement of NGOs like the IAW will promote that objective further. He mentioned that in many Asian countries, national co-
ordinating bodies or population commissions have been created to supervise
and co-ordinate the work being done, and suggested that the IAW may
wish to be involved in their activities.

The concluding addresses were given by the president of IAW, Edith
Anrep, and vice-president Laurel Casinader. The former spoke of the contribution that can be made to the subject of family planning by an NGO.

She explained the machinery by which the IAW worked with its affiliates and with the UN and its specialised agencies UNESCO, UNOP, ILO and FAO. "A responsibility of the Alliance", she said, "is the spreading of knowledge about international instruments adopted by the General Assembly affecting the status of women. In view of the fact that this year has been named by the UN as 'World Population Year' and next year, 1975, is 'International Women's Year', the affiliates should form a special committee to study the Declaration of Discrimination Against Women. Thirdly, as a member of an international organisation, it gives an affiliate added strength when it approaches the government or other authorities on a national level. The IAW gives guide-lines which the affiliate can adapt according to the pattern of its country, i.e. if revision of your family law is needed, then through the international headquarters, you can get information as to how another country has tackled the problem." Towards the conclusion she claimed that the Alliance was the first women's organisation to put family planning on its programme.

Laurel Casinader painted a picture which she entitled "The smaller family: traditions of yesterday—realities of today". Here is part of the picture. The scene is a typical Asian rural area:

"At the end of the child's first year, when perhaps he/she may be walking, No. 2 comes along; at the end of the second year, No. 3 comes along, and so on and on, but all the time the woman is important as wife and mother and social life centres around her. In a simple village community, where there are no other social amenities, these engagements relieve the tedium and drudgery of the work-a-day life, besides which, the more children there are, the more the husband takes pride in his virility."

The other aspect of the picture is dismal. "The mother's health is impaired by frequent child-bearing; the child tends to be neglected because of a new baby, and in countries where weaning foods, as known in the west, are non-existent, there is malnutrition with all its attendant evils. In other ages, another child was another pair of hands for work, another investment for old age, but in the context of present-day hardship, another child is also another mouth to feed."

This emphasis on family planning in the second of the three series of seminars was very appropriate in India with its vast population. In the following seminar, at Accra, Ghana, in West Africa in July 1974, although family planning appeared in the programme, it took its place with other important subjects like education and the economical potential of women, which formed the three main topics of the seminar; 35 participated from 10 countries: Ivory Coast, Dahomey, Gambia, Upper Volta, Liberia, Mali, Nigeria, Sierra Leone and Togo.

The first two sessions were devoted mainly to education, one section being concerned with the economic potential of women, the fifth and sixth with the right to plan a family, and the seventh was devoted to the role of women's organisations on which the director and the president of IAW, Irène de Lipkowski spoke. She was followed by Laurel Casinader who spoke on "fitting programmes to practical objectives".

An evaluation of the seminar was given by Helen Judd, who rather regretted the meaningless jargon of the general title, but in spite of this she said that discussion "was none the less intense and fruitful".

Among the recommendations of the seminar were the necessity for sex education, with indications of how this might be secured; the setting up of advice centres for health, nutrition and family planning; the abolition of ritual operations which lower the status of women; and a recommendation that there should be co-ordination of women's organisations at national and regional levels so as to share information and experience and constitute a more powerful force.

REFERENCES

1 See article in *IWN*—"Towards a new attitude in the role of women—IAW Memorandum on the influence of mass communication media" (Vol. 68, No. 2, March–April 1973). The account given is based on this article. The statements and opinions of affiliates are sometimes interpreted rather than quoted for the sake of clarity and unambiguous English.

2 The other three are (1) *Women in two large companies* by Isobel Allen; (2) *The Woman Director* by A. J. Allen and (3) *Women in the Administrative Class* by Patricia A. Walters. The studies were made under the direction of Michael P. Fogarty, Robert and Rhona Rapopert, published by George Allen and Unwin.

3 These keynote speeches in addition to Justice Iyer's were *Partnership in the Home* by Karin Ahrland of Sweden; *Family Law* by Chana Caplan of Israel; *Partners in the Economic and Social Field* by Annelise Truninger of Switzerland; *Partners in the Political Field* by Leela Damodara Menon of India; *International Partnership* by Irène de Lipkowski of France; *World Population Year* by Mehri Hekmati of United Nations Fund for Population Activities; *The Human Environment—Non-Governmental Organisation and their Contribution* by Mala Pal of India; and *The Role of Non-Governmental Organisations* by Louisa Giuriati, NGO Liaison Officer, Geneva.

4 Calculating from the Berlin Congress the IAW was then 69 years old, yet the Congresses are numbered from Washington 1902, which made it then 71.

5 Three booklets giving reports of the proceedings, addresses and discussions were published by the International Alliance of Women.

6 *Study on the Inter-relationship of the Status of Women and Family Planning.* Report of the special rapporteur for the twenty-fifth session of the Commission on the Status of Women. United Nations Economic and Social Council E/CN.6/575/Add.1.

CHAPTER TWENTY-TWO

1975–1976

International Women's Year and New York Congress

A group of women's non-governmental organisations, having consultative status with the United Nations Economic and Social Council, conceived the idea of an International Women's Year. As non-governmental organisations cannot introduce resolutions to a UN Commission, Florica Andrei, a government delegate of Romania, did so on the group's behalf at the 24th session of the Status of Women Commission early in 1972.

The proposal was adopted by the Commission because it found "that in spite of the existence of the Declaration on the Elimination of Discrimination against Women and other instruments of the United Nations and the specialised agencies, and in spite of the progress made in the matter of equal rights, women continue to be discriminated against in the political, cultural, economic and social fields".

The Commission therefore prepared a draft resolution for submission by ECOSOC to the General Assembly which gave the reasons for holding an International Women's Year. This was mainly an amplification of that already stated.

The proclamation of an International Women's Year would, it was stated, serve to intensify the action required to advance the status of women. The proposal was adopted by the General Assembly in its resolution 3010 of 18th December 1972. This proclaimed 1975 International Women's Year and requested the Secretary-general: "To prepare in consultation with member states, specialised agencies and interested non-governmental organisations, within the limits of existing resources, a draft programme for the Year, to be submitted to the Commission on the Status of Women at its 25th session in 1974."

A draft programme began with a declaration of the significance of the year, which was adopted by the working group appointed to study this by the Status of Women Commission for consideration at its 25th session in January 1974. The IWY is to be devoted to intensified action:

"(a) To promote equality between men and women;

"(b) To ensure the full integration of women in the total development effort, especially by emphasising women's responsibility and important role in economic, social and cultural development at the national, regional and international levels, particularly during the Second United Nations Development Decade;

"(c) To recognise the importance of women's increasing contribution to the development of friendly relations and co-operation among states and to the strengthening of world peace."

Objectives were formulated by the working group on the basis of the Secretary-general's draft classified under the three headings of Equality, Development and Peace. These were examined by the Status of Women Commission during the 25th session in 1974. Several amendments were made and the programme finally adopted.

Practically all the objectives had been repeatedly advocated in various forms at the many Congresses of the IAW. One of the most important and far reaching was that of "ensuring that women as well as men participate fully and as equal partners in policy formulation and decision-making at the local, national and international levels, including development planning, 'educational programming and questions of foreign policy such as disarmament, and the strengthening of friendly relations among states". Certainly an ambitious objective which would be very far-reaching in its realisation.

The principal event of International Women's Year 1975 was the international meeting in Mexico from 19th June to 2nd July (preparations for which meant a colossal world-wide task for the personnel of UN). It was in two sections: the Conference at the Gimnasio Juan de la Berrera and in the halls of the conference centre in the Plaza de la Tres Culturas for government delegates, and the meetings open to all, called the "Tribune", several miles away. The former was attended by over a thousand delegates from 125 nations, of whom about 30 per cent were men and the latter by over 6,000 women and men from all parts of the world, including representatives of 113 non-governmental organisations.

The conference of government delegates was opened by the UN Secretary-general, Kurt Waldheim, who said in his inaugural speech that "equality of opportunity between men and women is essential if we are to create a more equitable international economic and social system", and he stressed that the problems that confront the world are not capable of solution by individual nations, but only by combined international action. He was followed by President Echeverria of Mexico who spoke of the oppression of women in the past, and said that the trend towards a more rational and humane attitude with regard to women was part of a larger movement transforming the world. He implied the growing realisation that "the oppressed man who assumes attitudes of superiority towards women reproduces within the family the conduct of his oppressors" and thus "compromises the conduct of his oppressors".

Thirdly, Helvi Sipilä, the Secretary-general of the conference gave a spirited address in which she spoke of priority needs. "Education and training", she said, "are key issues which deserve priority consideration. Equally important is the question of women's legal capacity, particularly the legal provisions referring to marriage, inheritance and property rights. Economic independence, which enables women to determine freely their own destiny, is also a prerequisite to their participation in the life of society. There is also an urgent need for a radical change in attitudes of both men and women. Customs, traditions, and the unquestioned myths ingrained through centuries of prejudice still operate to prevent women from exercising their rights and benefiting from whatever opportunities are afforded them."

Only government delegates and participants were admitted to the conference, but during Helvi Sipilä's speech a group of banner-bearing demonstrators, including market women with their husbands and families, clamoured for admittance, and they were wisely permitted to listen. They applauded.

The Attorney-General of Mexico, Pedro Ojeda Paullada, was elected president of the Congress, and 46 vice-presidents and a rapporteur-general were also elected. It seemed a little surprising to some that a man was elected to what was essentially a woman's congress, and in reply to questions from the press on the matter he implied he was elected as a person, and that the UN called for the "equitable representation of both men and women". It was strictly irrelevant whether the president elected should be a man or woman; what was important was that a suitable person should be chosen. At the same time the choice of the Attorney-General of the host country inevitably prompted the question whether a more suitable choice could not have been made.

The conference and the officers elected formulated five main items for discussion:

1. The objectives and goals of the International Women's Year: present policies and programmes.
2. The involvement of women in strengthening international peace and eliminating racism, apartheid, racial discrimination, colonialism, alien domination and acquisition of territory by force.
3. Current trends and changes in the status and roles of women and men, and major obstacles to be overcome in the achievement of equal rights, opportunities and responsibilities.

4. The integration of women in the development process as equal partners with men.

5. World Plan of Action.

The plenary meetings for discussion during the two-week session were attended by the representatives of the 125 nations, of 36 inter-governmental
and non-governmental organisations, including many members of IAW
and its affiliates, specialised agencies and national liberation movements.
There appears to have been general agreement on one matter: the universal
discrimination against women. One representative said that "despite their
divergently different backgrounds, each speaker has made the same fundamental observation. Each has acknowledged the existence of the inferior
status ascribed to women", and another from Africa said that discrimination
against women was worse than other kinds of discrimination because it
was universal.[1]

Some poignant things were said in the discussions by government representatives and others. For example the Norwegian delegate to the conference contended that there will be no real progress in the status of
women until they make up half the government of their countries. This is
perhaps an overstatement, but it is obvious that a far greater proportion
of women in the parliaments of the world, much more than the existing
5 to 10 per cent, would be a major contribution. Olaf Palme, the Prime
Minister of Sweden, suggested that "The new economic order needs a
changed role for women which in turn requires a changed role for men.
A society built on inequality between men and women is a waste of human
resources."[2]

The conference did not progress without some disruptive incidents. For
example the Arab delegations walked out when Mrs Rabin, the wife of the
Israeli Prime Minister spoke, while there were many political digressions
on colonialism, imperialism, zionism and other such matters which rather
wasted the time of the conference. Conflicts and irrelevancies, however, occur
at many international conferences. A discipline which insists on concentration on the subject and purpose of a conference is an advantage.

The meetings of the Tribune, attended altogether by more than 6,000
women and men constituted perhaps a more vital and even virulent occasion
as so many of the exchanges between different viewpoints, customs, religions, from all parts of the world were often free of restrictive formalities.
There were, however, 35 formally convened meetings at which NGOs took a
conspicuous part. Irene de Lipkowski, president of the IAW presided at
one, and many members of the Alliance and their affiliates took a very
active part. There were in addition 192 informal meetings. The Tribune
was a cross section of the peoples of the world representing all shades of
opinion from different cultures, and social conditions, professions and
occupations.

There were complaints that the conference and the Tribune were not sufficiently related in the approach to the subject and in their activities. In response Helvi Sipilä explained to the Tribune audience that if a plan for action is adopted "the UN is ultimately powerless to see that it is applied. We cannot change your laws, your education, your economic plans. You have to do that" and she asked for co-operation to implement whatever comes from the conference.

The results of the international meeting at Mexico were the adoption of a (1) Declaration on the equality of women and their contribution to development and peace; (2) World plan of action for the implementation of the objectives of the International Women's Year; and (3) Resolutions which supplemented the Declaration and Plan of Action. As all three are mainly repetitious of what the International Alliance of Women had been advocating for the best part of a half century it is unnecessary to give the Declaration, Plan of Action and Resolutions in any detail; a selection of a few items of special significance must suffice. Not all were strictly pertinent to the main subject of equality of opportunity in all fields for women with men, some were concerned generally with development and peace, while a few were really political irrelevancies. The Declaration begins with an introductory preamble giving reasons for it, followed by the promulgation of 30 principles. The World Plan of Action consists of 219 paragraphs grouped in sections: Introduction, (1) National Action; (2) Specific areas for national action; (3) Research, data collection and analysis; (4) Mass communication media; (5) International and regional action; and (6) Review and appraisal. In the introduction it is stated in para. 15 that "This Plan of Action is intended to strengthen the implementation of the instruments and programmes which have been adopted concerning the status of women, and to broaden and place them in a more timely context. Its purpose is mainly to stimulate national and international action to solve the problems of underdevelopment and of the socio-economic structure which place women in an inferior position, in order to achieve the goals of International Women's Year". In para. 24 it is explained that "the aim of the plan to ensure that the original and multidimensional contribution—both actual and potential—of women is not overlooked in existing concepts for development action programmes and an improved world economic equilibrium." Recommendations for national and international action are proposed with the aim of accelerating the necessary changes in all areas, and particularly in those where women have been especially disadvantaged. In the section on national action it is pointed out (para. 26) that the "plan provides guidelines for national action over the 10 year period from 1975 to 1985 as part of a sustained, long-term effort to achieve the objective of IWY". It is stated in para. 42 that "implementation of this plan will require a redefinition of certain priorities and a change in the pattern of government expenditure", and it is suggested that (para. 45) "on the basis of his World Plan of Action, the UN Secretariat should elaborate a two-year plan of its own, aiming at the implementation of the World Plan of Action under the current control of the Commission on the Status of Women, and the over-all control of the General Assembly".

The Section on Specific Areas for National Action is divided under several sub-sections: (A) International co-operation and the strengthening of International Peace; (B) Political participation; (C) Education and training; (D) Employment and related economic roles; (E) Health and nutrition; (F) The family in modern society; (G) Population; (H) Housing and related facilities; and (I) Other special questions.

In the section on the family it is proposed (para. 132) that "Programmes of education for personal relationships, marriage and family life, health, including psycho-sexual development, should be integrated into all school curricula at appropriate levels and into programmes for out-of-school education, to prepare young people of both sexes for responsible marriage and parenthood. These programmes should be based on the ideals of mutual respect and shared rights and responsibilities in the family and in society. Child-rearing practices within each society should be examined with a view to eliminating customs that encourage and perpetuate ideas about superiority or inferiority on the basis of sex.

In the section on population some important comments are made on (para. 138) "The hazards of child-bearing, characterised by too many pregnancies, pregnancies at too early or too late an age and at too close intervals, inadequate pre-natal, delivery and post-natal care and resort to illegally induced abortions, resulting in high rates of maternal mortality and maternal-related morbidity. Where levels of infant and early childhood mortality as well as of foetal mortality are high, their reduction—a desirable end in itself—may also be a prerequisite of the limitation of the number of pregnancies that the average woman will experience, and of the society's adoption of a smaller ideal family size where this is a desired goal. Fewer pregnancies may be more easily achieved when there is a reasonable expectation that children born will survive to adulthood."

Family planning is referred to in para. 143 which says: "Family planning programmes should direct communication and recruitment efforts towards women and men equally, since successful fertility regulations requires their mutual understanding and co-operation. This policy would enable women to exercise equally with men their right to decide how many children they will bear and the timing of the births. Attainment of these goals requires the development of means of contraception and birth control that will be both efficient and compatible with cultured values prevailing in different societies. Family planning programmes should be integrated and co-ordinated with health, nutrition and other services designed to raise the quality of family life."

Under the section on mass communication media it is stated (para. 174) that "a major obstacle in improving the status of women lies in public attitudes and values regarding women's roles in society". The mass communication media have great potential as a vehicle for social change and could exercise, a significant influence in helping to remove prejudices and stereotypes, accelerating the acceptance of women's new and expanding roles in society, and promoting their integration into the development process as equal partners.

There were 34 resolutions which supplement the plan of action. One (9) refers to family planning and urges governments to provide family education and training plans, to offer family planning programmes within the broader context of complex maternal and child health care.

A much needed and welcome resolution is 19 which condemns the degrading exploitation of women as sex symbols and as vehicles for publicity and asks governments and responsible organisations to encourage a dignified and positive image of women.

National activities

The women's organisations of a large number of countries arranged activities in connection with International Women's Year. It is possible to mention only a few of the more notable celebrations.

In France, the country of the IAW president, the government held a Congress which was attended by two thousand women from many countries of Europe, and from the French speaking countries of Asia and Africa. The Congress was opened by the French President, M. Giscard d'Estaing with Mme Francois Giroud, Minister for Women's Affairs presiding. Giscard d'Estaing's speech was very sympathetic to the cause of women and dealt at some length with the themes indicated by the headings 'equality, development and peace'. The board of the IAW attended and enjoyed these celebrations and the generous hospitality of the French Government.

Following these celebrations the international committee of the IAW, consisting of the presidents of affiliates and board members, held several meetings in the buildings of the Senate and National Assembly, some of them plenary meetings in collaboration with the International Council of Women. One of these was addressed by the eminent French sociologist, Evelyn Sullerot, Director of the *Institut National pour la Promotion dans l'Industrie* who had organised a very successful course for the rehabilitation of women into employment after years of family care and domestic duties.[3] A board meeting of the Alliance followed at which it was decided to hold the 24th Congress in New York in July 1976.

The main celebrations of IWY in West Germany were organised by the *Deutscher Frauenring EV* and consisted mainly of conferences and seminars, the subjects of some of these were mass media; the motivation of young women towards political activities in the community; population, "planning your life as men and women", and several others. In addition a brochure entitled *Women want human rights* was published, which traces the history of the women's movement in Germany from the activities of Helene Lange in 1897. In East Germany a conference was held in celebration to which 2,000 women from 140 countries were invited. Freda Brown of Australia representing the International League for Peace and Freedom was active in its organisation and Helvi Sipilä, addressed the conference.

There were many celebrations in India. The significance of IWY was explained in many pamphlets, films, meetings, TV and radio; exhibitions were held, and awards were made to outstanding women.

In Iran, the principal activities were an international conference on participation of women and men in development planning and policy making, the organisation of research on the economic, social and cultural life of women; the inauguration of women studies at Tehran University, newspaper and magazine articles and radio and TV programmes and exhibitions of women's work in the arts and crafts. Most countries conducted some celebrations for IWY the most successful were generally those where women's organisations of considerable size were active and who obtained the co-operation of national and local government. They served to spread the influence of the main UN activity in Mexico.

A special publication of *International Women's News* in connection with IWY was devoted to the help being given to the education, especially literacy, and improved social conditions of women in developing countries. This was done in collaboration with UNESCO whose gift coupon scheme was explained. This is a facility to overcome currency or exchange difficulties in giving financial assistance in these projects. In this publication work of education and training of various kinds being given to women in many countries of Africa, Asia and South America was described. One of them, Guyana, was sponsored by the IAW.

Some months after the conclusion of the Mexico Conference on 15th December 1975 the General Assembly of the United Nations at its 30th session adopted the plan of action proposed at the conference in resolution 3520. Following the preamble giving reasons for the resolution it proclaimed "the period from 1976 to 1985 United Nations Decade for Women: Equality, Development and Peace, to be devoted to effective and sustained national, regional and international action to implement the World Plan of Action and related resolutions of the Conference" and "calls upon Governments, as a matter of urgency, to examine the recommendations contained in the World Plan of Action and related resolutions of the Conference" and then indicates in some detail the measures that governments should take. The long resolution concludes by announcing that UN decides to convene in 1980, at the mid-term of the Decade of Women "a world conference of all states to review and evaluate the progress made in implementing the objectives of the International Women's Year as recommended by the World Conference and where necessary to readjust existing programmes in the light of new data and research available".

Resolution 3521 is concerned with "equality between men and women and elimination of discrimination against women". In the preamble the results of the conference of IWY are welcomed. The resolution "calls upon all states that have not done so to ratify the international conventions and other instruments concerning the protection of women's rights . . . and to implement effectively the provisions of these conventions and other instruments". In this resolution the Commission on the Status of Women is requested to complete, in 1976, the elaboration of the draft Convention on the Elimination of Discrimination against Women". The Commission held its 26th session at Geneva in September resumed in December 1976 and after prolonged discussion adopted the Draft Convention on the Elimination of Discrimination against Women, consisting of 22 articles. Article 21 concerned with co-operation of non-governmental organisations was based on a proposal by the IAW (which was given consultative status to ECOSOC in category 1 in 1975) and other NGOs, as follows:

Non-governmental organisations concerned with the status of women shall have the right to submit to the Commission on the Status of Women information and recommendations relating to the observance to the provisions of the present convention. The Commission on the Status of Women shall consider these communications together with the comments, if any, of the state parties directly involved.

Other resolutions at this 30th session of the Assembly were concerned with: 3522 "improvement of the economic status of women for their effective and speedy participation in the development of their countries"; 3523 "women in rural areas"; 3524 "measures for the integration of women in development" and 3416 "employment of women in the secretariat" of United Nations.

What was accomplished by International Women's Year? and has all the effort put into the international and national efforts been worth while?

These questions have often been asked. The answers can only be given after there has been some assessment of the probable effects and results

in various countries possibly by the time of a second international conference in 1980 which is planned so as to evaluate how far the world has
succeeded in implementing the objectives of IWY 1975.

One result was the generation of a general awareness of the persistent
discrimination against women throughout the world, which created in
very many people, who thought about it for the first time, a feeling that it
was unjust. Even the male who had traditionally thought that women's
place is a subordinate one in the home began to doubt whether such thinking was entirely rational.

Some partial assessment of the effects were summarised by Helvi
Sipilä in an address given at the 24th Congress of the IAW in New York
a year later in July 1976, which was attended by affiliated societies from
25 countries. The participants at this Congress inevitably had IWY very
much in mind. (It was the first non-governmental organisation to hold its
inaugural meeting in the United Nations Building.) Presided over by the
president, Irène de Lipkowski (who was re-elected for a further term of
3 years) the opening address was given by Dr Kurt Waldheim, the UN
Secretary-general, who dwelt mainly on the decisions of the Mexico Conference. He said that the success of the United Nations Decade for Women
will depend very largely on the input of organisations such as the IAW.
This can be most effective in stimulating the continuing interest of governments, which in turn will influence the establishment of effective programmes. Among the points he made were that during International
Women's Year the need for full equality for women was recognised internationally as a moral and political imperative: "It was widely recognised", he said, "that no longer could the world afford to under-utilise
or impede, by custom, practice or law, the talents and potential contribution of half its citizens." He spoke "of our shortcomings" in the United
Nations Organisation, "with respect to the proportion of women staff
members . . . and I have personally given instructions", he added, "that
every effort should be made to increase the proportion of women pro-
fessionals".

Helvi Sipilä, in her keynote address, summarised the most important
achievements of IWY in eleven items. She pointed out that many things
have been accomplished internationally for the first time: "The world
as a whole has adopted a universal plan for the improvement of the situation of women which can have a crucial impact towards positive developments in our efforts to solve world-wide problems: the role of women has
been declared by the United Nations Assembly a key element in the development process and an integral part of the establishment of a new international economic order; the economic role of women has been recognised by
the General Assembly in their traditional activities and in such fields as
agriculture, industry, trade and science and technology; and for the first

Presentation of book to Helvi Sipilä
by presidents of women's international non-governmental organisations during International Women's
Year 1975. Left to right: Marion Dud-
ley, Zonta International; Olive Far-
quharson, Associated Countrywomen
of the World; Elizabeth May, International Federation of University
Women; Helvi Sipilä; Mahrangir Dala-
shahi, International Council of Women;
and Irène de Lipkowski, International
Alliance of Women.

time a more balanced division of labour between men and women in the
family and the society has been requested; all governments have been called
upon by the General Assembly to examine, as a matter of urgency, the
World Plan of Action and related resolutions in order to establish short,
medium and long-term targets and priorities, adopt national strategies,
plans and programmes for the implementation of the recommendations
within the framework of overall development plans, policies and programmes, to undertake regular reviews and appraisals of progress at the
national and local levels, and to report to the United Nations about the
implementation of the plan; all organisations in the United Nations system
have been asked to develop an inter-agency programme on the implementation of the World Plan of Action in order to co-ordinate and integrate
their activities."

The remaining items are concerned mainly with ways and means of achieving these objectives.[4]

The resolutions of the six commissions at the IAW Congress were to a considerable extent reaffirmations of previous decisions. IWY was inevitably referred to several times, and support was given to many of the recommendations. The United Nations Commission of the IAW was especially concerned that the effective functioning of the Commission on the Status of Women should be ensured in the new UN framework which is evolving, and that it should be maintained as the responsible body for the implementation of the World Plan of Action 1976–85 approved by a resolution of the General Assembly.[5]

REFERENCES

1 See *Meeting in Mexico—The Story of the World Conference of the International Women's Year*. United Nations, New York, 1975.
2 See article by Laurel Casinader, *International Women's News*. Vol. 70, No. 4, October–December 1975, p. 50.
3 This is described in an article entitled "French experiment aids women" by Dr Edith Young in an article in *International Women's News*. Vol. 69, No. 11, November 1974, pp. 59, 60, 62.
4 The items are given in full in the *International Women's News*. Vol 71, No. 4, October–December 1976, p. 44.
5 This is Resolution A3520 (XXX).

CHAPTER TWENTY-THREE

1976–1978

UNESCO and IAW. Seminars and Declaration of Human Rights

As must have been apparent in the course of this history, the International Alliance of Women has always worked as closely as possible with the league of Nations and its successor, the United Nations, primarily through the Economic and Social Council, with the United Nations Educational, Scientific and Cultural Organisation (UNESCO) and with the Status of Women Commission and later with the United Nations Fund for Population Activities (UNFPA). On 4th November 1976 UNESCO celebrated the thirtieth anniversary of its foundation, and the IAW took the opportunity, (*IWN*, Vol. 73, No. 1, February 1978) of recalling its contribution to and co-operation with the work of UNESCO in the sphere of the educational opportunities for women in the various countries of the world.

From the beginning in 1946 the IAW has studied the many aspects of UNESCO's work in relation to the aims of the Alliance for equal rights and opportunities in education for men and women. Andrée Lehmann was the representative of the IAW from 1946 when she was chairman of its Committee on Equal Civic and Political Rights, retaining the position until her death in 1970. She constantly insisted on equality in education for men and women and persuaded UNESCO to accept this not only in principle but in practice. She was much assisted by Amy Bush who succeeded her as chairman of the IAW Education Committee in 1952 and who continued as chairman until 1967, being succeeded in that year by Mme Lydie Boulle. They both continued the work of Andrée Lehmann in close collaboration with UNESCO.

As occasionally noted, collaboration between UNESCO and IAW resulted in a series of study courses and seminars beginning with that held in conjunction with the IAW Congress at Colombo in 1955 on the theme of equal access to opportunities for education. This was followed by a seminar on civic responsibilities preceeding the Athens Congress in 1958 and by seminars in Nigeria (1960), Pakistan (1968), India (1970), Tunisia (1972) and the three regional seminars on the "Implications of Women's Participation in Society" in Guyana (1972), in India, in connection with the Congress at Delhi (1973), and in Ghana (1974).

Illiteracy and the lack of access to all forms of education have been central themes of seminars for these have militated against women in the fight for equal status. The conviction held by many organisations that it is necessary to continue studying the subject, prompted a symposium at UNESCO headquarters in Paris in March 1977 on "Literacy and Life-Long Education in the context of a new Economic Order based on Justice and Equality", which was organised by IAW assisted by the Associated Countrywomen of the World and other non-governmental organisations. One of the main proposals resulting from this symposium was that there should be a joint project by UNESCO and national NGOs in the Year of the Child to study the needs of parents especially of the mother, because in some countries the mother lags far behind the father in literacy, vocational training and education generally, which, if rectified, would enable her to take her place on equal terms with her male counterpart.

Seminars 1976 1977 1978

In December 1976 the IAW sponsored a seminar in collaboration with the All India Women's Conference at Sri Sarada College, Salem, in the province of Tamil Nadu, South India, on the theme of providing continuing education for women to motivate and encourage them to take an active part in community and national development. In addition to delegates from India some attended from Bangladesh and Sri Lanka. Hilda Tweedy attended on behalf of IAW and produced a report for its journal (Vol. 72–2 –April 1977, pp. 14–15).

In this report Hilda Tweedy said that the main topics discussed were: The role of voluntary organisations in meeting the needs of women in adult education and female literacy; identification of women's rights; socio-environmental education and changing life styles; and the encouragement of women's participation in administration both at local and national level. It was suggested that voluntary organisations should become more professional in their work and that "talent banks" of women willing to use professional skills or technological expertise should be formed to help voluntary organisations. In the sphere of education in schools it was proposed that parents should be involved in the preparation of curricula, that part of each curriculum should be standard with, however, adequate allowance for innovations for different localities. Ethics it was advocated should be taught in addition to specific religious instruction, because the need for spiritual education for the full development of the person was stressed.

At the end of the seminar from 26th to 28th December, the golden jubilee of the All-India Women's Conference was celebrated and women from 400 branches came to the Sri Sarada College at Salem for the purpose. The AIWC had something to celebrate for in the 50 years of its life it has done much valuable educational work. It has been responsible for important educational projects, it has provided working women's hostels, orphanages, homes for deserted women, crèches, free legal aid, marriage counselling services, and many others. A new headquarters building has been erected in New Delhi to enable it to continue its valuable work with the utmost efficiency.

Seminars as employed by UN organisations and NGOs should ideally provide for the pooling of information and experience of economic, educational, political or cultural import in various countries and the discussion of these with the purpose of future action. The term seminar, derived from the Latin seminarium, rendered in English as seminary, originally meant seed-plot, and is a piece of ground where seeds are germinated and the plants cultivated in their early growth and transplanted. This is precisely the stages in seminars in which the IAW has been involved. Unfortunately the seeds for development were sometimes planted at a seminar, but were not always transplanted in the communities and countries which it was intended to benefit. Many active and progressive members of IAW had been conscious of this and it was considered how the discussions and resolutions at seminars could benefit the countries represented by the appropriate dissemination, so that the ideas generated are taken back by the participants to their countries to be further discussed and developed.

A scheme to conduce to this replanting was inaugurated at an East African regional seminar held in Mauritius in May 1977, which was organised by the IAW and sponsored by the United Nations Fund for Population Activities. The seminar was under the direction of Margaret Hardiman, among the participants were Irène de Lipkowski, President of IAW, Laurel Casinader who did the work of organisation, with Amy Bush as the seminar rapporteur. Members of the board of IAW who acted as resource persons at the seminar, visited one of the participating countries, met the participants and members of the national society, and arranged to return after the seminar to hold a workshop on its theme and to discuss starting a project.

The outline theme of the seminar was "population and the means of subsistence", and the aspect that received particular study was "The role of women in improving family life". Among the subjects studied and discussed were the problems of economic constraints to providing better diet and the better use of existing resources through health education; women's contribution to subsistence agriculture, their role in the production of cash crops, the employment of women outside the home and the family farm, and their position in the formal education system. Of particular significance was the continuing discussion between participants and the resource person who had visited their country to consider a suitable follow-up project. These projects were of a self-help nature to improve the economic status and welfare of women.

In May 1978 the IAW through its affiliate, the Hoda Charawy Association of Egypt, held its fifth regional seminar in Cairo on the theme of "The Promotion of Access to Equal Educational Opportunities for Girls and Women in Rural Areas". Co-operating were the International Planned Parenthood Federation (Regional Branch of the Family Planning Association in Egypt) and the International Co-operatives Alliance Participants. The Seminar was sponsored by UNESCO and supported by the UN Arab Bureau. Delegates attended from Morocco, United Arab Emirates, Kuwait, Sudan, Arab Republic of Yemen, Iran, Tunisia, Lebanon and the Arab Republic of Egypt. It was directed by Olive Bloomer, the treasurer of IAW and organised by Mme Malek Madkour. The president of IAW, Irène de Lipkowski, made a speech of welcome, and expressed thanks to the Egyptian Government for its support.

As indicated by the main theme of the seminar, it was devoted mainly to the interests of rural women and was divided into five sections: The first was on rural women's role in agricultural production. The limitations of rural women in their work were considered and the steps necessary to make available to them means of increasing production by modern methods, and at the same time enable them to take an active part in the civic responsibilities of their villages. The second was on the agricultural co-operative system and its role in rural life; the third on participation of rural women in public life, stressing the importance of citizenship and the strategic position of the rural woman in development; the fourth on the role of rural woman as housewife covering the necessity of training in modern hygiene methods and efficient management of her daily affairs; and the fifth on assisting rural women in the rearing and education of their children, involving the eradication of illiteracy at all levels and the provision of suitable educational programmes and extension services.

Several recommendations were made by the seminar on these lines among them the formation of co-operatives for rural women for production of diary produce and to assist them in the use of modern equipment, training, development of techniques for production, distribution and marketing; the establishment of centres to enable rural women to obtain information of scientific and technological progress, and to take part effectively in the public life of the community. The provision of vital public services, such as water supply, transportation and electricity to enable rural women more easily to undertake their various functions; and, very importantly, the organisation of propaganda campaigns to urge and encourage rural and Bedouin men to accept the participation of women in decision making and sharing in the public life of the community.

A meeting of the Board of IAW was held in Trinity Hall, Dublin, in September 1977. At the opening members were received by Dr Hillery, President of the Republic of Ireland in his presidential home. Among the matters agreed by the board at this meeting was the establishment of an IAW Day, which should be 3rd June (or any convenient day in the same week) as this was the day in 1904 when the Alliance was founded.[1] It was felt that this would provide an opportunity both for publicity and fund raising. 3rd June 1979 is the 75th anniversary.

Two applications were received for affiliation, one from the Canadian Alliance of Women and the other from *La Societe Feminines de Seychelles*. The former application was particularly gratifying as it was nearly fifty years since there was a Canadian affiliate and it is obviously valuable to re-establish such an old link with North America.

Mid-term of the Decade of Women

As stated in Chapter 22 (p. 275) the United Nations decided to convene in 1980, at the mid-term of the Decade of Women, a world conference to review and evaluate the progress made in implementing the objectives of the International Women's Year 1975 and to readjust existing programmes in the light of new data and research available. The Status of Women Commission at its 27th session held at New York in January and February 1978 considered preparations for the World Conference of 1980 and several requests and recommendations were made to the Economic and Social Council. It requested the president of the UN General Assembly to nominate a preparatory committee of 23 members on the basis of an equitable regional distribution taking into account the experience and the expertise of the members of the Commission on the Status of Women, and asked the Secretary-general to appropriate personnel and financial resources for the World Conference.

It also recommended a sub-theme: "Employment, Health and Education", and suggested that the conference should "place an emphasis on elaborating new strategies for integrating women into the developmental process, particularly by promoting economic and employment opportunities on an equal footing with men through, inter alia, the provision of adequate health and educational facilities, and that the preparatory work for the conference be carried out accordingly".

Member states, it is suggested, should be invited to select topics on which they have particular projects as well as giving information on other topics on the three subjects of employment, health and education. The topics listed are:

"Employment

(1) Training in technological methods of farming; (2) Training schemes, both elementary and advanced, for women employed in industry; (3) Vocational training; (4) Social support services to enable parents to combine employment and home care; (5) Income-generating projects for women living in urban slums or in rural or backward areas; (6) Promotion of and training in income-raising group activities for women living in rural areas and in urban slums; (7) Legal aid programmes.

"Health

(8) Basic services for women and children; (9) Promotion of education in the fields of health, nutrition and family planning; (10) Programmes to achieve functional literacy; (11) Accelerated courses of education; (12) Programmes to make both formal and non-formal education available to girls and women; (13) Promotion of education relevant to the needs of developing economies."

The commission discussed the participation of women in international conferences and recalled that the world conference of International Women's Year (resolution 31) requested the increase of such participation and that women should have equal opportunity with men to represent their countries in all international forums and particularly at meetings of UN organisations. It cited several international meetings shortly to take place such as the UN Conference on Technical Co-operation among developing Countries at Buenos Aires (30th August to 12th September 1978), the conference of WHO and UNCF at Alma Ata (September 1978), a conference of FAO on Agrarian Reform in July 1979, and the UN Conference on Science and Technology for Development at Vienna in 1979, and asks ECOSOC to urge all Governments to ensure:

"(a) That women are involved in the planning stages of international conferences and are included in the governmental delegates attending the above-mentioned conferences;
"(b) That the topic of women and development be included within the substantive discussions of the conferences and, where appropriate, be considered as a separate agenda item;
"(c) That the recommendations related to women and development emerging from the above-mentioned conferences be available for the Commission on the Status of Women at its twenty-eighth session and for the World Conference on the United Nations Decade for Women, to be held in Iran in 1980;
"(d) That national and regional forums and activities related to women and development be organised to provide an important input for consideration at the above conferences, in connection with which the participation

of both governmental and non-governmental organisations is recommended for the development of national and/or regional guidelines and programmes of action."

Declaration of Human Rights

The General Assembly of United Nations adopted the Universal Declaration of Human Rights on 10th December 1948. The Declaration was a statement of principles and did not have the force of law. It was necessary for the United Nations to transform the principles into treaty provisions which establish legal obligations on the part of each ratifying state. Because of differences in implementation of the various sections it was felt that two covenants were required, one dealing with civil and political rights and the other with economic, social and cultural rights. These covenants were drafted and, with the optional protocol, were adopted by the Assembly on 16th December 1966. It was necessary however, to secure ratifications of the covenants by 35 countries and these were obtained by 1975. The International Covenant on Economic, Social and Cultural Rights came into effect on 3rd January 1976 and that on Civil and Political Rights on 23rd March 1976 together with its optional protocol.² Part IV of the International Covenant on Civil and Political Rights, comprising articles 28 to 45 provides for the establishment of a human rights committee which shall consist of eighteen members and shall carry out the functions provided in the covenant. It shall be composed of nations of the states parties to the covenant (28), members of the committee shall be elected by secret ballot (29), and may not include more than one national of the same state (31), consideration shall be given to equitable geographical distribution of membership and to the representation of the different forms of civilisation and of the principal legal systems (31) and the committee shall submit to the General Assembly of the United Nations through the Economic and Social Council, an annual report on its activities (45).

This committee was duly elected in September 1976. Eva Kolstad of Norway, a member of the board of IAW writing in *International Women's News* (Vol. 72, No. 3, June 1977) states "18 men were elected. Brilliant experts in the field of hman rights, to be sure. But do they cover properly the special interests of women? Are they able to feel how discrimination on the grounds of sex is felt by women, who are mostly the persons who are victims of discrimination?

"The establishment", Eva Kolstad continues, "of an important international committee dealing with human rights and composed of men only, will for IAW, an association working for equal rights and equal responsibilities, be unsatisfactory, to use a mild word. We know only too well that comparatively few women today have sufficient competence in this

286 WOMAN INTO CITIZEN

field, because women have not had the same chance and stimulation as men to study, learn and work in such an area. An international committee working for non-discrimination of all kinds, should not only cover different legal systems or civilisations, with due regard to geography, it should be representing humanity, that is both men and women, to be able to fulfil its important task.

"Today we must face the fact that these 18 men have been elected. The term of 9 of them will expire at the end of the first two years.[3] What can we do in the meantime to make sure that the interests of women are kept in mind."

This evoked a reply from Helvi Sipilä, the UN Assistant Secretary General for Social Development and Humanitarian Affairs (*IWN* Vol. 73, No. 2, April 1978). Helvi Sipilä fully shared Eva Kolstad's disappointment at the election of eighteen men and no women in the first human rights committee. It is more than regrettable, she said, that "half of humanity, namely woman, has been completely forgotten in the course of this election". "It may not have been the purpose", she continued, "of those who nominated the candidates either.[4] The main thing is that women are still playing an invisible role in international affairs, except those explicitly related to women.

"One could argue that everyone should have taken into account the equal rights of men and women which is a principle among the very purposes of the United Nations. This is true and if those who make appointments and participate in elections would keep in mind that both sexes should always be represented, we would not be living in the unbalanced situation in international affairs which we are now experiencing.

"Women", she continued, "are the best agents of change for their own benefit and for the benefit of all in public affairs at any level. This is gradually taking place at the local and national level in many countries but not at the international level."

Helvi Sipilä concluded by recommending action. She suggested that women in all countries should "begin to study their role in decision-making and make concrete plans for the future. This implies gaining knowledge of international affairs, with which women may be least familiar. Women's organisations at the national level should begin a joint effort in order to familiarise themselves with current international issues and forthcoming events. They should inform themselves of the issues and the procedures and present candidates for appointment and election whenever possible. There is no problem area in the international field in which women could not become qualified candidates for any international meeting or any post in the secretariats of the United Nations or other organisations in the United Nations system."

The International Covenants on Human Rights are inevitably subject

Eva Kolstad, treasurer of IAW 1949–
1958 and president of Norsk Kvinnesaksforening.

to amendments in the light of future experience and change. It would be
logical and just, and in accordance with Helvi Sipilä's claim that, as equal
rights of men and women are among the purposes of the United Nations,
amendments should be made to Part IV of the International Covenant
on Civil and Political Rights.

For example, Article 29–2—states that "Each state party to the present
covenant may nominate not more than two persons. These persons shall
be nationals of the nominating state". It could be amended by adding
after persons: "preferably one of each sex". By using the term "preferably"
this does not make it obligatory, but the suggestion is there to combat
a traditional habit of thinking in terms of men only. It is true only one of
the two nominated will be elected but it gives women a better chance.
Article 31–2 could also be amended. It is stated that "in the election of
the committee, consideration shall be given to equitable geographical

distribution of membership and to the representation of the different forms of civilisation and of the principal legal systems". To make this more comprehensive it could be added after civilisation "and of the interests and welfare of both men and women therein".

This complete absence of women on the first UN Human Rights Committee demonstrates that it is still a long journey to reach a just equality of the sexes in the communities of the world. The IAW has still, therefore, much to do. But it must concentrate on this main objective and be wary of dissipating its energies into too many other channels. In this main objective it has, internationally a record second to none, and it must continue.

REFERENCES

1 The idea of such an alliance was really adumbrated in Washington in 1902 when the National American Woman Suffrage Association organised an International Woman Suffrage Conference as part of its annual convention in Washington in 1902 (see Chapter 1, p. ??) when it was decided to hold a second meeting of the IWSC as part of the meeting of the International Council of Women in Berlin in 1904, and it was then that the "International Woman Suffrage Alliance" was actually launched, changing its name at the Paris Congress in 1926 to "International Alliance of Women". The Congresses, however, have been numbered from the first meeting at Washington.

2 The full text of the covenants and protocol was published by the United Nations Office of Public Information in April 1976, from which copies are available.

3 Of the nine members elected in September 1978 five were already members of the committee and four were new, but there were still no women.

4 It is often just a habit of thinking, which does not include women. I was at one time on the executive committee of an important national voluntary organisation. We had a vacancy occurring on the committee and we tried to think of a suitable man to fill it (the existing committee were all men) and we considered one man after another without thinking of a suitable one. Then I said: "Why must we always think in terms of men, why not a woman." And several said immediately "a good idea". We thought of a woman who later joined the committee.

CHAPTER TWENTY-FOUR

RETROSPECT 1902–1979

To answer the question: what has been achieved for the emancipation of women in all fields of community life, political, cultural, economic and social, throughout the world during the present century would require, if answered in any detail, a book much longer than the present one. What can be said, however, is that the principle of the equality of the sexes has been accepted by the governments of many countries, completely by some, substantially by others and partly by the majority. Acceptance, however, by the people as a whole in various countries and the implementation of the principle in all fields cannot yet be said to have occurred in any country. In most countries there is still much to be done in education and propaganda before this is achieved. The most significant single circumstance is that in 1978 there were with the exception of the Scandinavian countries not more than 10 per cent of women in the parliaments of the world.

WOMEN ELECTED TO EUROPEAN PARLIAMENTS

Response to questionnaire sent by Karin Ahrland,
Regional Director, Europe, to IAW Affiliates.

Country	Parliament	Members	No of Women	Percentage of Women	Last Elections
Belgium	Senate	181	8	4·4%	10 Mar. 1974
	House of Reps.	212	14	6·6%	,,
Denmark	Parliament	179	29	16·2%	15 Feb. 1977
Finland	Parliament	200	47	23·5%	
France	Nat. Assembly	490	7	1·4%	11 Mar. 1973
	Senate	283	7	2·5%	1 Mar. 1975
Greece	Parliament	300	7	2·3%	17 Nov. 1974
Ireland	Senate	60	6	10·0%	20 Aug. 1977
	House of Reps.	144	6	4·1%	16 June 1977
Iceland	Parliament	60	3	5·0%	30 June 1974
Italy	Senate	315	11	3·5%	21 June 1976
	House of Reps.	630	47	7·5%	21 June 1976
Luxembourg	Parliament	59		4·3%	26 May 1974
Malta	Parliament	65	2		18 Sept. 1976
Netherlands	Senate	75	4	5·3%	
	House of Reps.	150	14	9·3%	29 Nov. 1972

Norway	Parliament	155	24	15·5%	10 Sept. 1973
Sweden	Parliament	349	80	22·9%	19 Sept. 1976
Switzerland	Senate	44	—	—	26 Oct. 1975
	House of Reps.	200	14	7·0%	,,
Turkey	Senate	150	ca. 20	3·3%	14 Oct. 1973
	House of Reps.	450			
Cyprus	Parliament	35	—		5 July 1970
West Germany	Parliament	496	35	7·1%	3 Oct. 1976
Great Britain	House of Commons	635	27	4·3%	10 Oct. 1974
Austria	House of Reps.	183	14	7·7%	5 Oct. 1975
	Senate	58	11	19·0%	—

Still, the widespread acceptance of the principle of equality in all fields of communal life is a remarkable achievement, especially when compared with the subjection of women in most countries of the world at the beginning of the century, and there is little doubt that history will record that among the most notable changes of the century was that of the position of women in political, cultural, social and economic life.

This has been brought about not by the activities of governments, but by the hard propaganda and educational work of women's international and national societies, and their support by individuals (including men) particularly of eloquent speakers and writers.

What is the part played by the International Alliance of Women, and what is the measure and significance of its contribution to this progress? The essence of its contribution, which is second to none, can be briefly indicated.

It could be claimed that the IAW has always been distinguished among international associations for being essentially far-seeing and progressive in its attitude to the improvement of the status of women in modern society. Much that is regarded in 1979 as advanced thinking in the matter of the equality of the sexes was advocated by the IAW fifty years ago. This has been especially apparent in such fields as employment, education, the nationality of married women and of woman's activities in relation to her traditional domestic vocation.

Some associations working on behalf of the interests of women in the early years of the century have, on occasion, been inclined to modify demands because of custom and habit and of what has universally obtained, and this led sometimes to a degree of crompromise. This attitude has frequently been met also in official bodies and committees of both the League of Nations and the United Nations. But IAW has never compromised in its demands; it has always been guided by strictly logical interpretation of equality of the sexes and this is perhaps the chief single factor in its consistently advanced thinking.

A few examples will demonstrate the validity of these claims. As far back as the Paris Congress of 1926 as part of the resolution for equal pay for equal work it was claimed that the right to work for all women should be recognised, and that no obstacle shall be placed in the way of married women who desire to enter and to continue in paid work. This was reiterated at successive congresses and occasionally amplified. Among the amplifications was that at the Istanbul Congress in 1935 which had formed the basis of a petition sent to the International Labour Conference on the subject. Points made were "that the essential rights of human personality are the same for a woman as for a man and are the same whether she is married or unmarried;" and "to deny a woman's right to earn because of marriage is to deny her one of the essential rights of human personality", while it was contended "that work itself suffers when employment is given on account of sex rather than capacity". This was very advanced thinking for 1935 when it is remembered that in most commercial and professional employment there was a prohibition on the employment of married women. It is advanced thinking in some countries in 1979.

Progressive recommendations were made in the field of education at the Zürich Conference held by the Alliance in 1937. They were based on the assumption that "every woman, married or not, has an indefeasible right to the same educational facilities, and the same access to professional work as a man under the same conditions". It was claimed that all schools, colleges, and universities, all professional and vocational training should be open to women on the same terms as to men.

When giving equality to men and women in all fields it is argued that these must necessarily be related to domestic ties. In its comprehensiveness the Alliance did not neglect any details in the application of the principles that it advocated. For example, the subject of conditions of work with equitable economic conditions in the home prompted a resolution at the Interlaken Congress in 1946. The question was posed whereby the combined functions of home-maker, wage earner and member of society is possible for the married woman. Several recommendations were made in this resolution, among them "the sharing of responsibility for the training and care of the children between both parents, so that while the special function of the mother is recognised, she shall be free to take part in the social and civic life of the community and in employment outside the home". In short, the work and responsibility in the home should be shared equally between husband and wife. That recommendation was made 33 years ago and is still very progressive in spirit.

There may have been occasional signs of flagging in this logical advanced thinking, but there are women still in the IAW who carry on the vigorous and imaginative work of the great pioneers of the Alliance, Carrie Chapman Catt and Margery Corbett Ashby, who are infused by their spirit— women like Edith Anrep, Eva Kolstad, Amy Bush and Laurel Casinader. It is to be hoped that younger women will be forthcoming to carry on the

work and spirit as there is still much to be done in getting principles widely accepted and their implementation extensively secured.

It is perhaps wise to remember that the essential aim is equal partnership with men and not antagonism to them which has sometimes befogged the activities of some women's organisations. As Judge Iyer said addressing the 25th Delhi Congress: "You must set your sights rightly and look beyond simple liberation. You must have a sense of correct perspective so that the new frontiers of human advance may be a joint achievement. You must shape your means not in hostility to man but hand-in-hand with him."

A similar sentiment was expressed by Dame Margery Corbett Ashby who, with the British Prime Minister, James Callaghan, and the leader of the Conservative Party, Margaret Thatcher, spoke on 3rd July 1978 at the opening of the exhibition at Westminster Hall to celebrate the fiftieth anniversary of equality of voting rights for men and women. She remarked that there will be no more spectacular victories, and equality will be gained little by little. It is much easier to change the law than to change the attitude of the community and the home. She concluded by saying that the more men and women work and play together the happier they will be.

Dame Margery Corbett Ashby in 1978 shortly after her 96th birthday on 19th April. The picture is of her aged 12 painted by a Danish artist, Nelly Erichsen. This period of 84 years witnessed the most active campaigning in the cause of equality of men and women in all fields of human activity with the result that it has been accepted in principle by most governments throughout the world.

APPENDIX I

Note on the extension of the franchise in the United Kingdom from the seventeenth century to the first world war, 1914

In the seventeenth and eighteenth centuries parliamentary representation in the United Kingdom was on the basis of ownership and holding of property of a certain value. Both counties and boroughs were each represented by two members. The borough representation was 374 and the county 90 members.

There was considerable agitation in the early nineteenth century for representation more in accordance with the changed distribution of population. While many small towns sent representatives to Parliament the growing industrial cities of the Midlands and the North, like Birmingham, Manchester, Leeds and Sheffield had no separate representation. In spite of all this agitation and the introduction of many bills nothing was achieved until the Reform Act of 1832. By this measure a considerable redistribution of seats was obtained, and the suffrage was extended to all householders in boroughs paying an annual rent of £10, to copyholders of £10 annual value, and annual tenants paying not less than £50. This increased the electorate to 750,000.

The country had to wait thirty-five years for a further extension of the suffrage. By the Reform Act of 1867, the suffrage was extended in boroughs to householders paying rates, whether directly or indirectly, and to lodgers paying £10 a year in rent; while in the counties it was extended to owners and tenants of property of £12 rateable value, while leasehold and copyhold qualifications were reduced to £5 a year. This gave a considerable advantage to the borough votes compared with the county, a matter that was set right by the Act of 1884 when the voting qualifications of county or rural householders were brought in line with those in the boroughs. This Act increased the electorate to about five million. It governed the male franchise up to the last elections in 1910 before the first world war, when all males above the age of 21 who were householders and paid rates directly or indirectly, and all lodgers paying more than £10 a year, were entitled to vote. A further Act of 1885 effected a redistribution of seats. Because of the increase in population the electorate had risen in the United Kingdom to 7,705,602 by 1911, of which 6,716,742 voted as householders and occupiers, the remaining 988,860 being accounted for by the plural voting by reason of the business premises vote and the university vote.

APPENDIX 2

Attitudes of women's organisations to the outbreak of war, 1914

(A) Manifesto drawn up by the International Woman Suffrage Alliance and delivered on 31st July 1914 at the Foreign Office and Foreign Embassies in London.

We, the women of the world, view with apprehension and dismay the present situation in Europe, which threatens to involve one continent if not the whole world, in the disasters and horrors of war. In this terrible hour, when the fate of Europe depends on decisions which women have no power to shape, we, realising our responsibilities as the mothers of the race, cannot stand passively by. Powerless though we are politically, we call upon the governments and powers of our several countries to avert the threatened unparalleled disaster. In none of the countries immediately concerned in the threatened outbreak have women any direct power to control the political destinies of their own countries. They find themselves on the brink of the almost unbearable position of seeing all that they most reverence and treasure, the home, the family, the race, subjected not merely to risks but to certain and extensive damage which they are powerless either to avert or to assuage. Whatever its result the conflict will leave mankind the poorer, will set back civilisation, and will be a powerful check to the gradual amelioration in the condition of the masses of the people, on which so much of the welfare of nations depends.

We women of twenty-six countries, having banded ourselves together in the International Women's Suffrage Alliance with the object of obtaining the political means of sharing with men the power which shapes the fate of nations, appeal to you to leave untried no method of conciliation or arbitration for arranging international differences which may help to avert deluging half the civilised world in blood.

Millicent Garrett Fawcett
First vice-president
Chrystal Macmillan
Recording secretary

(B) Extracts from article, (IWN) expressing the attitude of the National Union of Women's Suffrage Societies on the outbreak of war in 1914.

"In a war in which women have had no part or lot, their first thought everywhere has been to attend to their particular share of business—theirs to fill the men's places; theirs to keep the home; theirs to preserve the lives of infants and to heal the broken bodies of men; theirs to try and save some of the harvest from the trampling hoofs of barbarism. But suffragists will be unworthy of the political power which they have claimed as a human right in a civilised world if they do not now, while they are working to stem the torrent of misery, strive with all their mind and soul to understand the causes of this recurrent madness, so that they may heal it. We need be under no delusion that this healing can be accomplished in a day. Women themselves, millions in every country, are still taking their opinions and principles ready-made from men, and until women learn to *think* as women (and not merely *feel* as women), they will not effect much. 'Men must work and women must weep' wrote Charles Kingsley in his poem *The Three Fishers*. As long as men think that women must only weep for the errors of men, they will not trouble much. They are used to the tears of women; down the ages women have wept for the errors of men. The modern woman must drive back her tears; she has her work to do, as always, in meeting the situations created by men, but she has also a great new pioneer work to do in making her womanly thought prevail, in conquering the repulsive idea that womanly thought is cowardly thought, and the equally repulsive idea that it is womanly for a woman to echo the sentiments of men. . . .

"The National Union offered its services (and with 602 societies and branches all over the country, it will be seen that those services are worth having) for the relief and suffering caused by the war, and already a very large number of our women are on local relief committees, and are working as hard as they can on progressive lines. The response of the societies to the inquiries made by the executive was striking. Although the war broke out in the holiday season, when great numbers were away from home, answers poured in by hundreds and the unanimity and intensity of purpose were magnificent. Democratic institutions certainly justified themselves in the conduct of our union. We are pulling together with all the greater vigour because of our free and representative constitution; we are keeping our staff of secretaries and organisers, our offices and our weekly paper, the *Common Cause*, and we shall have endless opportunities, in the course of our relief work, of holding up suffragist ideals—ideals of civilisation and liberty.

"We have urged upon all our members the need for trying to maintain employment and for not buying up and hoarding gold or necessaries. The care of foreigners stranded in our midst has been a matter of conscience. We have endeavoured so to organise the work as to make relief effective and avoid overlapping. The active care of motherhood is a heavy responsibility upon the women, and it is hoped that a great work may receive the necessary impetus at this time. Another question that becomes acuter than ever in time of war is the increase in vice and disorderly living. The modern woman's newly won knowledge and determination should arm her in the conflict with this evil."

(C) Announcement by the Women's Social and Political Union of its attitude towards the war.

They believe that under the joint rule of enfranchised women and men the nations of the world will, owing to the women's influence and authority, find a way of reconciling the claims of peace and honour and of regulating international relations without bloodshed. The WSPU nevertheless believes also that matters having come to the present pass, it was inevitable that Great Britain should take part in the war; and with that patriotism which has nerved women to fight for the rights and duties of citizenship on behalf of the national good they ardently desire that their country shall be victorious. This because they hold that the existence of all small nationalities is at stake and that the status of France and Great Britain is involved.

Now that their political prisoners are released, and in view of the grave crisis in which the country is involved, the WSPU has decided to suspend hostilities and activities for the time being.

APPENDIX 3

IWSA and the appointment of a woman to the Permanent Mandates Commission of the League of Nations
Based on report by Margery Corbett Ashby—28th February 1921.

When the board of officers of the International Woman Suffrage Alliance met in London in December 1920, one of their immediate actions was to telegraph to the Assembly of the League of Nations, then in session in Geneva, asking that a woman should be appointed to the Permanent Mandates Commission.

In due course, Committee 6 on Mandates reported to the Assembly, and laid before that body a number of recommendations as to the constitution of the Permanent Mandates Commission. The second recommendation was "that at least one place in the commission be reserved for a woman". The Assembly accepted this and the other recommendations unanimously; but in the course of the debate, Mr Arthur Balfour (representative of Great Britain) pointed out that the Council of the League of Nations alone was responsible for the selection of the nine members who are to comprise the Permanent Mandates Commission; and that in the choice of these nine members—a majority of whom are to be nationals of non-mandatory powers—the Council would not be bound by any recommendation from the Assembly.

It was obvious, therefore, that it was necessary to bring all possible pressure to bear upon the Council to appoint a woman to the commission.

On 18th February, after consultation by letter and telegram with the other members of the board of officers, the headquarters committee sent the following letter to the Council of the League of Nations, and to the individual members of the Council, which comprised representatives of France (Leon Burgeois), Italy (Tacconi), Great Britain (A. J. Balfour), Belgium (Hymans), Spain (Quinones de Leon), Brazil (Gastao de Cunha), Japan (Viscount Ishi), China (Wellington Koo):

18th February 1921.

Sirs,—May we remind you of the recommendations unanimously accepted by the Assembly of the League of Nations on Saturday, 18th December 1920, namely: that there should be at least one woman on the Permanent Commission on Mandates.

The International Woman Suffrage Alliance speaks for the women of thirty-one countries who, through their delegates to the Geneva Congress of June 1920, showed their anxiety and interest in the conditions under which mandates are to be granted, and their conviction that women should be put on international bodies.

In all countries inhabited by races of different colours, the relations between the men of the governing race, and the women of the other are a source of difficulty and often an actual hindrance to good understanding. Unfair pressure may be put on men themselves through their family life, while again, questions of variation in standards of morals and customs call urgently for the representation of the woman's standpoint.

Success in administration must lie in developing what is already good in a race, and since women are the prime guardian of its traditions, we believe the addition of a suitable woman representative would be of essential and immense value to the commission.

They implore the Council to remember that the public opinion, both of men as shown in the Assembly of the League, and of women as shown in their International Conferences, is unanimously in favour of our request.

The board of officers of the International Woman Suffrage Alliance wishes to put forward the names of the following women, any one of whom would be eminently fitted to render valuable service as a member of the Permanent Commission on Mandates.

Anna Wicksell	... Sweden
Hennie Forchammer	... Denmark
Annie Furuhjelm, MP,	Finland
Elna Munch, MP	... Denmark
Paulina Luisi	... Uruguay
Aletta Jacobs	... Netherlands

Your faithfully,

Chrystal Macmillan
Vice president
Margery Corbett Ashby
*Secretary for League
of Nations Business*

Meantime headquarters had written to its auxiliaries in countries which were members of the League of Nations, urging them to petition the Council of the League of Nations to appoint a woman to the Permanent Mandates Commission, and to ask their governments also to make a similar recommendation to the Council of the League. The National Auxiliaries in France, Switzerland and Italy informed headquarters that they had taken action in the matter.

The Geneva Congress, 1920, had passed a resolution, which was forwarded to the League of Nations, urging that mandates should only be granted "for the administration of undeveloped countries, subject to the condition that within the mandatory territory there should be no regulation, segregation or official toleration of prostitution". Nor will the responsibility of the mandatory powers for the welfare of the women and children in the mandated areas end there. In Article 23 of the Covenant of the League, its states' members pledged themselves to "endeavour to secure and maintain fair and humane conditions of labour for men, women and children, both in their own countries and in all countries to which their commercial and industrial relations extend", and "to secure just treatment of the native inhabitants of territories

under their control". These pledges are as binding with regard to mandated areas as to any other; in short, the social, moral and industrial welfare of women and children in the mandated areas is a charge laid on every mandatory power. The necessity, therefore, for a woman to be a member of the Permanent Mandates Commission has been recognised by the whole Assembly of the League of Nations; it is recognised by the Aborigines Protection Society of Great Britain, which, at a representative conference held in London, passed a resolution urging the appointment of a woman; it is recognised by the Women's International League for Peace and Freedom; by the IWSA and its auxiliaries, and by the French and British League of Nations Unions. This demand for a woman on the Permanent Mandates Commission is backed by every progressive force. It was hoped that the Council of the League of Nations will recognise that demand and the urgent necessity on which it is based.

APPENDIX 4

Countries with women's organisations affiliated to the International Woman Suffrage Alliance, later, International Alliance of Women, 1904–1976 the year of the New York Congress

Argentina	1946–1949	Brazil	1923–1976
Australia	1904–1976	British Guiana	1958–1967
Austria	1909–1913; 1923–1935	Bulgaria	1908–1939
Bahamas	1961–1976	Cameroons	1967–1976
Bangladesh (as East Pakistan		Canada	1906–1939
1949–1971)	1973–1976	Ceylon—see Sri Lanka	
Barbados	1955–1976	China	1913–1920
Belgium	1909–1955	Cuba	1926–1935
Bermuda	1926–1939	Czechoslovakia	1920–1937
Bohemia	1911–1939	Dahomey	1976–1976

Denmark	1904–1976	Nigeria	1955–1976
Egypt	1923–1976	Norway	1904–1976
Ethiopia	1949–1976	Pakistan	1949–1976
Finland	1908–1976	Palestine—see Israel	
France	1909–1976	Peru	1926–1935
Germany	1904–1914; 1920–1939	Philippines	1952–1976
	1952–1976	Poland	1923–1939
Ghana	1958–1976	Porto Rico	1926–1935
Great Britain—see United Kingdom		Portugal	1913–1935
Greece	1923–1976	Romania	1913–1939
Guyana	1967–1976	Russia	1906–1914
Haiti	1952–1976	Sierra Leone	1961–1976
Hungary	1906–1914	Yugoslavia (formerly Serbia)	
Iceland	1911–1976	Yugoslavia 1911–1914; 1923–1939	
India	1923–1949; 1967–1976	South Africa	1908–1935
Indonesia—Perwari	1967–1976	Spain	1920–1946
Iran	1949–1976	Sri Lanka	1949–1976
Iraq	1949–1964	Sweden	1904–1976
Ireland	1923–1976	Switzerland	1904–1976
Israel	1923–1976	Syria	1946–1958
Italy	1906–1939; 1946–1976	Thailand	1952–1976
Ivory Coast	1976–1976	Tobago	1949–1976
Kenya	1964–1970	Trinidad	1949–1976
Jamaica	1923–1976	Tunisia	1967–1976
Japan	1926–1976	Turkey 1926–1935; 1949–1976	
Jordan	1955–1958	United Kingdom 1904–1976	
Lebanon	1946–1976	United States 1904–1949; 1923–1976	
Liberia	1958–1976	It has kept in close touch with the	
Lithuania	1923–1935	IAW with a corresponding Society	
Luxembourg	1926–1939	from 1958 to 1973. Two Societies	
Mauritius	1976–1976	then became affiliated and were	
Morocco	1973–1976	hosts at the New York Congress	
Nepal	1955–1976	1976.	
Netherlands	1904–1976	Upper Volta	1967–1976
Newfoundland	1926–1935	Uruguay	1920–1952
New Zealand	1904–1958		

APPENDIX 5

Summary of principal subjects of resolutions of Congresses 1906–1976

The four early Congresses from 1906 to 1911 concentrated on various as-pects of the one resolution: that on Suffrage for Women. From the Congress at Budapest in 1913 other subjects were added and between twelve and twenty were adopted at Congresses up to 1952 (Naples). In later years the principal resolutions were generally formulated by the five or six committees or commissions. (See note later). A brief indication of the sequence of principal resolutions is as follows:

1. *Enfranchisement of Women*—Copenhagen (1906), Amsterdam (1908), London 1909), Stockholm (1911), Budapest (1913), Geneva (1920), Rome (1923), Paris (1926), Berlin 1929), Istanbul (1935), Copenhagen (1939). As suffrage for women had been secured in most countries by 1945 it ceased to be a separate resolution and was merged in the more general subject of *Political Rights* in the first Congress after the second world war at Interlaken in 1946.

2. *Equal Moral Standard or Rights, Prostitution and related matters*—Became important themes for resolutions from the Congress at Budapest (1913) when "White Slave Traffic" was the subject of a resolution. Two resolutions at the Geneva Congress (1920) were on "Prostitution and Venereal Disease", and "Deported and Slave Women". At Rome (1923), "Moral Questions—Education and Instruction" was the theme; and "Equal Moral Standard" and "Traffic in Women" were subjects of resolutions at Paris (1926), Berlin (1929), Istanbul (1935), Copenhagen (1939), Interlaken (1946), Amsterdam (1949), Naples (1952), Colombo (1955), Athens (1958), Dublin (1961), Trieste 1964), and London 1967). In resolutions of

later Congresses the word moral was no longer used, and the subject was absorbed into other related themes.

3. *Peace and the League of Nations*—This first became the subject of resolutions in the first Congress after the world war at Geneva in 1920. The subject continued to be a prominent one for resolutions at the Congresses at Rome (1923), Paris (1926), Berlin 1929), Istanbul (1935), and Copenhagen (1939). At the first Congress after the Second World War Peace was the subject of the first resolution, and again at Amsterdam (1949). Then at Naples (1952) and Colombo (1955) the resolution was entitled "Peace and Human Relations" then to become "International Understanding" at all subsequent Congresses.

4. *Equal Economic Rights*—This became the subject of a resolution under various titles, first at Geneva (1920). At Rome (1923) the theme was entitled "Equal Pay and Right to Work"; at Paris (1926) "Like Conditions of Work for Men and Women", repeated at Berlin (1929) and the theme continued to produce resolutions at each subsequent Congress.

5. *Equal Educational Rights*—This first became the subject of resolutions at the Naples Congress in 1952, and a resolution under the above title was adopted at the Congresses at Colombo (1955), Athens (1958), Dublin (1961), Trieste (1964) and revived at Königstein (1970) and Delhi (1973).

6. *The Nationality of Married Women*. This was the subject of a resolution at the Congress in Rome (1923), Paris (1926), Berlin (1929) and Copenhagen (1939).

7. *Slavery*—This was the subject of resolutions at the Congresses at Rome (1926) and Istanbul (1935).

8. *Democracy*—The resolution on this subject was adopted at the Congress at Interlaken (1946) immediately after the war when it was felt that it was desirable to be quite clear on the just and logical interpretation of democracy that would provide the best conditions for a good quality of life for women equally with men.

As previously indicated, from the Geneva Congress in 1920 to the Naples Congress in 1952 many resolutions, between twelve and twenty, were made at each Congress, which arose partly from the work of the International Committees or Commissions and partly from discussions at the Congresses. From the Colombo Congress in 1955 up to that in New York in 1976, with the exception of that at Trieste in 1964, which reverted to the pre-Colombo pattern, the resolutions arose mainly from the work of the International Commissions or Standing Committees (the titles seem to have alternated) and resolutions were given under the titles of the Committees. The subjects of the Committees were:

Equal Civil and Political Rights
Equal Economic Rights
Equal Educational Rights
Equal Moral Standard
Peace and Human Relations

Athens Congress 1958—The same as in 1955 except that the Committee on Peace and Human Relations became International Understanding. Most of the resolutions under each heading were reaffirmations of previous resolutions, often with different wording. Sometimes a new aspect was introduced resulting from current trends.

Dublin Congress 1961—The same as in 1958.

Trieste Congress 1964—The committees remained the same as at the two previous Congresses, which made resolutions, but in addition adopted resolutions on the Status of Women Commission, on the Economic and Social Consequences of Disarmament and the need for a National Bill of Human Rights.

London Congress 1967—The committees were the same as in 1958–64. There was an additional resolution, an emergency one, asking that non-governmental organisations in consultative status interested in human rights shall be invited to participate in the International Conference on Human Rights at Teheran 1968.

Königstein Congress 1970—The "committees" were called "commissions" at this Congress and were entitled:

Civil and Political Rights Commission
Economic Commission
Education Commission
International Understanding Commission
Social Commission with Sub-commission on Slavery
United Nations Commission

Delhi Congress 1973—The commissions remained the same as in 1970, except that the sub-commission of the Social Commission was on Slavery and Prostitution.

New York Congress 1976—Commissions were the same as in 1973.

APPENDIX 6

Chronological table of the principal events in the history of the women's movement from 1696–1979

1696 Publication of *A Serious Proposal to the Ladies for the Advancement of their true and greatest interest. In Two Parts. By a Lover of her sex*—Mary Astell (1668–1731). Part I 1696, Part II 1697.
Mary Astell's "proposal" was the establishment of a women's college, a proposal which very nearly succeeded.

1739 Publication of *Woman Not Inferior to Man or a short and modest vindication of the natural Right of the Fair Sex to a perfect Equality of Power, Dignity, and Esteem with the Men.* By Sophia, A Person of Quality.
This was replied to by *A Gentleman* with a pamphlet entitled *Man Superior to Woman* which brought forth a spirited reply from Sophia published in 1743 entitled *Woman's Superior Excellence over Man.*

1791 *Declaration of the Rights of Women and Citizenesses* by Olympe de Gouges published in Paris.

1792 *A Vindication of the Rights of Women* by Mary Wollstonecraft, published in London.

1799 Publication of *The Female Advocate, or an attempt to recover the rights of women from male usurpation* by Mary Radcliffe.

1802 Publication of *Ueber die Bestimmung des Weibeszur höhern Geistesbildung* by Holst.

1804 *Code civil des Francais* became law. In 1801 it was called *Code Napoléon.* It was framed entirely in the interests of men and incorporated the subjection of women.

1807 Association for the Improvement of Female Prisoners in Newgate Prison, founded by Elizabeth Fry.

1818 Jeremy Bentham supported Women's Suffrage in his *Resolutions on Parliamentary Reform.*

1819 Reform Bill agitation to Peterloo in which women shared.

1825 *An appeal of one half the human race, Women against the pretentions of the other half, Men, to retain them in political and thence in civil and domestic slavery: in reply to a paragraph of Mr James Mill's celebrated Article on Government* by William Thompson. Mr Mill was the father of John Stuart Mill.

1828 Caroline Herschell and Mary Somerville elected members, Royal Astronomical Society.

1831 Article advocating women's suffrage by Mrs Mylne published in Westminster Review.

1832 First Reform Act, Great Britain. This is the first time the word "male" was inserted before "person" in an Act of Parliament, thus excluding women from the right to vote.

1835   Municipal Reform Act. As in the Reform Act of 1832 the word "male" was inserted in front of "person" so as to exclude women.

1836   Caroline Norton published series of pamphlets on a Mother's Right to the Custody of her Infant Children.

1838   Chartist Movement began. In the first draft of the Charter of Rights and Liberties Women's Suffrage was included, but was withdrawn because several thought that it might retard the extension of the suffrage for men.
Women's Political Associations formed as part of the Chartist Movement.

1839   Infants' Custody Act, which gave women some rights in their children where they formerly had none. The act enabled mothers against whom adultery was not proved to have the custody of their children under seven with right of access to others at stated times.

1842   Act forbidding the employment of women in mines.

1842   Unmarried women and widows in Norway granted licence for trading.

1843   Report of Commission on Conditions of Employment of Dressmakers and Milliners.
A Plea for Women by Mrs Henry Reid published. Report of the Second Commission on the Employment of Women and Children.

1845   Sons and daughters given equality in Sweden in matters of inheritance.

1846   First Women's Suffrage leaflet circulated by Ann Knight of Chelmsford.

1847   Act limiting working hours of women and children in Factories (called the Ten Hours Act).

1848   First Women's Convention in the USA held at Seneca Falls, New York, 19th and 20th July.
Queen's College for Ladies opened in London.

1849   Bedford College for Women founded.
Letters from Clara Rafael published. This has been regarded as the beginning of the women's movement in Denmark.

1849   Elizabeth Blackwell received a medical degree from the medical college in Geneva, New York. "She was the first woman to practice medicine in America. She founded the first school of nursing in 1857 in America: The New York Infirmary College in 1866; and in 1871 the National Health Society in England—an organisation for teaching health habits, and the prevention of disease." *The First Woman Doctor: The story of Elizabeth Blackwell, MD*, by Rachael Baker (NY 1944: 17th printing, 1962).

1850   North London Collegiate School founded by Miss Buss.
Women's Convention, Worcester, Massachusetts.
Equal rights of inheritance given to sons and daughters in Iceland.

1851   Petition for Women's Suffrage from Female Political Association at Sheffield presented to House of Lords by Lord Carlyle.

1854   Barbara Leigh Smith (Mme Bodichon) published *A Brief Statement of Laws Concerning Women*.

1854   Equal rights of inheritance given to sons and daughters in Norway.
The Governor's Daughter, by Camilla Collett, published in Norway, a feminist novel inspiring many later great writers, among them Henrik Ibsen.

1855   Young Women's Christian Association of Great Britain founded.

1857   First Marriage and Divorce Act making divorce possible for women in certain cases.
Englishwomen's Journal began publication.
Society for the Promotion of the Employment of Women formed.
First High School for Girls founded in Russia.

1859   Society for Promoting the Training of Women formed.
Dr Elizabeth Blackwell (of USA) admitted to British Medical Register (register then closed to holders of foreign degrees).

1860   Elizabeth Garrett entered Middlesex Hospital as a nurse with permission to attend medical lectures: subsequently permission withdrawn.

1861   Vassar College founded (USA) the first fully endowed college for women.

1863   Girls admitted (informally) to take Oxford and Cambridge Local Examinations.
Women of Sweden, paying taxes to the amount of 500 kroner, given Municipal Franchise.

1863   Unmarried women given majority status in Norway.

1865   Communal vote conferred on women who were property owners and tax payers.
Oxford and Cambridge Local Examinations formally opened to girls.
Elizabeth Garrett passed Society of Apothecaries examination and obtained licence to practise medicine. (Women subsequently refused admission to this examination).
Allegemeine deutsche Frauenverein (Association of German Women) founded in Leipzig.

1866   London Society for Women's Suffrage founded. (This later became the Fawcett Society).
Petition to House of Commons for Women's Suffrage presented by J. S. Mill and Henry Fawcett.

1867   Amendment to the Representation of the People Bill moved by John Stuart Mill to substitute the word "persons" for "men". Resulted in debate on women's suffrage.

1867   First woman student (medicine) at University of Zurich.
Demand by Mathilde Champ Renaud for women's rights—liberté du travail, egalité des droits, fraternité humaine—during an international congress in Geneva.

1868   Foundation of "Union Internationale des Femmes" by Marie Groegg of Geneva.

1868   Demand for women's suffrage during the revision of the constitution of Zürich.

1869   J. S. Mill published "The Subjection of Women".

Municipal Franchise extended to women householders.

First Women's College founded temporarily at Hitchin.

National Women's Suffrage Association formed in USA.

Women given the Franchise in the territory of Wyoming, USA, thus the first country in the modern world in which there was equality of franchise of men and women. This was confirmed when Wyoming became a state, and admitted to the Union in 1890.

1869 Association pour les droits des "femmes" founded in France by M Léon Richer.

Journal des Femmes founded by Marie Groegg-Pouchoulin in Geneva. Later combined with "Droit de Femmes".

1869 Varvara A. Kashevarova-Rudnova received her degree in medicine in St Petersburg, and became the first woman medical doctor in Russia.

1870 Foundation of women's society at Herzogenbuchsee (near Berne) by Amalie Moser.

1872 Foundation of "Solidarité"—association pour la défense des droits de la femmes.

1873 First woman elected a member of British Medical Association. Although women medical students began to be accepted by Zürich University in 1867, the University was legally open to women in 1873.

Mrs Nassau Senior appointed first woman Poor Law Inspector in England.

1878 Neuchatel University open to women.

1882 Women admitted as students to the University of Kristiania (now Oslo), Norway.

1883 Establishment of Medical Women for India Fund, to bring fully qualified women doctors to India; to open medical schools to Indian and other women for medical training and to raise money to set up a hospital for women and children, staffed entirely by women.

1884 Society of Norwegian Women founded.

Finnish Women's Association founded.

1884 Norsk Kvinnesaksforening (Norw. Society for the Rights of Women) founded—with a man as first president.

1885 First co-education school founded in Kristiania, Norway.

1885 Women's Suffrage Society founded in Norway.

1885 Petition asking for Women's Suffrage presented to French Government by Madame Hubertine Auclert.

Society of Swiss Women founded.

Women's Suffrage League founded in Melbourne, Australia.

1886 The Cama Hospital for Women and Children in Bombay was officially opened, with Edith Pechey as Senior Medical Officer, her official title being First Physician. This was the first hospital in India with a staff consisting entirely of women.

1886 The Grant Medical College in Bombay admitted Indian women for the very first time.

1886 Lausanne University open to women.

1887 Women admitted to Dental Schools.

1888   First woman elected to British County Councils.

1888   Married women given restricted majority status in Norway.

1889   The Women's Suffrage League of South Australia formed.

Women's Trade Union League formed by British Trade Union Congress.

The Voice of Woman journal first issued in Bulgaria.

1890   Basel University open to women.

1892   British Medical Association admitted women to membership.

Scottish universities admitted women to membership.

Women's Alliance founded in Finland.

1893   Franchise given to women on equal terms with men in Colorado, USA.

Suffrage extended to women in New Zealand—the first sovereign state in the world in which women had parliamentary vote.

1893   Miss May Abraham and Miss May Paterson first women appointed as Factory Inspectors in England.

1894   University Examinations (without degrees) opened to women students at Oxford.

Extension of suffrage to women in South Australia.

Women's Suffrage Association started in the Netherlands.

Bund deutscher Frauenvereine (Union of German Women's Associations) founded.

1895   Royal College of Surgeons admitted women to membership.

National Council of Women of Great Britain founded.

Women suffrage in the state of Idaho, USA.

1897   National Union of Women's Suffrage Societies founded in Britain.

The journal La Fronde founded, first edited by Madame Durand.

1898   Suffrage Association started in Denmark by Fru Norlund and Fröken Luplan.

National Woman Suffrage Association started in Norway.

1898   Miss Bessie Charles first woman in England to qualify as an architect.

1899   Extension of suffrage to women in Western Australia.

Legislation in Iceland giving married women the right to their own property.

Women admitted to examinations in medicine in Germany.

1900   Congrès des Œuvres et Institutions Feminines and the Congrès de la Condition et des Droits des Femmes held in Paris.

1901   The right to vote and be elected to local councils in Norway given to women who were tax-payers.

1902   Parliamentary franchise extended to women in Australia and in New South Wales.

German Society for Women's Suffrage founded.

Stockholm Society for Women's Suffrage founded.

Women's Suffrage League founded in Natal.

1903   Formation of Women's Social and Political Union (Militant Suffrage Society) by Mrs Emmeline Pankhurst and her daughter Christabel.

Parliamentary franchise extended to women in Tasmania.

1904   Resolution on Women's Suffrage carried in British House of Commons. No subsequent progress.

First public meeting in Finland to promote Women's Suffrage, organised by Women's Alliance Union.

Women students admitted to the Universities of Heidelberg and Freiberg.

1906   First Women's Suffrage candidate at by-election (Wigan). Defeated.

In Finland 19 women of a total of 200 deputies were elected to the Diet.

Italian National Women's Suffrage Society founded.

Women admitted to Russian Universities.

1907   First Women's Suffrage procession in London (Mid March).

Comitato Nazionale per il Suffragio Femminile founded in Italy.

Women's Suffrage Association founded at Reykjavik (Iceland).

Women's Suffrage Congress held at Frankfurt.

Women's Enfranchisement League founded, Cape Colony. The right to vote and be elected for Parliament in Norway given to women who are tax-payers, or married to man with adequate income

1908   First British Woman Mayor (Mrs Garrett Anderson at Aldeburgh).

Municipal suffrage extended in Denmark to all tax-payers (men and women) whose income mounted to 800 kroner in Copenhagen and a little less in country districts.

In Finland 25 women deputies were elected to the Diet.

In the Netherlands the leaders of four of the seven political parties declared in a debate in Parliament in favour of women's suffrage.

In Germany women were for the first time allowed to be members of political parties.

Women admitted as students to Prussian Universities.

1908   Legislation in Germany ending the legal restrictions which prevented women from taking part in public meetings and founding associations.

1909   British Men's League for Women's Suffrage formed.

Women's Freedom League formed in Britain and also many special WS societies such as Catholic Women, Jewish Women, Artists, Actresses, etc.

National French Union for Women's Suffrage founded.

Women's Suffrage Association founded in Switzerland.

Women's Suffrage in Victoria. This means that by that date women in all the Australian states had the vote.

1910   Formation of the Conciliation Committee (Britain) and the promotion of a Conciliation Bill based on household suffrage for both sexes.

Women's suffrage obtained in Washington, USA.

Unrestricted municipal suffrage for women in Norway.

1911   Women's suffrage in California, USA.

First woman takes seat in the Parliament (Storting) of Norway.

1912   Defeat of the Conciliation Bill on 28th March in the British House of Commons by an adverse majority of 14 votes. Act admitting women in Norway to all public appointments except military and ecclesiastical.

1913   Full parliamentary suffrage for women in Norway.

Intensification of militancy in Britain. Mrs Pankhurst sentenced to 3 years' penal servitude.

"Cat and Mouse" Act passed in Britain to require suffragette prisoners to complete sentences, after temporary release on hunger strike.

1914 to 1918   European War. Activity of women throughout Great Britain in every type of war work. Great success of women in such work and strong swing of popular sentiment in favour of their right to vote.

1915   National agreements to protect men's Trade Union rates of pay by paying substitute women at same rates.

Women granted parliamentary vote in Denmark.

Women over 40 granted parliamentary vote in Iceland. Age limit reduced to 25 and in 1920 was on equal terms with men.

1916/17   Formation in Britain of Women's Legion, Women's Army Auxiliary Corps, Women's Royal Naval Service, Women's Royal Air Force Service, Women's Land Army, etc.

1916   Question of new Parliamentary Register discussed in British Parliament. Women's claim for inclusion admitted. Speaker's Conference appointed by Prime Minister to draft Bill.

Order of Dames of the British Empire instituted.

1917   Franchise for Women in union of Soviet Socialist Republics.

1918   Women householders and the wives of householders over 30 enfranchised in Britain.

Franchise for Women in Germany.

1918   Act enabling women to be elected to British House of Commons.

Affiliation Orders Act (increasing maximum payment by fathers of illegitimate children to 1/- a week).

Countess Markievicz elected (first woman) to British House of Commons—did not take her seat.

1919   First woman to British House of Commons the Viscountess Astor. Countess Markievicz appointed Minister of Labour in Irish Dail.

Sex Disqualification Removal Act, Great Britain (admitting women to legal profession, jury and magistrate service, police, the Home Civil Service and all Incorporated and Chartered Societies).

Franchise extended to women in Austria.

Franchise extended to women in the Netherlands.

Franchise extended to women in Poland.

1920   Vote granted to women in the USA by the 19th amendment to the federal constitution stating that "the right of citizens of the United States to vote shall not be denied or abridged by the United States or by any State on account of sex".

1920   British House of Commons

Resolution for equal entry and conditions of women in Civil Service passed.

Matrimonial Orders Enforcement Act.

First women magistrates appointed in Britain (169 in England, 21 in Wales and 42 in Scotland).

Oxford University admitted women to degrees and membership of the University

1922 First woman included in Great Britain delegation to League of Nations.

Married Women's Maintenance Act (allowing payments for children as well as wives in cases of legal separation).

Criminal Law Amendment Act (raising age of consent to 16).

Law of Property Act (giving mothers and daughters same position as fathers and sons in cases of intestacy).

Dr Ivy Williams first woman called to English Bar.

1923 First woman chairman of British Trade Union Congress (Margaret Bondfield).

Matrimonial Causes Act (establishing equal grounds for divorce for men and women) in UK.

1924 First 2 women hold office in Government as Parliamentary Secretaries.

Women appointed fully attested police constables.

Admission of women to open competitive examination for Administrative Class of Civil Service.

1925 Equal Guardianship of Infants' Act.

Separation and Maintenance Act.

1928 Representation of the People Act, giving Women's Suffrage on equal terms with men in United Kingdom.

1929 Age of Marriage Act (raising age of marriage to 16 for both sexes).

First woman Cabinet Minister (Margaret Bondfield, Minister of Labour).

1929 Women granted the vote in the Commonwealth of Puerto Rico.

1930 Parliamentary suffrage for women in South Africa.

1931 Parliamentary suffrage for women in Spain.

1932 Parliamentary suffrage for women in Brazil and in Turkey.

1933 Parliamentary suffrage for women in Thailand.

1934 British Nationality and Status of Aliens Act (to prevent loss of nationality when woman does not by marriage acquire nationality of her husband).

1935 Law Reform Act (to put married women in same position as single in regard to debt, bankruptcy, etc.).

1936 Hours of Employment Act.

1937 Divorce Act (to allow new grounds of divorce equally for men and women).

1937 Parliamentary suffrage for women in the Philippines.

1944 Parliamentary suffrage for women in France.

1945 Parliamentary suffrage for women in Italy, Japan and Yugoslavia.

1947 Parliamentary suffrage for women in Bulgaria and China.

1948 Parliamentary suffrage for women in Israel.

1949 Rose Heilbron and Helena Normanton became first women

King's Counsel.

1955 Parliamentary suffrage for women in Indonesia.

1959 Mrs Sirimavo Bandranaike of Sri Lanka becomes the world's first woman Prime Minister.

1961 Parliamentary suffrage for women in Paraguay.

1963 Parliamentary suffrage for women in Iran.

1966 Indira Gandhi, became Prime Minister of India. She remained in office until 1977.

1969 Golda Meìr became Prime Minister of Israel. She remained in office until 1974.

1969 Family Law Reform Act where wives can have financial and legal contracts in their own right.

1970 Equal Pay Act.

1971 Parliamentary suffrage for women in Switzerland.

1973 British Guardianship Act giving equal rights of guardianship of children to both parents.

1973 Parliamentary suffrage for women in Jordan.

1974 Ella Grasso elected Governor of Connecticut the first woman to become a Governor of an American State.

1974 Maria Peron of Argentina—the first woman to become President of a Republic

1975 Margaret Thatcher became the first woman leader of a principal political party in Great Britain.

1975 Sex Discrimination Act which makes discrimination by reason of sex unlawful in employment, education, training and provision of services to the public

1975 United Nations International Women's Year.

1977 Tina Anselmi became Italy's first Woman Cabinet Minister.

1977 Dr Emilie Lieberherr became Switzerland's Minister for Women's Affairs. She was the first woman to be elected to the City Council of Zürich in 1970.

1978 Appointment of Mme Pelletier as the first Minister of Women's Affairs in the French Government.

1979 Election of Dame Diana Reader Harrison as first Woman Chairman of the Council of the Royal Society of Arts.

BIBLIOGRAPHY

Selected bibliography of works in English

There are numerous books in English which give the history of the women's movement from the national standpoint, but few that give a world picture. The most complete record of the early struggles is the History of Woman Suffrage in six volumes published in USA with a brief record in the last volume of progress in other countries. Most of the books in the following list are national in character and are mainly American and British. To give books on the woman's movement in other countries would make a very long list and would occupy too much space to be included here.

A few works devoted to special groups and activities are mentioned in the notes at the ends of chapters, and are not with few exceptions, repeated here.

Evelyn Acworth: *The New Matriarchy*. London 1965 (Gollancz).

Susan B. Anthony, Elizabeth Cady Stanton and Matilda Joslyn Gage, (edited by): *The History of Woman Suffrage*, in six volumes. The first four volumes were published by Susan B. Anthony in New York (1881–1902) and the last two by the National American Woman Suffrage Association (1922) Vol. 1, 1884–1861; Vol. 2, 1861–1876; Vol. 3, 1876–1885. These first three were edited by the women given above. Vol. 4, 1883–1900 edited by Susan B. Anthony and Ida Hursted Harper; Vol. 5, and Vol. 6, 1900–1920, both edited by Ida Hursted Harper.

Simone de Beauvoir: *The Second Sex*. London 1953 (Jonathan Cape).

Helen Blackburn: *Women's Suffrage—a record of the women's suffrage movement in the British Isles with biographical sketches of Miss Becker*. London 1902 (Williams and Norgate).

Lyon Bleaze: *The Emancipation of Englishwomen*. London 1910.

Lynn Z. Bloom, Karen Coburn and Joan Pearlman. *The New Assertive Woman*. New York 1975 (Delacorte Press).

C. S. Bremner: *Education of Girls and Women in Great Britain*. London 1897 (Sonnenschein).

Vera Brittain: *Lady into Woman—a history of women from Victoria to Elizabeth*. London 1953. (Andrew Dakers). *Pethick-Lawrence—A Portrait*. London 1963 (Allen & Unwin). No Englishman of the present century did more for the emancipation of women than Lord Pethick-Lawrence, and his contribution to the cause is sympathetically recalled in this biography.

Gertrude Bussey and Margaret Tims: *Women's International League for Peace and Freedom, 1915–1965*. A record of fifty years work. London 1965 (Allen & Unwin).

Mayra Buvinic with Cheri S. Adams, Gabrielle S. Edgcomb, and Maritta Koch-Weser: *Women and World Development—an annotated Bibliography*. Some 381 works with notes on each are included. It is divided into nine sections:

1. General studies on women in development.
2. The impact of society on women's roles and status.
3. The individual in society: women's behaviour patterns and customs.
4. Socio-Economic participation of rural women.
5. Education and women.
6. Women's work and economic development.
7. Women and health, nutrition and fertility/family planning.
8. Women's informal and formal associations.
9. Women, Law and Politics.

The bibliography was produced under the auspices of the American Association for the Advancement of Science. 1976.

William H. Chafe: *The American Woman—her changing social, economic and political role 1920–1970*. New York 1972 (Oxford University Press).

Millicent Garrett Fawcett: *Women's Suffrage—a short history of a Great Movement*. London 1913 (T. C. & E. C. Jack). A short informative account in "The People's Books" series.

International Women's News—the official journal of the International Alliance of Women continuously published—1906 to 1979, contains a wealth of information on the activities of women to secure equality of men and women in all spheres of political, economic, cultural and social life.

G. W. Johnson: *The Evolution of Women from Subjection to Citizenship*. London 1926.

Josephine Kamm: *Hope Deferred—Girls' Education in English History*. London 1965 (Methuen). *Rapiers and Battle-axes—the women's movement and its aftermath*. London 1966 (Allen & Unwin). This was published on the occasion of the centenary of the Fawcett Society.

Beatrix Kempf: *Suffragette for Peace, the life of Bertha von Suttner*. Austria 1964. English translation London 1972 (Oswald Wolf).

John Stuart Mill: *The Subjection of Women*. London 1869.

Kate Millet: *Sexual Politics*. London 1971 (Rupert Hart-Davis).

David Mitchell: *Women on the Warpath—the story of the Women of the First World War*. London 1966 (Jonathan Cape).

William L. O'Neill: *The Woman Movement, Feminism in the United States and England*. London 1969 (Allen & Unwin).

Christabel Pankhurst: *Unshackled—the story of how we won the vote*, edited by Lord Pethick-Lawrence. London 1959 (Hutchinson). This was published posthumously and is a personal, often emotional narrative, which gives a vivid picture of women's struggle to get the vote.

Emmeline Pankhurst: *My Own Story*. London 1914.

E. Sylvia Pankhurst: *The Suffragette, the history of the Women's Militant Suffrage Movement 1905–1910*. London 1911 (Gray & Hancock).

Mary Gray Peck: *Carrie Chapman Catt—A Biography*. New York 1944 (H. W. Wilson Co.). Mrs Catt was one of the great international leaders in the women's movement and this biography gives much information of the movement, especially in America.

Emmeline Pethick-Lawrence: *My part in a Changing World*. London 1938 (Victor Gollancz).

Political and Economic Planning: *Women in Top Jobs. Four Studies in Achievement*. London 1971 (Allen & Unwin). The studies are of women in two large companies by Isobel Allen: The Woman Director; A. J. Allen: Women in the B.B.C. and women in the Administrative Class of the Civil Service by Patricia A. Walters.

Political and Economic Planning: *Sex, Career and Family*, by Fogarty, Rapopert and Rapopert. London 1971 (Allen & Unwin). This study includes an International Review of Women's Roles.

Constance Rover: *Women's Suffrage and Party Politics in Britain 1866–1914*. London 1967 (Routledge & Kegan Paul).

Constance Rover: *Love, Morals and the Feminists*. London 1970 (Routledge & Kegan Paul).

Andrew Sinclair: *The Better Half—the Emancipation of the American Woman*. London 1966 (Jonathan Cape).

Mary Stott: *Organization Woman—The story of the National Union of Townswomen's Guilds*. London 1978 (Heinemann). A good objective account to celebrate the jubilee of the Guilds.

Ray Strachey: *The Cause—A short history of the women's movement in Great Britain*. One of the best books on the subject, vividly written. 1935. Reprinted 1975.

E. Sulleiot: *Women, Society and Change*. London 1971 (Weidenfeld and Nicolson). English translation from a French work.

Mary Wollstonecraft: *A Vindication of the Rights of Women*. London 1792.

Ethel M. Wood: *The Pilgrimage of Perseverance*. London 1949 (The National Council of Social Service).

Alice Zimmern: *Women's Suffrage in Many Lands*. London 1909. A short summary of the women's movement up to 1909 in 22 principal countries of the Western World.

INDEX

References in italics denote illustrations

Gourd (*cont.*)
for the IAW, 153, 154; Death of,
154
Graff, Ester, 10, 173, 174; Becomes
president of IAW (1952), 173; Por-
trait, *176*; Presidential address at
Athens Congress (1958), 182; Resig-
nation of presidency of IAW, 184
Great Britain, 32
Grinberg-Aupourrain, Mme, 139
Grinberg, Suzanne, 71
Guardian, The, (British Newspaper),
237
Guthrie d'Arcis, 110
Gutteridge, Prof. H. C., 131

Hailsham, Lord, British delegate to
disarmament conference, 109
Haiti, 170
Halsey, Elizabeth, secretary of IAW,
207; On Swiss women's prospect of
the vote, 212
Hamilton-Smith, Elisabeth, relin-
quishes editorship of *International
Women's News* (1952), 174
Hamm-Brucher, Hildegard, 227
Harburn, Miss, and women police in
Cologne, 74
Hardiman, Margaret, 281
Hayman, Sylvia, 151
Health, part of sub-theme for World
Conference, (1980), 284
Heinzelmann, Dr G., 210
Hesselgren, Miss, 131
Hillery, Dr, receives IAW board
(1977), 283
Hodge, Margaret, 54
Horsburgh, Florence, 196
Human Rights, advisory commission
to ECOSOC, 187
Human Rights, Declaration of, 285;
Covenants of, 285
Human Rights, United Nations Uni-
versal Declaration of, 164; Sum-
mary of its provisions, 164, 165
Hungary, 32
Hunt, Orator, MP, 20

IAW, see International Alliance of
Women
Idaho, and women's suffrage, 18;

state seal designed by Emma Ed-
wards, 18
India, 19
India, Woman's movement in, 55
Infants Custody Bill, 1839, 23
Ingledew, Margaret, article in *IWN* on
"Women's use of the Vote", 235,
236, 237
Innes, Mrs, 108
Inter-Allied Suffrage Conference, 71
International Alliance of Women, 10,
11, 12, 13, 16, 30, 34, 128; New
name of International Woman Suffrage Alliance, 94, 100 (ref.); Congress at Berlin, 101–105; Economic
Depression (1930–35), 117–120;
Board meeting of London (1932),
118; Proposed fusion with International Council of Women, 127;
and status of Women, 128; Meeting of Board, Amsterdam (1936),
128; Zürich Study Conference,
134–136; Copenhagen Congress
(1939), 136–145; Status of Women,
Copenhagen Congress, gives main
points to League of Nations, 142–
144; During second world war,
147–150; Attitude to second world
war, 147; Revival of after second
world war, 152; Board Meeting at
Geneva (1945), 153; Interlaken Congress, 154–161; Further change of
title (1945), 154; Granted consultative status to United Nations,
163; Conference at Beirut (1949),
Five, Commission of, 167; Congress
at Naples (1925), 170–174; Extension of influence to Near and Far East,
177; Congress at Colombo (1955),
177–179; Congress at Athens,
(1958), 181–185; Congress at Dublin (1961), 191–193; Congress at
Trieste (1964), 199–201; Congress
in London (1967), 212–214; Congress at Königstein (1970), 225–
234; Congress at New Dehli (1973),
250–259; Congress at New York
(1976), 276; Collaboration with
UNESCO, 279
International Co-operative Women's
Guild, 114
International Council of Women, 31,